Clarence Gallagher: CANON LAW AND THE CHRISTIAN
COMMUNITY

Analecta Gregoriana

Cura Pontificiae Universitatis Gregorianae edita
Vol. 208. Series Facultatis Iuris Canonici: Sectio A, n. 8

CLARENCE GALLAGHER S.J.

CANON LAW
AND THE CHRISTIAN COMMUNITY

The Role of Law in the Church According to the
Summa Aurea of Cardinal Hostiensis

UNIVERSITÀ GREGORIANA EDITRICE
ROMA 1978

CLARENCE GALLAGHER S. J.

CANON LAW
AND THE CHRISTIAN COMMUNITY

The Role of Law in the Church According to the
Summa Aurea of Cardinal Hostiensis

UNIVERSITÀ GREGORIANA EDITRICE
ROMA 1978

IMPRIMI POTEST

Romae, die 18 septembris 1978

R. P. Carolus M. Martini, S.I.
Rector Universitatis

Con approvazione del Vicariato di Roma
in data 21 settembre 1978

TYPIS PONTIFICIAE UNIVERSITATIS GREGORIANAE — ROMAE

PREFACE

This study of the *Summa Aurea* was presented in 1970 to the Canon Law Faculty of the Gregorian University, Rome, in fulfilment of the requirements for the doctorate in canon law. To make all the revisions that I would now like to make would involve writing a different book, so the thesis is being published substantially as it was presented in 1970.

A large part of Chapter Seven has already been published in the *Heythrop Journal* (July and October issues for 1971), and I am grateful to the editor for his permission to reproduce it here. I would also like to thank Fr Olis Robleda, S.J. for his kindness to me and encouragement while directing the thesis and Mgr Charles Lefebvre who first suggested the topic to me.

Clarence Gallagher S.J.

TABLE OF CONTENTS

	Page
PREFACE	5
TABLE OF CONTENTS	7
BIBLIOGRAPHY	9
INTRODUCTION	15

CHAPTER I: *Cardinal Hostiensis: His Life and Work* 21

1. The Importance of Hostiensis 21
2. Brief Biography of Hostiensis 26
3. The Writings of Cardinal Hostiensis 40

CHAPTER II: *The Juridical Background* 47

1. Canonical Legislation in the Twelfth and Thirteenth Centuries 47
2. Views of Canonists and Popes on the Role of Law . . 55
3. The Practical Concerns of Medieval Canon Law . . . 60

CHAPTER III: *The General Approach of Hostiensis* 65

1. His Attitude to his Readers 65
2. His Method in Argumentation 68
3. The Relationship between Canon Law and Theology . . 73
4. On the Role of Canon Law in General 81

CHAPTER IV: *Canon Law and the Promotion of Order and Harmony* 87

1. Security against Fraudulence 87
2. Promotion of Harmony through Juridical Order 89
3. Canon Law and Papal Primacy 94
4. Protection for Ecclesiastical Interests and Institutions . . 113
5. Directions for the Administration of the Sacraments . . 117

CHAPTER V: *Delineation of Rights and Duties and Due Process* . 125

1. The Primacy of Justice and Equity 126
2. Delineation of Duties and Rights 138
3. Due Process of Law 154

Page

CHAPTER VI: *Canon Law as a Guide and as a Deterrent* . . . 163

1. The Law as a Guide to Christian Living 165
2. The Law as an Instrument of Moral Reform 176
3. The Law as a Deterrent against Heresy 184

CHAPTER VII: *Evaluation* 203

1. Summary 203
2. Hostiensis and the Medieval Legal Tradition 207
3. Evaluation 215
4. General Conclusion 239

BIBLIOGRAPHY ***

A. Medieval Sources

Cardinal Hostiensis, *Summa Aurea super Titulis Decretalium*, Lyon, 1556 (Two other editions were also used: Lyon, 1568, and Venice, 1570).
――――, *In I-VI Decretalium Libros Commentaria*, Two Volumes, Venice, 1581 (also referred to as the *Apparatus* or *Lectura*).
Bernardus Parmensis, *Glossa Ordinaria in Decretales*, Venice, 1514.
Corpus Iuris Canonici, edited by A. Friedberg, Two Volumes, Leipzig, 1879.
William Durandus, *Speculum Iudiciale*.
Goffredus Tranensis, *Summa in Titulos Decretalium*, Venice, 1586.
Innocent IV, *Commentaria in V Libros Decretalium*, Venice, 1578.
Ivo of Chartres, *Prologus in Decretum*, Migne, P. L., 161, 47-60.
Matthew Paris, *Matthei Parisiensis, monachi Sancti Albani, Chronica maiora*, edited by H. R. Luard (*Rerum Britannicarum Medii Aevi Scriptores*), Volumes III and IV, London, 1877.
Paucapalea, *Die Summa des Paucapalea*, edited by J. F. von Schulte, Giessen, 1890.
Quinque Compilationes Antiquae, edited by A. Friedberg, Leipzig, 1882.
Rolandus Bandinelli, *Die Summa Magistri Rolandi*, edited by F. Thaner, Innsbruck, 1874.
Rufinus, *Die Summa Decretorum des Magister Rufinus*, edited by H. Singer, Paderborn, 1902.
Thomas Diplovatatius (1468-1541), *De Claris Iurisconsultis*, edited by H. Kantorowicz and F. Schulz, Berlin, 1909.

B. Modern Works

Allen, Carleton Kemp, *Law in the Making*, 7th ed., Oxford, 1964.
Barraclough, Geoffrey, *The Medieval Papacy*, London, 1968.
Bellini, P., ' "Denunciatio evangelica" e "denunciatio iudicialis privata" ', *Ephemerides Iuris Canonici*, 18 (1962), pp. 152-210.
Benson, Robert, 'Rufin', *Dictionnaire du Droit Canonique*, Volume 7, Paris, 1965.
――――, *The Bishop-Elect. A Study in Medieval Ecclesiastical Office*, Princeton University Press, 1968.
Bévenot, Maurice, S.J., 'The Inquisition and Its Antecedents I-IV', *Heythrop Journal*, 7 (1966), pp. 257-268; 381-393; 8 (1967), pp. 52-69; 152-168.
Biechler, James E., (Editor), *Law for Liberty. The Role of Law in the Church Today*, Baltimore, 1967.

―――――――――

*** This bibliography is a list of only those books or articles which have been referred to in the text or the notes of this study.

Broomfield, F., (Editor), *Thomae de Chobham Summa Confessorum* (*Analecta Mediaevalia Namurcensia*, volume 25), Louvain, 1968.

Brown, Peter, *Augustine of Hippo*, London, 1967.

Brundage, J.A., 'The Crusader's Wife: A Canonistic Quandary', *Studia Gratiana*, XII (1967), pp. 425-441.

——, 'The Crusader's Wife Revisited', *Studia Gratiana*, XIV (1967), pp. 241-251.

——, 'The Votive Obligations of Crusaders. The Development of a Canonistic Doctrine', *Traditio*, 24 (1968), pp. 77-118.

Calendar of the Close Rolls of the Reign of Henry III (1242-1247), Record Publications, London, 1916.

Calendar of the Patent Rolls preserved in the Public Record Office (1232-1247), London, 1906.

Cantini, J., *De autonomia iudicis saecularis et de Romani pontificis plenitudine potestatis in temporalibus secundum Innocentium IV*, Excerptum e dissertatione ad Lauream, Romae (Salesianum), 1962.

Caron, P.G., '"Aequitas" romana, "Misericordia" patristica ed "Epicheia" Aristotelica nella dottrina Decretalistica del duecento e trecento', *Studia Gratiana*, XIV (1967).

——, 'Ostiense (Enrico da Susa), *Novissimo Digesto Italiano*, 3rd ed., volume XII, Turin, 1965, pp. 283-285.

Coing, H., 'English Equity and the Denunciatio Evangelica of the Canon Law' *Law Quarterly Review*, 71 (1955), pp. 223-241.

Conway, J.D., 'Law and Renewal', *Jurist*, 26 (1966), pp. 413-425.

Didier, Noel, 'Henri de Suse en Angleterre (1236?-1244)', *Studi Arangio-Ruiz*, volume II, Naples, 1952, pp. 333-351.

——, 'Henri de Suse, prieur d'Antibes, prévôt de Grasse (1235?-1245)', *Studia Gratiana*, II (1954), pp. 595-617.

——, 'Henri de Suse, évêque de Sisteron (1244-1250)', *Nouvelle revue historique de droit français et étranger*, XXXI (1953), pp. 244-270; 409-429.

Dodd, C.H., *Gospel and Law*, Columbia University Press, New York, 1951.

Duggan, C., *Twelfth-Century Decretal Collections*, London, Athlone Press, 1963.

——, 'Decretals', *New Catholic Encyclopedia*, New York, 1967, volume 4.

Eschmann, I.T., O.P., 'St Thomas Aquinas on the Two Powers', *Mediaeval Studies*, 20 (1958), pp. 177-205.

Fedele, Pio, 'Primato pontificio et episcopato con particolare riferimento alla dottrina dell'Ostiense', *Studia Gratiana*, XIV (1967), pp. 351-367.

Forest, A., F. Van Steenberghen, and M. de Gaudillac, 'Le Mouvement Doctrinal', Fliche-Martin, *Histoire de l'Eglise*, volume 13, Paris, 1950.

Fuchs, Joseph, S.J., 'Theologia Moralis Perficienda', *Periodica*, LV (1966), pp. 499-548.

Gaudemet, J., 'La Doctrine des Sources du Droit dans le Décret de Gratien', *Revue de Droit Canonique*, I (1951), pp. 5-31.

——, 'Contribution à l'Etude de la Loi dans la Doctrine Canonique du XIIᵉ siècle', *Ius Canonicum*, 1967.

Ghellinck, J. de, S.J., *Le Mouvement Théologique du XIIᵉ Siècle*, 2nd ed., Brussels, 1948.

Gilchrist, J.T., 'Canon Law Aspects of the Eleventh-Century Gregorian Reform Programme', *Journal of Ecclesiastical History*, XIII (1962), pp. 21-38.

Glorieux, P., 'James of Viterbo', *New Catholic Encyclopedia*, New York, 1967, volume 7.

Granfield, P., O.S.B., 'The Right to Silence', *Theological Studies*, 27 (1966), pp. 401-420.

Hackett, J.H., 'State of the Church: A Concept of the Medieval Canonists', *The Jurist*, 23 (1963), pp. 259-290.

Hart, H.L.A., *The Concept of Law*, Oxford, 1961.

Haughton, R., 'The Changing Church: The Ending of the Law', *Doctrine and Life*, 18 (1968), pp. 86-90.

Hazeltine, Harold Dexter, 'Roman and Canon Law in the Middle Ages', *Cambridge History*, volume V, 1926, pp. 697-764.

Hellsig, O., 'Ein bisher übersehene Schrift des Henricus Hostiensis', *Deutsche Zeitschrift für Kirchenrecht*, series III, XIV (1904).

Helmholz, Richard, 'Canonists and Standards of Impartiality for Papal Judges Delegate', *Traditio*, 25 (1969), pp. 386-404.

Huizing, P., S.J., 'The Reform of Canon Law', *Concilium*, 8 (1965).

Kantorowicz, Hermann, 'Note on the Development of the Gloss to the Justinian and the Canon Law', in B. Smalley, *The Study of the Bible in the Middle Ages*, 2nd ed., Oxford, 1952, pp. 52-55.

——, 'Die Allegationen im späteren Mittelalter', *Archiv für Urkundenforschungen*, 13 (1933), pp. 15-29.

Kay, Richard, 'Hostiensis and Some Embrun Provincial Councils', *Traditio*, 20 (1964), pp. 503-513.

Kelly, J.M., *Roman Litigation*, Oxford, 1966.

Kemp, J.A., S.J., 'A New Concept of the Christian Commonwealth', *Proceedings of the Second International Congress of Medieval Canon Law*, Rome, 1965.

Kemp, E.W., *Counsel and Consent. Aspects of Church Government*, (The Bampton Lectures for 1960), London, 1961.

Knowles, David, *The Religious Orders in England*, Volume One, Cambridge, 1956.

Kuttner, S., *Repertorium der Kanonistik (1140-1234). Prodromus corporis glossarum I*, (Studi e Testi, 71), Vatican City, 1937.

——, 'Liber Canonicus. A Note on Dictatus Papae c. 17', *Studi Gregoriani*, Volume Two, Rome, 1947, pp. 387-401.

——, 'The scientific investigation of medieval canon law, the need and the opportunity', *Speculum*, XXIV (1949), pp. 493-501.

——, 'Some Considerations on the Role of Secular Law and Institutions in the History of Canon Law', *Scritti in Onore di Luigi Sturzo*, Volume Two, Bologna, 1953.

——, 'Methodological Problems concerning the History of Canon Law', *Speculum*, 30 (1955), pp. 539-549.

——, *Harmony from Dissonance. An Interpretation of Medieval Canon Law*, (Wimmer Lecture X), Pennsylvania, 1960.

——, 'Pope Lucius III and the Bigamous Archbishop of Palermo', *Medieval Studies Presented to Aubrey Gwynn, S.J.*, Dublin, 1961, pp. 409-453.

——, 'The Code of Canon Law in Historical Perspective', *The Jurist*, 28 (1968), pp. 129-148.

Landgraf, A.M., 'Diritto canonico e teologia nel secolo XII', *Studia Gratiana*, I (1953), pp. 371-413.

Le Bras, Gabriel, 'Canon Law', *The Legacy of the Middle Ages*, (Edited by C. G. Crump and E. F. Jacob), Oxford, 1926, pp. 321-361.

——, *Prolégomènes*, Paris, 1955.

——, *Institutions ecclésiastiques de la Chrétienté Médiévale: Préliminaires et Première Partie, Livre I*, (*Histoire de l'Eglise*, edited by Fliche et Martin) Volume XII, Paris, 1959.

——, 'Le droit classique de l'Eglise au service de l'homme', *Congrès de Droit Canonique Médiévale, 1958*, Louvain, 1959, pp. 104-110.

——, 'Théologie et droit romain dans l'oeuvre d'Henri de Suse', *Etudes historiques à la mémoire de Noel Didier*, Grenoble, 1960, pp. 195-204.

——, C. Lefebvre, and J. Rambaud, *L'Age Classique, 1140-1378. Sources et Théorie du Droit.* (Histoire du Droit et des Institutions de l'Eglise en Occident, Volume VII), Paris, 1965.

Lecler, Joseph, *Histoire de la Tolérance au Siècle de la Réforme*, Paris, 1955.

Lefebvre, Charles, 'Hostiensis', *Dictionnaire du Droit Canonique*, Volume V, 1953, col. 1211-1227.

——, ' "Aequitas canonica" et "periculum animae" dans la doctrine de l'Hostiensis', *Ephemerides Iuris Canonici*, 8 (1952), pp. 305-321.

——, 'La doctrine de l'Hostiensis sur la préférence à assurer en droit aux intérêts spirituels', *Ephemerides Iuris Canonici*, 8 (1952), pp. 24-44.

——, 'Rigueur et équité chez Innocent IV et Hostiensis', *Ephemerides Iuris Canonici*, 17 (1961), pp. 200-230.

——, 'Hostiensis', *New Catholic Encyclopedia*, New York, 1967, Volume 7.

Legendre, P., 'Le droit romain, modèle et language. De la signification de l'Utrumque Ius', *Etudes d'histoire du droit canonique dediées à Gabriel Le Bras*, Paris, 1965, Volume II, pp. 913-930.

——, *La Pénétration du Droit Romain dans le Droit Canonique Classique, 1140-1254*, Paris, 1964.

Lesage, G., *La Nature du Droit Canonique*, Ottawa, 1960.

Lombardia, P., 'Canon Law Today', *The Furrow*, September, 1969, pp. 444-453.

Lottin, O., *Psychologie et Morale aux XIIe et XIIIe Siècles*, Volume 1-6, Louvain-Gembloux, 1942-1960.

Lyonnet, S., *St Paul, Liberty and Law*, Rome, 1962.

Maccarone, M., *Chiesa e Stato nella Dottrina di Papa Innocenzo III*, Rome, 1940.

McKenzie, John, *The Power and the Wisdom*, London, 1965.

Michaud-Quantin, Pierre, *Sommes de Casuistique et Manuels de Confession au Moyen Age (XII-XVI Siècles)*, Analecta Mediaevalia Namurcensia, 13, Louvain, 1962.

Morey, A., *Bartholomew of Exeter, Bishop and Canonist*, Cambridge, 1937.

Nolin, J. B., [Dom Denys de Sainte-Marthe], *Gallia Christiana*, Volume Three, Paris, 1876.

O'Mahoney, D., 'Canon Law in the Seminary Today', *Irish Theological Quarterly*, 1967.

Orsy, L., S.J., 'Towards a Theological Conception of Canon Law', *The Jurist*, 24 (1964), pp. 383-392.

——, 'Quantity and Quality of Laws after Vatican II', *The Jurist*, 27 (1967), pp. 385-412.

Palazzini, P., 'Il diritto strumento di riforma ecclesiastica in S. Pier Damiani', *Ephemerides Iuris Canonici*, 11 (1955), pp. 361-408; 12 (1956), pp. 9-58.

Panziroli, Guido, *De Claris Legum Interpretibus*, Leipzig, 1721 (republished by Gregg, England, 1968).

Paul VI, *Allocutio ad E.mos Patres Cardinales et ad Consultores Pontificii Consilii Codici Iuris Canonici recognoscendo*, A.A.S., 1965, pp. 986-989.

Plucknett, T. F. T., *A Concise History of the Common Law*, 5th ed., London, 1965.

——, *Early English Legal Literature*, Cambridge, 1958.

Pollock, F., and F. W. Maitland, *The History of English Law*, 2nd ed., Cambridge, 1898, (Reissued with a new introduction and bibliography by S. F. C. Milsom, Cambridge, 1968).

Post, Gaines, *Studies in Medieval Legal Thought*, (Public Law and the State, 1100-1322), Princeton University Press, 1964.

Powicke, F. M., *Henry III and the Lord Edward*, Two Volumes, Oxford, 1947.

Rivera Damas, A., *Pensamiento Politico de Hostiensis*, Zürich, 1964.

Rodes, R. E., 'A Suggestion for the Renewal of Canon Law', *The Jurist*, 26 (1966), pp. 272-307.

——, 'The Canon Law as a Legal System — Function, Obligation, and Sanction', *Natural Law Forum*, 9 (1964), Indiana, 1964, pp. 45-94.

Russell, J., S.J., *The Sanatio in Radice before the Council of Trent*, Rome, 1964.

Russo, F., 'Pénitence et excommunication: étude historique sur les rapports entre la théologie et le droit canon dans le domaine pénitentiel du 9e au 13e siècle', *Recherches de Sciences Religieuses*, 1946.

Ryan, J. J., *St Peter Damian and His Canonical Sources: A Preliminary Study of the Gregorian Reform*, (Studies and Texts, 2), Institute of Medieval Studies, Toronto, 1956.

Sarti, M., & M. Fattorini, *De Claris Archigymnasii Bononiensis Professoribus a saeculo XI usque ad saeculum XIV*, (Edited by C. Albicinius Foroliviensis and C. Malagola), Bologna, 1888-96.

Schulte, J. F. von, *Die Geschichte der Quellen und Literatur des canonischen Rechts von Gratian bis auf die Gegenwart*, Three Volumes, Stuttgart, 1875-1877.

Sheehan, M. M., 'Canon Law and English Institutions', *Proceedings of the Second International Congress of Medieval Canon Law*, Rome, 1965, pp. 391-397.

Sohm, Rudolph, *Kirchenrecht*, Band I. *Die Geschichtlichen Grundlagen*, Leipzig, 1892.

Southern, R. W., *The Making of the Middle Ages*, London, 1953.

——, *Western Society and the Church in the Middle Ages*, (The Pelican History of the Church, Volume Two), Penguin Books, 1970.

Stickler, A., 'Concerning the Political Theories of the Medieval Canonists', *Traditio*, 7 (1949-51), pp. 450-463.

——, *Historia Iuris Canonici Latini. I. Historia Fontium*, Turin, 1950.

Tierney, Brian, *Foundations of the Conciliar Theory*, Cambridge, 1955.

——, 'Papal Political Theory in the Thirteenth Century. Some Methodological Considerations', *Medieval Studies*, XXVII (1965), pp. 227-245.

——, 'Some Recent Works on the Political Theories of the Medieval Canonists', *Traditio*, 10 (1954), pp. 594-625.

——, 'Hostiensis and Collegiality', *Proceedings of the Fourth International Congress of Medieval Canon Law*, Rome, 1976, pp. 401-409.
——, *Medieval Poor Law. A Sketch of Canonical Theory and Its Application in England*. University of California Press, 1959.
Ullmann, Walter, *Law and Politics in the Middle Ages*, London, 1975.
——, *Medieval Papalism. The Political Theories of the Medieval Canonist*, London, 1949.
——, *A Medieval Idea of Law*, London, 1946.
——, *The Growth of Papal Government in the Middle Ages*, London, 1955.
——, 'The Significance of Innocent III's Decretal "Vergentis"', *Etudes d'Histoire du Droit Canonique*, Paris, 1965, Volume One, pp. 729-741.
Van Hove, A., *Prolegomena*, 2nd ed., Malines-Rome, 1945.
Van de Kerckhove, M., 'La Notion de Juridiction chez les Décretistes et les Premiers Décrétalistes (1140-1250), *Etudes Franciscaines*, 49 (1937), pp. 420 ff.
Vereeke, L., 'Moral Theology, History of', *New Catholic Encyclopedia*, New York, 1967, Volume 9.
Villey, M., *La Croisade*, Paris, 1942.
Vinogradoff, Paul, *Roman Law in Medieval Europe*, 3rd ed., Oxford, 1961.
Watt, J. A., 'The Term "Plenitudo Potestatis" in Hostiensis', *Proceedings of the Second International Congress of Medieval Canon Law*, Rome, 1965, pp. 162-187.
——, 'The Theory of Papal Monarchy in the Thirteenth Century. The Contribution of the Canonists', *Traditio*, 20 (1964), pp. 179-317. (Also published separately as a book under the same title by Burns and Oates, London, 1965).
——, 'Medieval Deposition Theory: A Neglected *Consultatio* from the First Council of Lyons', *Studies in Church History*, 2 (1965), pp. 197-214.
——, 'The Constitutional Law of the College of Cardinals: Hostiensis to Joannes Andreae', *Mediaeval Studies*, 33 (1971), pp. 127-157.
Wretschko, A. von, 'Ein Traktat des Kardinals Hostiensis mit Glossen betreffend die Abfassung von Wahldekreten bei der Bischofswahl', *Deutsche Zeitschrift für Kirchenrecht*, 3rd series, XVII (1907), pp. 73-88.

INTRODUCTION

In the present climate of criticism of law within the Church and the widespread distaste for anything that savours of a juridical approach to religion, a canonist cannot but ask himself what his place in the Christian community should be. Has he a useful role to play in the modern Church? To be able to answer this question implies, of course, that a satisfactory answer can be given to the more fundamental question about the role that law itself should play in the Christian community. What precisely is the function of law in the life of the Church? This question has particular importance today because unless it is clear what the law is trying to accomplish, really meaningful reform of the law will be difficult if not impossible.

Canon law tends to be despised and rejected by many today. Those who reject it are often deeply convinced Christians who see law as leading inevitably towards a sort of pelagianism and the self-satisfaction of that morality of law which was condemned so vehemently by St Paul. The very term 'juridical' has become in some quarters a synonym for all that is narrow, rigid, reactionary and closed to growth and development of any kind. Some years ago Professor Kuttner described the situation in these words:

> To many of us, clergy or lay, the law of the Church appears as no more than a sum of dry technical rules for ecclesiastical administrators and judges, the rubrics, as it were, of ecclesiastical routine, or even worse, a stifling instrument of regimentation. [1]

In short, many Catholics look upon canon law not as a guide, but as a straitjacket, and they dismiss it as, at best, irrelevant to the modern Church.

What lies behind this rejection of canon law? Many factors have contributed to the situation but among the more important of these is the irrelevance to modern life of many canons in

---

[1] S. Kuttner, *Harmony from Dissonance. An Interpretation of Medieval Canon Law*, Pennsylvania, 1960, p. 5.

the present Code.   The large number of *latae sententiae* censures, and the failure to be specific about the rights of the laity are examples of the defects which need to be remedied.   Perhaps even more important than the shortcomings of the Code itself have been the formalism and narrow-mindedness of a number of canon lawyers who studied and taught the law in a formalistic way and applied it woodenly without reference to the *ratio legis*. Some critics go so far as to say that there is no place for law within the Christian community as such because the guidance of the Holy Spirit has replaced all need for it.   There is, it has been argued, an opposition between Gospel and Law.[2]

There are others who reluctantly agree to keep *some* law in the Church, but only because this is considered a necessary evil, an external restraint needed because of man's sinful state. As one recent American writer puts it; 'Law is for the *ungodly* and it becomes functional to the extent that the option to live a life of Christian liberty is not seized upon'.[3]

The implication of such remarks as this would seem to be that there is and must be a real opposition between the Spirit of God and any kind of external law.   It seems to presume that the transforming power of the Spirit *cannot* be fully operative in anyone whose actions are 'constrained' by an external law.   To follow any kind of law is to be shackled in some way; it is to be unfree.   Fr Lyonnet's interpretation of St Paul's teaching on freedom from the law adopts this view and it is shared by many modern Catholics.[4]   Whether it is what St Paul himself meant in those well-known passages is quite another question and one that cannot be investigated here.[5]

---

[2] Cf. for example, John McKenzie, *The Power and the Wisdom*, London, 1965, p. 227.   This approach recalls the views of Rudolph Sohm who held that canon law contradicts the very nature of the Church. 'Das Wesen der Kirchenrechts steht mit dem Wesen der Kirche in Widerspruch'.   The organisation of the Church, he maintained, should be charismatic, not juridical.   It should be a uniquely sacramental organisation.   Cf. R. Sohm, *Kirchenrecht, Band I.   Die geschichtlichen Grundlagen*, Leipzig, 1892, p. 26 and p. 700 (quoted by G. Lesage, *La Nature du Droit Canonique*, Ottawa, 1960, p. 8 and p. 24).

[3] J. E. Biechler (Editor), *Law for Liberty*, Baltimore, 1967, p. 135.

[4] S. Lyonnet, *St Paul, Liberty and Law*, Pontificio Istituto Biblico, Rome, 1962.

J. McKenzie, *The Power and the Wisdom;* R. Haughton, 'The Changing Church: The Ending of the Law', *Doctrine and Life*, February, 18 (1968) pp. 86-90.

[5] Cf. C. H. Dodd, *Gospel and Law*, Columbia University Press, New York, 1951.

Along with this rejection of the rigidity and restrictions imposed by canon law there has however, also been a movement demanding more law, or rather, a different sort of law. There has been a demand for better legal protection in a variety of circumstances. An example of this can be seen in the open letter signed by a number of eminent theologians asking that freedom for research and theological inquiry should be guaranteed by law.[6] These men want to see the basic rights and duties of the Christian written into the law of the Church, including the right to protection from arbitrary denunciation, the right to be heard and to be able to defend oneself and so on. Catholics in the United States are particularly concerned with the importance of 'Due Process' for the law of the Church.

The Church has already moved some way towards meeting these demands. The reform of the old Holy Office provides an example of this. The Index of prohibited books has been abolished, the strict secrecy of the past has been modified and provision has been made for the defence of writers whose work has been attacked.[7] The revised code will, it is hoped, contain many other examples. Enough has been said, however, to show that the question about the role of law in the Church is by no means simply an academic exercise. It does have some bearing on the well-being of the whole Christian community.

It was this current concern with the function of law in the Church that suggested an inquiry into the medieval Church. What did the canonists of the Classical Period think the role of canon law should be? How do their problems compare with those of today? An examination of the views of canonists of the period when canon law was at the height of its power and prestige might produce information that would be of help in the attempts to solve modern problems. What then did medieval canonists think about the function of law in the Church? The function of canon law was not, of course, in the Middle Ages the problem that it is today. Ecclesiastical authority was accepted as essential to the idea of Christendom. There were, it is true, a variety of views on how the Church and the State should be related with each other in the government of countries and these differences frequently developed into violent conflicts. But the conflicts were concerned mainly with the relative posi-

---

6 Cf. *Herder Correspondence,* 6 (1969), 46-49.

7 Cf. Motu Proprio, *'Integrae Servandae',* of December 7, 1965, in *A.A.S.* LVII (1965), p. 952-955.

2

tion of the authorities of Church and State. They did not affect
the fundamental acceptance of the law of the Church as a force
that bound all the members of Christendom. Both the law of
the Church and the law of the State were looked upon as
integral constituents of medieval society and were respected as
such. In these circumstances canon law was not the object
of passionate questioning that it has become today. That it
had important functions to perform for society in general was
simply taken for granted. Consequently we shall look in vain
for long and formal treatises by medieval lawyers on the role
of canon law. Other more practical problems occupied their
attention. They did not, however, leave the question unmen-
tioned even if they touched on it only briefly and, as it were,
en passant. To uncover what the medieval canonists thought
was the role or function of canon law in the Church (though
they formulated the question somewhat differently), one has to
a certain extent to read between the lines of their voluminous
commentaries. Their idea of the function of law might perhaps
be gleaned from their concept of the nature of law. If, for
example, canon law was held to be an authoritative declaration
of God's will for the Christian community, then its function
would be to specify, to clarify, to make explicit God's will for
man. Further light too might be gained by considering carefully
what the law was actually doing for the community and what
society expected it to be doing. All this, of course, involves
more than a glance at the medieval collections of canon law as
well as a study of the commentaries on these.

What role did medieval canonists think that canon law
should play in the Church? This is the question to which a
clear answer is desirable, and yet to obtain a fully adequate
answer would involve a detailed study of the principal canonists
of the Classical Period. A start has, however, to be made some-
where and the careful examination of the writings of *one* of
the most distinguished thirteenth-century canon lawyers — Cardinal Hostiensis — will, it is hoped, provide the beginnings of
an answer to our question and form a positive contribution to
the current discussion about the function that law should have
in the Christian community. It is this that is being attempted
in these pages.

The first chapter of this work provides a brief description
of the life and writings of the thirteenth-century canonist, Henry
of Susa (c. 1200-1271), together with an explanation of why this
particular writer has been chosen as the subject of the investiga-

tion.   Secondly, since it is important to see the *Summa Aurea* within its medieval context, a chapter has been added giving an outline of the thirteenth-century juridical background and a short account of the canonical tradition that Hostiensis inherited. This is followed by a detailed examination of the views on canon law which Hostiensis expressed in his *Summa Aurea* in an attempt to discover what precisely he took to be the function or functions of canon law within the Christian community. The scheme for the investigation has been taken from a short passage in the preface to the *Summa* in which Hostiensis himself indicates seven functions of law.   These seven functions provide the divisions of the dissertation.

First of all, the law's provision for stability, security and concord in society is examined in detail.   This is followed by a discussion of Hostiensis' views on how the law fulfilled the role of delineating rights and duties and how it provided protection for these rights by means of due legal process.   Chapter Six gives an account of Hostiensis' thought on the role of canon law as a guide to Christian living, as an instrument of moral reform within the church and as a deterrent against the evils of heresy.   Finally, by way of a general conclusion, a brief summary is given of the results of the whole investigation and a comparison is drawn between the views of our medieval canonist and the current approach to canon law in the church.

CHAPTER ONE

CARDINAL HOSTIENSIS: HIS LIFE AND WORK

1. *The Importance of Hostiensis*

Henry of Susa, better known as Cardinal Hostiensis, has been chosen as the subject of this investigation for a variety of reasons. First of all, the period when he lived coincided with the Golden Age of Classical Canon Law. His activity as a canon lawyer stretched from around 1230 until 1271 and so he was able to profit from the legal renaissance and the rapid development of canon law that took place in the late twelfth and early thirteenth centuries. In Roman law Azo's influential *Summa Codicis* had been published in the first quarter of the century and his pupil, Accursius (d. 1260), was compiling what was soon to become the *glossa ordinaria* for Roman law. In 1234 Pope Gregory IX's historic compilation, the *Decretales*, had been produced by Raymond of Peñafort and within ten years or so Bernard of Parma's commentary had become the *glossa ordinaria* for the decretal collection, just as some years earlier the *glossa ordinaria* on the *Decretum* had been published by Bartholomaeus Brixiensis in his revision of the work of John Teutonicus. By 1241 Goffredus Tranensis, a curial cardinal, had produced the first *Summa in Titulis Decretalium*.

Henry of Susa was, therefore, in a position to draw on the decretist and decretalist publications which had been produced since the appearance of Gratian's *Decretum* almost a century earlier. His *Summa Aurea*, completed around the year 1253, was thus produced at a time when the best thirteenth-century legal work was readily available, and it provides what is probably the most comprehensive survey of decretalist thought of that period when classical canon law was at its height. Hostiensis was also able to benefit from the remarkable renaissance in theology that took place in the first half of the thirteenth century. [1]

---

[1] J.A. Watt has drawn attention to this aspect of his work: 'As an

He was too a prolific writer and when he discussed a problem he generally did so at considerable length.   He himself
acknowledged this several times in his work, and in his own
defence he was fond of quoting a saying of an old teacher of
his to the effect that deep and important problems cannot easily
be dealt with briefly, and that when he tries to be brief he
becomes obscure.[2]   J. A. Watt sees in this comprehensiveness
an added reason for paying special attention to Hostiensis:

> Hostiensis wrote with considerable clarity and at length, even
> verbosely.   After the laconic commentary of Innocent IV, in
> whose writing ambiguities are often caused as much by his
> omissions as by any inherent complexity of the matter at
> issue, the repetitiveness of Hostiensis is a welcome aid to
> understanding.[3]

The writings, therefore, of Henry of Susa provide as complete
a survey of medieval jurisprudence as one could hope to find
in the work of any single medieval canonist.   There are, moreover, quite a variety of early printed editions of his books
readily available in university libraries.
    Another reason for choosing Hostiensis lies in the great
influence that he exerted both in his own lifetime and on later
canonists.   He is one of the best known of thirteenth-century
canonists, was highly esteemed by his contemporaries and influential for a long time after his death.   This is clear from
the glowing tributes paid to his work by contemporary canonists and later writers.   William Durandus (1237-1296), for
example, himself a distinguished canon lawyer of the second
half of the thirteenth century, was an ardent admirer of Hostiensis, whom he regarded as his master, and at the beginning

---

academic he ranks as the first to furnish a great synthesis of ecclesiastical
jurisprudence; his works denote the final achievement of its maturity
as an autonomous sacred discipline, nourished by both theology and
Roman law, but yet consciously distinct from them.   His political views
reflect this balance of canon law between theology and law: they are
themselves distinctively canonist in their expression, but Hostiensis did
not hesitate to borrow from theologians and especially civilians if his
positions might thereby be strengthened'.   J. A. Watt, 'The Theory of
Papal Monarchy in the Thirteenth Century', *Traditio* 20 (1964), p. 281.
    [2] ' Sed sic dicebat dominus meus, nequeunt de facili magna et ardua
verba brevibus expedire, et dum brevis esse laboro obscurus fio', *Summa*,
I, *Prooemium*, n. 2. Cf. also *Apparatus*, V, 38, 3, s.v. *longum esset*.
    [3] J. A. Watt, 'The Theory of Papal Monarchy', *Traditio*, 20 (1964), p. 282.

of his own canonical commentary he lists Hostiensis and Innocent IV as by far the two greatest canonists of the century:

> Novissime autem due stelle lucidissime nostris temporibus ruti-
> larunt, videlicet sanctissime recordationis dominus Innocentius
> Papa IV ..., pater iuris, et reverendus pater dominus meus
> Henricus Dei gratia Hostiensis episcopus, lumen iuris, quorum
> veneranda memoria fulget ut splendor firmamenti perpetui
> velut stelle in eternitates permansure ...; cum in hoc cunctos
> incomparabiliter transcenderint cuiusque magnitudinem maiori
> excellentia obumbrantes ..., sicut eorum opera indicant eviden-
> ter. Quicquid namque alibi circa iuris theoricam quaeritur in
> eorum scriptis perfectissime reperitur.[4]

This reputation was maintained among later writers who could
refer to Hostiensis in such terms as 'pater canonum et doctor
supremus', 'fons et monarcha iuris', and so on.[5]   Eighteenth-
century historians of Bologna numbered him among the most
distinguished jurists that university had ever produced,[6] and
his commentary on the Decretals was classed with those of
Innocent IV and Joannes Andreae as carrying greater weight
than any other commentaries on canon law.[7] It would seem
too from Dante's *Paradiso* that the phrase, 'to be a follower
of Hostiensis', was used as an equivalent for the study of canon
law.[8] This mention by Dante is itself a clear indication of how
green the memory of Hostiensis remained some fifty years after
his death.

    Among modern historians too the reputation of Henry of
Susa has remained undimmed.   He is described as 'the most

---

[4] William Durandus, *Speculum iudiciale*, in *Prooemio*.

[5] Thomas Diplovatatius, (1468-1541), *De claris iuris consultis*, (Edited
by H. Kantorowicz and F. Schulz), Berlin, 1909, p. 141.

[6] Cf. M. Sarti et M. Fattorini, *De Claris Archigymnasii Bononiensis
Professoribus* (1888 edition), Bononiae, Volume I, pp. 439 & 443:
'Ab his doctoribus in academia nostra eruditus, docere ipse coepit
tanto plausu, ut inter professores juris canonici superiorem habuisse
non videatur'. 'Quemadmodum dum viveret ob doctrinae praestantiam
summo in honore habitus est et ad amplissimas dignitates postulatus,
ita post mortem perennis eius fama fuit, nec umquam eius memoria
extincta est; quod paucis contigit. Pater canonum, fons et monarcha
iuris, stella ac lumen lucidissimum decretorum appellatus est.'

[7] Thomas Diplovatatius, *op. cit.*, p. 145.

[8] Dante, *Paradiso*, Canto XII, v. 82:
> 'Non per lo mondo, per cui mo s'affanna
> Di retro ad Ostiense e a Taddeo,
> Ma per amor della verace manna.'

famous canonist of the century', [9] 'the best canon lawyer of the day', [10] and 'l'un des plus illustres juristes du moyen âge'. [11] Professor Tierney lists the writings of Innocent IV and Hostiensis among 'the supreme achievements of medieval canonistic science'. He continues:

> These two great masters, whose forceful and sometimes conflicting views on ecclesiastical authority dominated the canonistic speculations of the second half of the thirteenth century, retained the attractive vitality and intellectual adventurousness of their predecessors but combined these qualities with a more mature scholarship which gave an added depth and precision to their works. No inquiry into medieval theories of Church government can afford to neglect the views of such eminent and influential masters. [12]

Referring to Hostiensis' mastery of Roman as well as canon law, Mgr C. Lefebvre describes the *Summa Aurea* as 'l'aboutissement de l'effort scientifique des glossateurs et des canonistes du siècle anterieur; elle est l'élément de base du *ius commune* en voie de formation'. [13] Professor P. G. Caron concurs with this and regards the *Summa Aurea* as the most complete synthesis available of Roman and canon law, and maintains that it represents 'una delle più alte vette del pensiero giuridico'. [14] The *Summa* also provides, in the view of Lefebvre, a fine synthesis of both decretist and decretalist legislation:

> Le developpement rigoureusement logique des institutions jusqu'à la législation grégorienne est mis en relief avec une clarté dont ses prédécesseurs n'ont pu faire preuve à un tel dégré. [15]

These modern scholars also agree that Hostiensis may be taken as a typical representative of what is best in medieval

---

[9] F. M. Powicke, *Henry III and the Lord Edward*, Oxford, 1947, vol. I, p. 273.

[10] R. W. Southern, *Western Society and the Church in the Middle Ages*, Penguin, London, 1970, p. 128.

[11] N. Didier, 'Henri de Suse, Prieur d'Antibes', *Studia Gratiana*, II (1954), p. 595.

[12] B. Tierney, *Foundations of the Conciliar Theory*, Cambridge, 1955, p. 17.

[13] C. Lefebvre, in Le Bras, Lefebvre and Rambaud, *L'Age Classique*, Paris, 1965, p. 313.

[14] P. G. Caron, '*Aequitas* romana, *Misericordia* patristica ed *Epicheia* Aristotelica nella dottrina Decretalistica del duecento e trecento', *Studia Gratiana*, XIV (1967) p. 316.

[15] Lefebvre, *L'Age Classique*, p. 313.

canonistic writing. This is the declared view of eminent historians of medieval canon law of the calibre of Mgr. Charles Lefebvre and Professor Le Bras and it is shared by other modern writers. Lefebvre describes the *Summa Aurea* as 'L'une des plus représentative du droit médiéval',[16] and Le Bras considers Hostiensis as probably *the* representative of the decretalist compilers of *summae*.[17] He is also included by Le Bras among the four doctors of the classical age of canon law, — the other three being Bernard of Parma, Innocent IV and William Durandus.[18] Finally, Dr J. A. Watt thinks of Hostiensis as typifying the canonistic writing of the thirteenth century.[19] 'He wrote with an unrivalled knowledge and understanding of earlier canonist literature and was thus a truly representative product of the canonist tradition.'[20]

Enough evidence has now been given to show that the writings of Cardinal Hostiensis — and particularly his *Summa super Titulis Decretalium* — are of outstanding importance for the student of medieval canon law and merit special attention. Further justification for the choice of the *Summa Aurea* as the subject of this investigation would seem then to be unnecessary. There is, however, another reason which has not yet been mentioned.

A glance at the three large folio volumes that together make up the *Summa Aurea* and the *Apparatus*, — comprising more than 5,000 folio columns of closely printed text in the sixteenth-century editions, — might produce the impression that we are dealing with the work of a man who spent his life in scholarly retirement. Nothing could be further from the truth. In his lifetime he was respected both as a canonist and as a diplomat by popes and kings. He won the respect of Pope Innocent IV and was the trusted counsellor of Alexander IV and of Urban IV who made him a cardinal and appointed him to the most distinguished post in the Roman Curia, the bishopric of Ostia. But it was not only in ecclesiastical circles that his

---

[16] Lefebvre, *L'Age Classique*, p. 312.

[17] Le Bras, *L'Age Classique*, p. 25, note 4.

[18] G. Le Bras, 'Théologie et droit romain dans l'oeuvre d'Henri de Suse', *Etudes Historiques à la memoire de Noël Didier*. Grenoble, 1960, p. 195.

[19] J. A. Watt, 'The Theory of Papal Monarchy ...', *Traditio*, 20 (1964), p. 281.

[20] J. A. Watt, "The Use of the Term 'Plenitudo Potestatis' by Hostiensis", in *Proceedings of the Second International Congress of Medieval Canon Law*. (Edited by S. Kuttner and J. J. Ryan), Vatican City, 1965, p. 162.

influence was felt. He was on friendly terms with King Henry III of England and, as will be seen shortly, was employed
by him on a number of important diplomatic missions. He was
also respected and consulted by King Louis IX of France. It is
not then surprising to find him regarded by some modern writers
as among the most interesting of thirteenth-century canonists.
There were few who combined so signally an active life both
pastorally and diplomatically in the highest European political
circles with such high academic distinction. This is a factor
that gives his views on the law a particular interest.

> Based on an extremely thorough knowledge of canonist and
> civilian literature, they were written by a man with long and
> intimate experience of political affairs both in the curia and
> outside. There is therefore a vein of actuality running through
> his work which gives it an immediacy often felt to be lacking
> in more purely academic writers of the period. [21]

Clearly Henry of Susa was a man of outstanding ability,
experience and influence who was closely involved in the highest
ecclesiastical and political affairs in the middle of the thirteenth
century. The views of such a man on the role of canon law
in the Church are certainly worth serious consideration. But
before these are examined something must briefly be said about
his life.

2. Brief Biography of Hostiensis

a) Early Years

About the boyhood and youth of Cardinal Hostiensis very
little is known. [22] He himself informs us that he was born in

---

[21] J. A. Watt, 'Theory of Papal Monarchy ...', *Traditio*, 20 (1964), p. 282.
[22] This brief summary of the life of Hostiensis in greatly indebted
to the following works, in particular to the three masterly studies by
Professor Noel Didier who unfortunately did not live to take his biography
beyond the year 1250.
N. Didier, 'Henri de Suse, prieur d'Antibes, prévôt de Grasse (1235-1245)',
    Studia Gratiana, II, (1954), pp. 595-617.
N. Didier, 'Henri de Suse en Angleterre (1236?-1244)', *Studi Arangio-Ruiz*,
    Naples, 1952, Volume II, pp. 333-351.
N. Didier, 'Henri de Suse, Evêque de Sisteron (1244-1250)', *Nouvelle revue
    de droit français et étranger*, XXXI, 1953, pp. 244-170; 409-429.
Matthew Paris, *Matthei Parisiensis, monachi Sancti Albani, Chronica
    majora.* Edited by H. R. Luard (*Rerum Britannicarum Medii Aevi
    Scriptores*), vols. III and IV, London, 1877.

Piedmont in the town of Secusia, or Susa as it is now called, not far from Turin.[23]   And he is referred to as 'Henricus de Secusia' in a letter of Pope Innocent IV in 1244.[24]   The date of his birth is not known with certainty but he was probably born in the year 1200 or perhaps a few years earlier.   He may have come of a noble family for he is sometimes referred to by later writers as Henricus de Bartholomaeis.   He studied law at Bologna about the same time as Sinibald Fieschi, later to become Pope Innocent IV, and his teachers were Jacobus de Albenga, in canon law, and Jacobus Balduino and Homobono, in Roman law.   There is a tradition that he also taught at Bologna for a spell but, though Schulte thought this very probable, there is no clear evidence for it.

Nor is it known when he moved from Italy to Provence and Paris.   The Counts of Savoy had a residence at Susa and it may be that the young canonist was quite early befriended by the family and taken into their service.   What is certain is that Henry was throughout his life a close friend and adviser of Beatrice of Savoy who married Raymond Berengar, Count of Provence, in 1220.   So it may have been the Countess who introduced Henry to Provence and supported the advancement of his career in both Church and State.   The Countess Beatrice was undoubtedly to be a friend with unusual influence in Europe.   Her two eldest daughters became the queens of France and England, her third married Henry III's younger brother, and Sanchia, the youngest, was to become the wife of Charles of Anjou in 1246 and the new Countess of Provence.   To be a friend of such a family could not but brighten anyone's prospects for promotion.   This connection would explain how Henry of Susa came to be employed by the Count of Provence on a

---

Calendar of the Patent Rolls preserved in the Public Record Office, Henry III (1232-1247), London, 1906.

Calendar of the Close Rolls of the reign of Henry III (1242-1247), London, 1916.

C. Lefebvre, 'Hostiensis' in Dictionnaire du Droit Canonique, vol. V, col. 1211-1227.

J. F. Schulte, Die Geschichte der Quellen und Literatur des canonischen Rechts, Stuttgart, 1875-1880, volume II, pp. 123 ff.

M. Sarti et M. Fattorini, De claris archigymnasii Bononiensis professoribus a saeculo XI ad saeculum XIV, (new edition by C. Albicinius and C. Malagola), Bologna, 1888-96, volume I, pp. 439-445.

[23] Cf. Summa Aurea, I, De rescriptis, n. 23: 'de Secusia oriundum'; see also Apparatus, I, 3 (de rescriptis), 28, n. 7: 'a Secusia unde originem duxi'.

[24] Cf. Didier, 'Henri de Suse, prieur d'Antibes ...', Studia Gratiana, II, p. 600.

number of important missions and how he appears to have
acted for a time as a sort of liaison between Provence and the
court of Henry III of England.

Henry must have begun lecturing at Paris around the early
thirties of the thirteenth century, but again clear evidence is
lacking. In a passage in the *Summa Aurea*, which can be dated
to the year 1239, he states that it was he himself who could
be identified as the person who was archdeacon of Paris, who
lectured on the Decretals and who held benefices both in England and in Provence.[25] How long he held this teaching post
in Paris is not known but his lectureship there could not have
lasted for long after 1239 on account of the other business
that claimed his time and attention. Yet his teaching at Paris
was to have extremely important results since it was there that
he began both the *Summa Aurea* and the *Apparatus* on the
Decretals.

b) *Provost of the Cathedral Chapter (1234-1245)*

Professor Didier has argued persuasively that Henry of Susa
must have become prior of the cathedral chapter of Antibes
in southern Provence sometime before 1234 or 1235.[26] There
was at this time a dispute between the canons and the bishop
over the diocesan property which was jointly owned by bishop
and chapter. The canons pressed for a division but the bishop
would not agree. Finally, in 1239, both parties agreed to submit
the matter to the arbitration of the metropolitan, Aymar, Archbishop of Embrun. At this point, however, proceedings were
suspended because of the departure of the prior to England
on business, and it was not until two years later that the matter
was resumed and the archbishop — with the agreement of both
bishop and chapter — entrusted Henry of Susa with the task
of dividing the diocesan property. This provides a clear indication of the esteem which the canonist enjoyed both inside
and outside the diocese. The business was completed in September, 1242.

At this same time the metropolitan reorganised the diocese
of Antibes. The canons were to be distributed between the
churches of Antibes and Grasse, and Henry of Susa was made

---

[25] *Summa*, I, De rescriptis, n. 23. For the dating of this passage, see
Didier, 'Henri de Suse, prieur d'Antibes ...', *Studia Gratiana*, II, pp. 606-607.

[26] Didier, 'Henri de Suse, prieur d'Antibes ...', *Studia Gratiana*, II,
p. 610.

provost of the reconstructed chapter with a residence in both towns. It is as provost, rather than prior, that Henry appears in a document, dated 21 September, 1242, in which Count Raymond Berengar, in return for services rendered, confirms him in the possession of the 'château de La Moute'.[27] This is but one example of the many such papers in which the name of Henry of Susa is linked with that of the ruling family of Provence. He was clearly *persona grata* there.

Nothing further is known of Henry's activity in Antibes until the summer of 1244 when Innocent IV transferred the episcopal see from Antibes to Grasse. The provostship of Antibes became then the provostship of Grasse and remained in the hands of Henry. That same year new diocesan statutes were drawn up by bishop and provost which gave the provost and the chapter a greater degree of independence than they had previously enjoyed. Henry and the chapter were in fact later accused of ruining the old bishop who, when he died a short time later, did not leave enough money even to cover his funeral expenses.[28] There may be some truth in the report. The reforms had given greater independence to the chapter and improved the position of the provost, but it was the old bishop who was blamed for the pitiful state of the diocese — both materially and spiritually — in a letter to his successor from Innocent IV in 1245. The diocesan records show that new regulations were drawn up for Grasse in 1246, when Henry had left the diocese, in which the duties of the provost were defined in terms which suggest that the previous holder of that office had acted somewhat too independently of both the bishop and the rest of the chapter. By this time, however, Henry had become Bishop of Sisteron and was frequently with Innocent IV at the papal court in Lyons. The new provost of Grasse was Otto Fornari who had perhaps been given the benefice by Henry himself by virtue of an apostolic commission he had received from Innocent IV.[29]

While holding his teaching post in Paris and his benefice in Provence Henry of Susa seems to have spent a considerable time in England. It is probable that he first came to England towards the beginning of 1236 in the entourage of Eleanor of

[27] *Ibid.*, p. 612.

[28] Didier, 'Henri de Suse, prieur d'Antibes ...', *Studia Gratiana*, II (1954), p. 614, n. 99.

[29] *Ibid.*, p. 613.

Provence who married Henry III of England in that year.
Eleanor was the second daughter of Raymond Berengar, Count
of Provence, and Beatrice of Savoy; her elder sister had married Louis IX of France several years previously. Henry of
Susa, the Savoyard prior of Antibes in Provence, as has been
suggested above, would have been already well known to the
ruling family of the county. It is not unlikely that he held
an important place among the followers of the new queen's
uncle, William of Savoy, bishop-elect of Valence, who was soon
to become a close and influential friend and adviser of Henry III.
It may have been this connection that led to his playing a
leading role in the dramatic conflict between the king and
William Raleigh over the see of Winchester.

By the early thirties of the thirteenth century the Devonshire lawyer, William Raleigh, had spent many years in the
king's service and had become the leader of the king's judges. [30]
Around the year 1238 he decided to retire from the Bench and
he expected that his service to the king would be rewarded by
the grant of a bishopric. At this point Winchester, one of the
most opulent of English dioceses, became vacant and the chapter
wished to elect Raleigh as the new bishop. Henry III was opposed to this and made it plain that he wanted William of
Savoy to be the new bishop of Winchester. The chapter, however, refused to elect the Savoyard and postulated instead Ralph
Nevill, Bishop of Chichester and Chancellor of England. This
infuriated the king who appealed at once to the pope against
the postulation and sent two lawyers to the papal court to
state his case. Henry of Susa may have accompanied the royal
delegation since he is known to have been at Arles in August,
1239, and back in Antibes in December of the same year. Pope
Gregory IX allowed the king's appeal and appointed William
of Savoy to the see of Winchester, while Raleigh had to content
himself with the bishopric of Norwich.

This settlement of the problem was, however, short-lived.
William of Savoy died suddenly in October, 1239, leaving Winchester once again without a bishop. In May of the following
year the chapter went ahead with its own plans and postulated
William Raleigh. The king again objected, encouraged, it would
appear, in his opposition by Henry of Susa who was by this

---

[30] Cf. F. Pollock and F. W. Maitland, *History of English Law*, 2nd edn.,
1898 (re-issued with a new introduction by S. F. C. Milsom, 1968), vol. I,
p. 196.

time back in England. Since Raleigh was already bishop of
Norwich his translation to Winchester required papal approval
and this gave the king an opportunity to send another delegation to Rome. But before any settlement was reached Gregory
IX died in August, 1241. His successor, Celestine IV, died a
few weeks after his election, and, because of the difficulties
raised by Frederick II, it was almost two years before a new
pope was elected. During this time Raleigh continued as bishop
of Norwich and the king collected the revenues of the vacant
see of Winchester, with his own nominee as prior.

Meanwhile Henry of Susa improved his position at court
and was the recipient of a number of royal favours. He was
drawing a salary from the exchequer in 1240 and in the following year he was appointed prior of the Hospital of St Cross
near Winchester which yielded a substantial annual income.[31]
In this appointment Henry is described as a 'royal clerk'. In
the spring of 1242 the king sent a new delegation to the papal
court which included Master Henry of Susa. A variety of business had to be dealt with. The election of Boniface of Savoy
as Archbishop of Canterbury required papal confirmation, and
there was the Winchester problem to be settled. There was
other business too to be transacted, for in July, 1242, Henry
of Susa was present at Tarascon to witness to the marriage
agreement between Richard of Cornwall, the king's brother, and
Sanchia, the third daughter of Count Raymond Berengar. A new
pope was at last elected in June, 1243, and one of his first
official acts was to consider the petition of Henry III concerning
Winchester. He rejected the king's appeal and confirmed the
postulation of William Raleigh, transferring him from Norwich
to Winchester.[32] It was clear that Henry III could not expect
Innocent IV to be as accommodating as Gregory IX had been.

When Raleigh received news of the papal confirmation he
at once renounced the see of Norwich and proceeded to take
over his new duties as bishop of Winchester. The king refused
to accept the papal judgment and informed Raleigh that it was
unlawful to take possession of a bishopric without the royal
assent. To which Raleigh replied that he was simply acting
in accordance with the command of the pope. Henry III's reac-
tion was to treat Raleigh as a usurper and order that he should

---

[31] Didier, 'Henri de Suse en Angleterre', *Studi Arangio-Ruiz*, vol. II,
p. 341.
[32] *Ibid.*, p. 340.

be refused entry to Winchester. On Christmas Eve, 1243, Raleigh
presented himself barefoot before each of the city gates.   He
was refused admittance and a short time later he put Winchester
under interdict, excommunicated those who opposed him and
fled to France where, as Matthew Paris put it, he was received
like another Thomas Becket. [33]   Grosseteste of Lincoln and a
number of the other bishops appealed to the king on Raleigh's
behalf, but they were told to await the outcome of a new mission
that he was sending to the papal court.   It would appear from
the chancery rolls that a leading role in the whole Winchester
controversy was played by the canonist, Henry of Susa. [34]   Professor Powicke writes:

> In the maintenance of his cause, Henry relied upon a very
> distinguished canonist, Henry of Susa ... He acted as the king's
> agent at Rome and also in negotiations with the former justice
> at Winchester. He advised Henry at each step and prepared
> his case. It was a very interesting case. Henry of Susa
> contended that the new pope, himself a great canonist, had
> been deceived by the bishop-elect and that his decision was
> open to correction on the ground of "exceptions" which Henry
> had sent to Gregory IX and which, when he was made aware
> of them, Innocent IV, in view of canonical precedents, ought
> to consider. There was no appeal against the pope, yet there
> had been a miscarriage of justice, for Henry's case had not
> been heard. The whole point turned on the moral, if not
> legal, obligation of the pope to review his decision in the
> light of the exceptions; in other words, to reopen the case. [35]

Henry of Susa was unsuccessful in his attempt to persuade
Raleigh to cooperate in an impartial review of the king's ob-
jections and postpone his claim to Winchester.
     The new royal delegation to the court of Innocent IV was
led by Henry of Susa and Thibaut, prior of Hurley. It failed
to persuade the pope to change his mind, and in February, 1244,
Innocent IV addressed a bull to Henry III in which he defended
his action over William Raleigh and confirmed his election as
bishop of Winchester. 'Pope Innocent wrote in firm but friendly

---

[33] *Ibid.*, p. 344, note 67.
[34] Cf. *Calendar of Patent Rolls* (1232-1247), 377, 409-11, 437-42.
[35] F. M. Powicke, *Henry III and the Lord Edward*, Oxford, 1947, vol. I,
p. 272. Powicke points out that the whole story has to be reconstructed
from the Patent and Close Rolls, with the prejudiced aid of Matthew
Paris who was opposed to the important part that foreigners — in
particular, Savoyards, — were playing in the realm.

terms. He deplored Henry's assertion that his consent to the postulation of a bishop was necessary before the temporalities could be restored. The supreme authority which the popes have received from God could not submit to the judgment of princes in such matters'.[36] Henry III at last realised that he had lost his case and that further opposition was useless; so he acquiesced in Raleigh's election and sent Hugues de Saint-Cher to him in France to effect a reconciliation. Raleigh returned to England to take possession of his see in April, 1244. From Henry of Susa's point of view, of course, his mission to the pope had been a failure and he decided not to return to England. 'So ended a curious episode in the life of the most famous canonist of the century.'[37]

In spite of this set-back, however, the canonist did not forfeit the favour either of the king of England or of the pope. Later in that same year, 1244, Innocent IV, in a letter to the king, commended the zeal that Henry of Susa was showing in his service to the king. And years later, as archbishop of Embrun, he was given further important missions by Henry III. It was also in 1244 that he obtained a dispensation from Innocent IV on the accumulation of benefices, and later in the same year he became a papal chaplain. Clearly his diplomatic failure had not undermined his prospects for promotion in the Church, though it does seem to have put an end to his career in England.

---

[36] Powicke, *op. cit.*, p. 273.

[37] *Ibid.* Did Hostiensis know that other famous Devonshire lawyer, Henry of Bracton? It seems very likely that he did. We know that Bracton began to draw a substantial salary for service to the king in 1240. So it would appear that the two distinguished lawyers entered the service of Henry III within a couple of years of each other. They must then have been at court at the same time. Professor Plucknett has argued that Bracton before entering the king's service was probably a clerk to William Raleigh. It would seem that Henry III took over this able lawyer into his service when Raleigh retired from the Bench in 1239. But Bracton's devotion to his old master remained and he was probably of great service to Raleigh throughout the Winchester dispute. 'During the fierce feud with the king Raleigh almost certainly must have used the good offices of his old servant, who was now the king's, and who could speak with more effect since he was not yet involved in the tangled personal politics of Henry III's court'. (Cf. T. F. T. Plucknett, *Early English Legal Literature*, Cambridge, 1958, pp. 43 ff.). It is interesting to think of Hostiensis being opposed by the greatest authority on English law during this controversy.

c) *Bishop of Sisteron (1244-1250)*

Matthew Paris, who was no friend of Savoyards, relates that Henry of Susa, having failed to win the king's case at the papal court, proceeded to misappropriate funds belonging to Henry III in order to acquire a bishopric in his own country. [38] The fact that Henry of Susa continued to be employed by the king does not support this story, nor is it confirmed by what is otherwise known about Henry's appointment as bishop of Sisteron in northern Provence. When Rudolph, bishop of Sisteron, died in 1241 a dispute arose between the chapters of Sisteron and Forcalquier over who had the right to elect his successor. After a long controversy both chapters seem to have reached a compromise agreement by which Zoen Tencarari, bishop of Avignon and papal legate, should be asked to appoint the new bishop. Tencarari agreed and towards the end of 1243 he designated Henry of Susa as bishop of Sisteron. Apart from Henry's acknowledged reputation, his selection for this bishopric in Provence can be well explained without having to invoke bribery or simony. Tencarari happened to be the righthand man of Count Raymond Berengar of Provence who would be particularly interested in the bishopric of Sisteron since his family had a residence in that city. Henry's relationship with the ruling family of Provence would, therefore, be an influential factor. There is also the fact that Tencarari and Henry of Susa had been at Bologna at about the same time. [39]

It would appear that Henry was in no hurry to accept the nomination. He was at this time fully occupied with the Winchester controversy. In May, 1244, he was addressed as Provost of Antibes by Innocent IV who does, however, allude to his designation as bishop of Sisteron. [40] Henry had clearly won the esteem and friendship of the canonist who had become Pope Innocent IV. He became a papal chaplain and was attached to the papal court. When, at the end of 1244, Innocent fled from Italy and took up residence at Lyons Henry of Susa would have been among the faithful supporters who surrounded the pope in exile. At the Council of Lyons in the following year he would have met many of the prelates he had known in England: Grosseteste, Raleigh, and Boniface of Savoy, among

[38] Matthew Paris, *Chronica Maiora*, vol. IV, p. 352.

[39] Didier, 'Henri de Suse, Evêque de Sisteron', *Nouvelle revue historique de droit français et étranger*, 1953, pp. 246-248.

[40] *Ibid.*, p. 249.

others. He would also have met again the Dominican theologian, Hugues de Saint-Cher, who had been made a cardinal in 1244. Perhaps also it was at Lyons that he became acquainted with Fra Salimbene who praised him highly in his chronicle. [41]

There is no mention of the bishop of Sisteron in the documents of the First Council of Lyons, but then no complete list of the participants has come down to us. As a papal chaplain he must have been quite close to the pope during the council, and this might explain some passages in his writings. In the *Apparatus*, for example, he reports a memorandum that was drawn up by a certain bishop on the papal right to depose an emperor. He himself may have been the bishop responsible. [42] If one can accept a letter attributed to Henry of Susa, King Louis IX, when he was trying in 1248 to effect a reconciliation between pope and emperor, consulted Henry about the problem of the deposition. [43] The canonist was in fact highly thought of by the king of France and he was later invited to intervene in serious family disputes.

In the years following the council Henry must have spent quite a lot of his time at the papal court at Lyons. In a number of places in the *Summa* and the *Apparatus* he refers to his experience 'in curia', and frequently cites the customs of the church at Lyons. [44] In August, 1248, Innocent IV granted Henry a personal indult on his own request according to which no delegate of the Holy See could pronounce against him a sentence of suspension, interdict or excommunication without a special mandate from the pope mentioning this indult. It is not known what Henry was afraid of at this particular time, but the very existence of the indult implies that he had enemies in high places. [45]

In spite of his absences in Lyons, however, Henry does not seem to have neglected his own diocese of Sisteron, and

---

[41] *Ibid.*, p. 251, where Didier quotes Salimbene's praise of Henry of Susa 'in scientia et in cantu et in litteratura et in honesta et sancta vita'.

[42] *Ibid.*, p. 251, note 41, where Didier quotes from *Apparatus*, I, fol. 60, col. 2. See also J.A. Watt, 'Medieval Deposition Theory: A Neglected Canonist *Consultatio* from the first Council of Lyons', *Studies in Church History* 2 (1965), pp. 197-214.

[43] Didier, 'Evêque de Sisteron', p. 252.

[44] *Ibid.*, pp. 251-252.

[45] *Ibid.*, p. 254, and p. 424, n. 6 where the indult is printed. It reveals the papal esteem for Henry of Susa: '... Personam tuam speciali debcmus honore prosequi, que ad hoc intenta esse dignoscitur ut grata nobis et ecclesiae, per sincere devotionis studium, habeatur ...'.

there were quite a number of problems to be resolved there that required all his talents as canonist and diplomat. There was the important dispute over the rights of episcopal election between the chapter of Forcalquier and that of Sisteron, but this was only settled in 1249 when Henry was about to leave Sisteron for Embrun. The chapter at Sisteron granted Henry land for the construction of an episcopal palace in Sisteron, — they were clearly keen to have their bishop in residence in their own city. In 1246 another mark of favour was shown him by these canons when they granted him the personal privilege of having a voice in their capitular deliberations 'tamquam canonicus'.[46] During the whole time that Henry was bishop of Sisteron the papal court was at Lyons. This proximity of the pope was turned to the advantage of the church of Sisteron, for the bishop obtained for his church three papal bulls which bestowed apostolic protection and confirmed the possessions of the church. One of these, dated 1247, was drawn up with great solemnity and contains the papal signature and monogram and the signature of six cardinals together with that of the Vice-chancellor. This type of document had apparently become quite rare under Innocent IV, and the fact that one was drawn up for Sisteron provides perhaps added proof of the esteem in which Henry of Susa was held at the papal court.[47]

Several events show that the bishop of Sisteron was quite concerned about his income. From the plurality of benefices that he regularly held, of course, it is clear that Henry of Susa was interested in having sound financial resources. And a number of the dispensations that he received on this score have been recorded. In Sisteron itself there was a dispute between Henry and his chapter concerning payments due to the bishop when he visited his cathedral church.[48] There was also a conflict between the diocese of Sisteron and the Hospitallers of St John of Jerusalem in which Henry appeared as a vigorous upholder of the rights of the diocesan bishop. The Hospitallers had acquired several parish churches in the diocese. One of these had a fashionable cemetery where many of the local notables chose to be buried. According to the custom of the time this meant that considerable sums came to the Hospitallers by way of legacies from those who were buried in their cemetery.

---

[46] Didier, 'Evêque de Sisteron', p. 258.
[47] *Ibid.*, pp. 259-260.
[48] *Ibid.*, p. 258.

Henry of Susa, as bishop of the diocese, claimed that he had a right to the 'portio canonica' of all such pious bequests that were made within his diocese. He was later to defend this episcopal right strenuously both in the *Summa* and in the *Apparatus*. It was not, however, acknowledged by the Hospitallers and Henry took the case to court and papal delegates were appointed to settle the dispute. The bishop was demanding a considerable sum of money for he was laying claim to the 'portio canonica' on all burials that had taken place in the cemetery since the death of Count William II in 1209. The case dragged for some years and before a variety of judges, and it was only finally settled in 1251 by arbitration. The Hospitallers were acquitted but agreed to pay a lump sum to the bishop, while the chapters of Sisteron and Forcalquier consented to make no further claims.[49] But by this time Henry of Susa was no longer their bishop.

Throughout these years Henry remained the trusted friend and adviser of the Countess of Provence, Beatrice of Savoy, who appears to have spent much of her time at Sisteron after the death of her husband in 1246 and the accession of Charles of Anjou as the new Count of Provence.[50]

One of the last things that Henry of Susa did before leaving Sisteron was to draw up a settlement of the dispute between the canons of Forcalquier and those of Sisteron over the rights of episcopal election. In 1249 he issued new regulations, recognising the Forcalquier chapter's right to participate in the election and laying down the procedure that should be followed. The designation of his own immediate successor, however, was to be made by Cardinal Hugues de Saint-Cher or the bishop of Fréjus. Everything else was to be worked out by the new bishop.

In the *Summa Aurea*, as will be seen later, Henry of Susa propounded an exacting doctrine on the pastoral duties of the diocesan bishop. It would be interesting to know how he himself lived up to this ideal in his own diocese, but there is very little information available. He seems to have been frequently absent at the papal court; but then Lyons is not very far from Sisteron and he could easily have been in regular contact with his diocese while staying there. Almost all that is known of

---

[49] For a fully documented discussion of this case, see N. Didier, 'Henri de Suse, Evêque de Sisteron', pp. 262-270.

[50] *Ibid.*, pp. 409-412.

his pastoral activities as bishop of Sisteron is contained in a set of diocesan statutes which were promulgated by him in 1249. [51]   This was basically a manual already drawn up by two Dominicans to which Henry added his own expansions and modifications, and although, according to Didier, it bears the stamp of Henry's strong personality, it does not really tell us much about his pastoral work in the diocese.

It is not unlikely that while he was bishop of Sisteron he continued to work on the *Summa* and the *Apparatus*.   The first draft of the *Summa* may have almost reached completion before he left Sisteron in 1250.   He himself tells us that this was partially destroyed in a fire shortly after he moved to Embrun, but much of his earlier work must have been salvaged since his new version was ready for publication by the end of 1253, and this in spite of the fact that he had had to take up his new duties as archbishop and had also spent a year in Germany with the papal legate, Hugues de Saint-Cher. [52]

d) *Archbishop of Embrun (1250-1262), Cardinal Hostiensis (1262-1271).*

It was unlikely that a man of Henry's distinction and con-nections should remain for long as the ordinary of a small diocese.   And so towards the beginning of 1250 he was trans-ferred to the metropolitan see of Embrun, a city in Dauphiné about 120 miles south of Lyons and about half that distance from his native town of Susa.   One of his first acts as arch-bishop would appear to have been the summoning of a provin-cial council.   He refers to this council in the *Summa Aurea* where he argues that a special statute can be made in a pro-vincial council to unite a number of churches for the purpose of contributing to the expenses of a metropolitan visitation, — 'sicut et fecimus in provinciali concilio quod nuper celebravi-mus apud Dignam'. [53]   Henry also accompanied Hugues de Saint-Cher when the cardinal was sent as papal legate to Germany from April 1251 until April 1252.   It was during this mission that the archbishop of Mainz, having been deposed by the legate, accused the legate's *socius*, Henry of Susa, as the one respon-

---

[51] Didier, 'Henri de Suse, Evêque de Sisteron', pp. 414-416.

[52] *Ibid.*, p. 417.

[53] *Summa*, I, De Officio Archidiaconi, n. 5.   For a discussion of the date of this council, see Richard Kay, 'Hostiensis and Some Embrun Provincial Councils', in *Traditio*, 20 (1964), pp. 503-13.

sible for this measure, alleging that he had been bribed to secure the deposition by Gerhard who succeeded to the archiepiscopal see. There does not, however, seem to be any other evidence to support the accusation.[54] It was apparently also on this mission that he met Jacques de Troyes, archdeacon of Laon, — an interesting fact, since Jacques de Troyes was elected to the papacy ten years later, taking the name of Urban IV, and among the first cardinals he created was the archbishop of Embrun.[55]

While archbishop of Embrun Henry seems to have returned to his old diocese of Sisteron from time to time. He encountered considerable opposition from the citizens of Embrun over something or other; so much so that in 1254 he put them under interdict.[56] There is a record of a meeting he held in Sisteron in the spring of 1255 to discuss affairs with some of his Embrun subjects. These men objected to the location for the meeting on the grounds that the archbishop had too many friends in Sisteron, particularly the dowager Countess, Beatrice of Savoy, — 'domine dicte civitatis, amicissime dicti domini archiepiscopi'.[57]

As archbishop his talents as jurist and diplomat continued to be used by the rulers of France and England. In 1258/9 he was charged by Henry III with an important mission at the court of Alexander IV.[58] His relations with the new pope seem to have been similar to those he had with his predecessor, Innocent IV, and there is a story that it was Alexander IV's encouragement that led him to keep up his work on his commentary on the Decretals. In 1259 he received a bull from Alexander IV confirming his rights of patronage in Embrun, and that same year he was sent as papal legate for northern Italy to try to combat the influence of the late emperor's illegitimate son, Manfred. The mission does not appear to have been very fruitful and the legate was left free to remain in Lombardy or return to the curia.[59]

In 1257 he had been witness to an arbitration settlement between King Louis IX and his brother, Charles of Anjou.[60]

---

54 Didier, 'Henri de Suse, Evêque de Sisteron', p. 418.
55 C. Lefebvre, 'Hostiensis', *DDC*, vol. V, col. 1213.
56 *Ibid.*, col. 1214.
57 Didier, 'Henri de Suse, Evêque de Sisteron', pp. 411 and 418.
58 Lefebvre, *DDC*, vol. V, col. 1214.
59 *Ibid.*, col. 1214.
60 Didier, 'Henri de Suse, Evêque de Sisteron', p. 252.

Some five years later Louis IX wanted both Henry of Susa and the Archbishop of Narbonne to come and resolve the differences between Queen Margaret and Charles of Anjou on the subject of Provence. The new pope, Urban IV, refused to allow this on the grounds that he required the services of both these men for the government of the Church. In 1261 the Archbishop of Narbonne was created a cardinal (he became Pope Clement IV in 1265) while in May of the following year Henry of Susa became Cardinal-bishop of Ostia, the see with which later generations would always associate him, calling him simply, Hostiensis. [61]

Very little is known about the last years of his life or of his activities as a cardinal, though his name appears in a number of documents and in the papal registers. In November, 1268, he took part in the famous conclave which assembled at Viterbo to elect a successor to Clement IV. This dragged on for almost three years and in the course of it Hostiensis was compelled to renounce his rights as an elector and ask to be excused on grounds of ill health. He left the conclave in June, 1270. These facts are mentioned in the *Apparatus* which he must have completed within the next year. [62] In his will, dated 30 April, 1271, he states that there were four exemplars of this *Apparatus*, one of which had already been sent to Bologna to be copied.

Cardinal Hostiensis died at Lyons towards the end of 1271 and was buried there in the Dominican convent. He had had a long and extremely active life and ranks among the most outstanding churchmen of the thirteenth century. It was, however, his mastery of the law that kept his memory green and his reputation was built upon the lengthy canonical expositions that he left to posterity.

3. *The Writings of Cardinal Hostiensis*

a) *The Summa Aurea*

A *summa*, as the name implies, was a compendious and systematic exposition of the main aspects of a subject, whether moral, theological or legal. A great variety of these were composed in the Middle Ages, — *summa confessorum, summa theo-*

---

[61] Lefebvre, *DDC*, vol. V, col. 1214.

[62] *Apparatus*, I, 9 (de renuntiatione), 10, n. 32; I, 41 (de in integrum restitutione), 5, n. 2.

logica, summa in Decretum, and so on.[63]   Among medieval Roman lawyers the term was used to distinguish a systematic legal exposition from an exegetical commentary on the actual text of the law, but the earlier canonical *summae* on the *Decretum* often included exegetical commentary along with the juridical exposition.   The decretalists, however, in their *summae* generally omitted commentary on particular legal texts and restricted themselves to the systematic exposition of the legal aspects of the problem that was being dealt with.   These canonical manuals followed the order of the *tituli* in the Gregorian collection of decretals and were known as *summae titulorum.*[64]

The *Summa Aurea* of Cardinal Hostiensis, or, to give it its full title, the *Summa super Titulis Decretalium,* was published towards the end of 1253, when Henry of Susa had been for several years archbishop of Embrun.   Hence it is often referred to as the *Summa Archiepiscopi.*[65]   The work clearly owes much to the commentary of Goffredus Tranensis which had been published more than a decade earlier and which Hostiensis quotes frequently; but, as Mgr Lefebvre has demonstrated, the *Summa Aurea* marks a considerable advance beyond Goffredus both in clarity and comprehensiveness.[66]   First of all, Hostiensis did not keep to the 185 *tituli* that had been chosen by Raymond of Peñafort for the *Liber Extra.*   To these he added more than fifty supplementary titles of his own in order to provide a clearer and more complete exposition.   Quite a number of the original *tituli* he divided into subsections for the sake of clarity.   New titles were also added to take account of the juridical development that had taken place since the publication of the *Decretales* in 1234.   Hence, for instance, *De recusatione ludicis dele-gati* is separated from the title dealing with the powers and duties of the judge-delegate.   Hostiensis, who was writing a manual for practitioners, was obviously trying to keep up to date with current court practice.   His interest in Roman law was another factor that led him to add to the *tituli* of the *Decretales.*   He was, after all, known as the 'monarcha utriusque

---

[63] Cf. A. Van Hove, *Prolegomena,* 2nd edition, Mechliniae-Romae, 1945, p. 433.

[64] *Ibid.,* p. 447.

[65] The latest act cited in the *Summa Aurea* is dated September 9th 1253.   For the evidence for this dating of the *Summa* see Lefebvre, 'Hostiensis' in the *Dictionnaire du Droit Canonique,* vol. V, cols. 1215-1216.

[66] Mgr Lefebvre has provided a detailed comparison of the *Summa Aurea* with the *Summa Goffredi* in the article cited in the preceding note.

iuris' and his *Summa* contains an abundance of passages which
are straight Roman law.

In short, Hostiensis in his *Summa Aurea* used the structure
of the *Liber Extra* as a framework round which he constructed
a systematic account of all law — both canonical and Roman —
which concerned ecclesiastical interests. He quotes freely and
extensively from the writings of his predecessors, usually acknowledging his source, but rarely taking over the views of
another lock, stock and barrel. He usually has his own comments to add.[67] The *Summa Codicis* of Azo is the work most
frequently quoted by Hostiensis from Roman law just as the
Summa Goffredi is his most frequent canonical source. 'Ma,
rispetto a questi scrittori,' writes Professor Caron, 'l'Ostiense
mostra maggiore chiarezza, distingue elementi fino allora confusi, e — ciò che contraddistingue in modo inconfondibile la
sua opera — si adopera per realizzare una sintesi fra il diritto
romano e il diritto canonico mai tentata prima d'allora'.[68] As
Hostiensis himself advises the reader in the preface:

> Qui ergo diversa scripta utilia in unum volumen quo ad utrum-
> que ius fideliter redacta habere desiderat, ad scribendam hanc
> Summam accedat intrepidus et securus, quam ego post studium
> utriusque diutinum et longum exercitium, adiutorio Dei in
> omnibus praecedente, suffultus composui.

Mgr Lefebvre maintains that Henry of Susa's whole conception of the *Summa* differed greatly from that of his predecessors. His work is more systematic and clearer than that
of Goffredus. Moreover, he aimed at presenting a practical
manual which would give a comprehensive account of all legislation concerning ecclesiastical matters. A synthesis, in fact,
of both canon and Roman law. This is one of the reasons for
the great prestige the *Summa Aurea* enjoyed during the following centuries right up to the Council of Trent and beyond.

---

[67] Schulte has made a list of all the canonists and Roman lawyers
cited by Hostiensis. It is an impressive one and includes all the principal
lawyers of the century. There are seventeen Roman lawyers mentioned
and fifteen canonists. Cf. J. F. Schulte, *Die Geschichte der Quellen*,
Volume II, p. 126, note 24. It has also been shown that the *titulus
De feudis*, is but an enlarged edition of the treatment by Pillius de
Medicina, a Roman lawyer of the late twelfth century. Cf. R. Seckel, in
Zeitschrift der Sav. Stift. für Rechtsgeschichte. Rom. Abt. XXI (1900), p. 252.
[68] P. G. Caron, 'Ostiense', *Novissimo Digesto Italiano*, 3rd edn. Turin,
1965, vol. XII, p. 284.

Another factor that made his book popular was his practical approach. He indicated current practice and mentioned local and regional customs. His experience as bishop, archbishop, and counsellor of kings and popes provided ample opportunity for illustrating legal principles by practical examples of cases in which he himself had taken an active part.

Later historians, as has been seen, were generous with the praise they lavished on the writing of Hostiensis. His *Summa* was described as 'aureum sane opus, quo nullum ante illud tempus utilius prodierat',[69] and it came to be for canonists what the *Summa Codicis* of Azo had been for Roman lawyers. The large number of extant manuscripts and printed editions of the *Summa Aurea* tends to support this judgement. In Mgr Lefebvre's phrase, 'this treatise became the vade mecum of canonists until the 17th century'.[70]

b) *The Apparatus or Lectura in Quinque Libros Decretalium Gregorii IX*

Shortly after the publication of the *Summa Aurea* Henry of Susa produced a commentary on a number of the decretal letters of Pope Innocent IV,[71] as well as a small treatise on episcopal elections.[72] It was not, however, until just before he died, in 1271, that he completed his second major canonical work, the *Commentaria vel Lectura in Quinque Libros Decretalium Gregorii IX*. This *Lectura* — or *Apparatus*, to use the term that Hostiensis himself applies to it, — has been described as an 'opus praestantissimum'[73] and ranks among the most important canonical works of the Middle Ages. It provides an exegetical commentary on each of the decretals contained in

---

[69] Sarti & Fattorini, *op. cit.*, p. 444.

[70] C. Lefebvre, 'Hostiensis', *New Catholic Encyclopedia*, 1967, vol. 7, p. 170. Schulte listed manuscripts of the *Summa* from eighteen different cities on the continent and ten printed editions between 1473 and 1612. For the *Apparatus*, on the other hand, he listed only four manuscripts and three printed editions between 1512 and 1581. This is a good indication of the relative influence of the two works. The British Museum Library Catalogue enumerates six copies of the *Summa Aurea*, but none of the *Apparatus*. Cf. Schulte, *Geschichte der Quellen*, vol. II, p. 126.

[71] Cf. Lefebvre, 'Hostiensis', *DDC*, vol. V, col. 1220, where it is shown that this must have been produced around 1253. Printed versions can be found in the Paris and Venice editions of the *Apparatus*.

[72] Cf. A. von Wretschko, 'Ein Traktat des Kardinals Hostiensis mit Glossen betreffend die Abfassung von Wahldekreten bei der Bischofswahl', *Deutsche Zeitschrift für Kirchenrecht*, Series III, XVII, 1907, pp. 73-88.

[73] A. Van Hove, *Prolegomena*, p. 478.

the Gregorian Collection. Like the *Summa Aurea* this too must
owe its origin to the days when Henry of Susa was lecturing
in Paris. Schulte has argued that it was undertaken at the
request of Henry's pupils who, having seen his commentaries
on some of Innocent IV's decretals, wanted a complete exposition of the *Decretales*. There is also the story that it was Pope
Alexander IV, the protector of Thomas Aquinas and Bonaventure, who asked the archbishop to carry out this work, but
we possess little evidence for this. Perhaps he had begun the
work much earlier but had had to abandon it under pressure
of more urgent business. It was composed after the pontificate
of Innocent IV; Hostiensis is critical of some of that pope's
ideas and makes this plain from time to time. [74] He must have
continued working on the *Apparatus* right to the end of his
life since, as we have already seen, he mentions the death of
Clement IV in 1268 and his own part in the conclave which
followed and which he had to abandon because of ill health in
1270. In his will dated April, 1271, he mentions four exemplars
of the work and names their possessors. [75]

The *Apparatus* is almost twice as long as the *Summa Aurea*,
comprising two volumes with more than three thousand folio
columns of printed text. This is not surprising, of course, since
in the *Apparatus* Hostiensis is attempting to provide a commentary on all the Gregorian decretals, some of which are extremely detailed. This commentary was highly esteemed when
it first appeared in the thirteenth century. Later canonists judged
it to be on the same level as the commentaries of Innocent IV
and Johannes Andreae. [76] The number of extant manuscripts

---

[74] 'There is an independence of mind about a commentator who can
conclude a gloss with the remark that what he has just said was the
view of Innocent IV "cuius est hec tota glossa incerta, inutilis et confusa".'
J. A. Watt, in 'The Use of the Term "Plenitudo Potestatis" by Hostiensis',
Proceedings of the Second International Congress of Medieval Canon Law,
Vatican City, 1965, p. 162.

[75] The actual terms of his will are: '... Tertio commentum meum super
Decretalibus, quod misi Bononiam conscribendum, studio Bononiensi relinquo. Aliud vero ejusdem commenti volumen quod scripsit Molinarius
scriptor, relinquo ecclesiae Ebredunensi: ita tamen quod antequam redda-
tur ipsi ecclesiae, mittatur Parisius ad corrigendum quod ibidem misi ...'.
Cf. 'Testamentum Henrici Archiepiscopi olim Ebredunensis Ostiensis Car-
dinalis' in *Gallia Christiana*, vol. III, col. 180.

[76] 'Nihil attinet dicere quam probata ea fuerint iuris canonici stu-
diosis, quae scilicet eodem in pretio fuerunt ac Innocentii IV et Joannis
Andreae commentaria. Ea non semel typis edita sunt et manu exarata

and printed editions, however, is much smaller than that for the *Summa Aurea*, [77] which suggests that it was neither as well known nor as influential as the earlier work. Its very length, of course, tended to make it a work for the scholar. Diplovatatius mentions that in fact a compendium of the *Apparatus* was produced 'quia propter prolixitatem dicte lecture fructus ipsius sive utilitas in pluribus ignoratur' [78]. This commentary of Hostiensis, however, is still regarded as important and the 1581 Venice edition has been recently reprinted. [79]

---

passim reperiuntur inter antiquos bibliothecarum codices'. Sarti et Fattorini, *De claris archigymnasii Bononiensis professoribus*, p. 444.

[77] Cf. F. von Schulte, *Geschichte der Quellen*, vol. II, p. 126.

[78] Diplovatatius, *De claris iuris consultis*, p. 144. Von Schulte mentions an abridged edition of the *Apparatus* that was published by Samson de Calvo Monte in the first third of the fourteenth century. Cf. Von Schulte, *op. cit.*, p. 204.

[79] Produced by the Bottega d'Erasmo, Turin, 1965.

CHAPTER TWO

THE JURIDICAL BACKGROUND

This inquiry is primarily concerned with the *Summa Aurea.* However, to provide the context for the detailed investigation into the teaching of Cardinal Hostiensis and to give some idea of the canonical tradition that he inherited, a preliminary chapter has been included at this point. The aim is to give a brief outline of the state of canonical legislation and canonistic science when Hostiensis was writing his *Summa.* The views of some medieval popes and canonists on the function of the Church's legislation will also be briefly considered.

1. *Canonical Legislation in the Twelfth and Thirteenth Centuries.*

a) *The Juridical Renaissance*

The canon law which governed the Roman Catholic Church from medieval times until 1918 was contained primarily in the two volumes of the *Corpus Iuris Canonici,* a collection of ecclesiastical legislation that we owe principally to the popes and canonists of the twelfth and thirteenth centuries. This period was, of course, the classical age of canon law in the Church but it was also an age of intense juridical thought and activity in the civil sphere as well. Irnerius had founded the school of Roman law at Bologna towards the end of the eleventh century and from that time onwards the *Corpus Iuris Civilis* had increasingly become the object of critical examination and commentary. A school of glossators was born and Bologna became the leading law school in Christendom where for the next two centuries a succession of distinguished glossators added lustre to its reputation. Bulgarus (d. 1166), Placentinus (d. 1192), Vacarius (d. 1200), Azo (d. 1220) and Accursius (d. 1263) are only some of the famous Roman lawyers of this period.[1] It was a

---

[1] Cf. P. Vinogradoff, *Roman Law in Medieval Europe,* Oxford Univer-

lawyer's world. As historians have observed: 'In no other age, since the classical days of Roman law, has so large a part of the sum total of intellectual endeavour been devoted to juris-prudence'.[2] A similar interest and activity were to be seen in the field of canon law. Within a comparatively short time the *Corpus Iuris Civilis* was to have its canonical counterpart in a *Corpus Iuris Canonici*, consisting of Gratian's *Decretum* and three official collection of papal decretals, — the Gregorian De-cretals of 1234, the *Liber Sextus* of 1298 and the *Decretales Cle-mentinae* of 1317. This was a large body of legislation to have grown up in little more than a century and a half. How did it develop? Gabriel Le Bras has pointed out that from the earliest times the Church had found it necessary to draw up rules of government and to define the obligations of her mem-bers in order to preserve her unity, to maintain her worship, to ensure the exercise of charity and the practical application of the evangelical virtues.[3] Through this gradually developing law she prescribed a discipline for Christian society and she instructed her members in their duties and their rights. Holy Scripture and the traditions of the Early Church were the foun-dations of these laws. To these were added down the centuries the decrees of General Councils and the legislation of individual popes. The law developed according to the demands of the times and in response to current problems. Laws were intro-duced, for instance, to protect Church property and to safeguard the privileges that had been granted to the clergy. Until the eleventh century, however, the development was haphazard. The local Churches looked after their own needs and compiled their own collections of Church laws. There was no universally ac-cepted and authoritative body of ecclesiastical law. In the elev-enth century the Gregorian reformers tried to remedy this situa-tion and clear up the confusion by establishing a body of law

sity Press, 1961[3], p. 56 f. H. Kantorowicz, 'Note on the Development of the Gloss to the Justinian and the Canon Law,' in Beryl Smalley, *The Study of the Bible in the Middle Ages*, Oxford, 1951[2], pp. 52-55. P. Fournier, 'Un tournant de l'histoire du droit (1060-1140)', *Nouvelle Revue hist. de droit français et étranger*, 1917. H. D. Hazeltine, 'Roman and Canon Law', *Cambridge Medieval History*, vol. V, 1926, 697-764. W. Ullmann, *Law and Politics in the Middle Ages*, London, 1975, Ch. 3 'The Scholarship of Roman Law', pp. 83-116.

[2] F. Pollock & F. W. Maitland, *The History of English Law*, Cambridge, 1968[2], vol. I, p. 111.

[3] Gabriel Le Bras, 'Canon Law', in *The Legacy of the Middle Ages*, edited by C. G. Crump and E. F. Jacob, Oxford U. P., 1926, p. 322.

which would be binding upon the whole Church. This legal revival was not motivated by a desire for centralisation and concentration of power, though this was in fact one of the results of their reforms. What Hildebrand and those who supported him in the eleventh century were striving after was the radical reform of the Church. They looked to canon law to help them in their efforts to rid the Church of corruption and bring it back to the pristine practice of the Christian ideals. Their declared intention was for a spiritual and interior reform through the restoration of the Christian discipline of the early Church. The law was to be an instrument of this restoration. With this in mind they searched out patristic and conciliar texts which they hoped would be received as authoritative by all Christians and which would support the primacy of the pope and protect the rights of the Church against the growing claims of temporal kings and princes. The fact that spurious documents found their way into the collections is not surprising nor does it affect the sincerity of the reformers. One of the main aims of their revision of law was to rid the Church of the evils that had arisen from the practice of lay investiture. The reformers were out to secure the independence of the spiritual from feudal subjection to temporal rulers and allow the clergy the free exercise of their spiritual duties. They also aimed at enforcing by law the traditional ideal of the Western Church in the matter of clerical celibacy. Another glaring abuse that Pope Gregory VII was anxious to remove was the practice of simony, the buying and selling of spiritual offices. In all this movement of reform within the Church it was for the law clearly to define the rights of the Church and provide legal sanctions against those who refused to obey the pope. The reformers tried to show that all this was solidly based on the traditional teaching of the Church. But how was one to define this traditional teaching? One way was to collect the early authorities of the Church and show how these revealed the ancient Christian discipline. These commonly accepted authorities would show what had once been the common law of Christianity. Hence the quest for a consistent and authoritative collection of early texts by those eleventh century canonists who supported Pope Gregory VII. Professor Kuttner has drawn attention to another important aspect of this search: when these reforming canonists wished to refer to the rules that obtain in the Church, 'they did not speak of any book or books, but of *canonicae traditiones, decreta sanctorum patrum, auctoritas*

4

canonum, sanctorum patrum privilegia, canonum statuta, and the like'.[4]   The terminology underlines the point that their search was for the restoration of pristine Christian ideals.   It was, then, this desire for a radical reform of the whole Church that led to the series of canonical collections that appeared continuously throughout the century that preceded Gratian's collection.   These collections of *auctoritates* were not official texts in the sense that they were officially promulgated by papal authority, but they were used by papal legates as 'manuals for reform' throughout the entire Church and as such they exercised great influence.

b) *The Decretum of Gratian*

The *Decretum Gratiani* or, to give it its full title, *Concordia Discordantium Canonum,* published in 1141, was the best of these canonical collections and it soon superseded all that had gone before.   Gratian made great use of the collections his predecessors had compiled but, by a careful arrangement of authorities according to subject-matter, he added an order and clarity that the others had lacked.   The result was a masterly compilation of almost all the important legal texts from the first millenium of Christianity along with a concise commentary.   Gratian himself was not a Church official.   He was probably only a professor of canon law in the University of Bologna.   His book had no official status in the Church but it was such an advance on the collections that had hitherto been in use that it rapidly became the standard text-book in the schools and was treated as an authority in the ecclesiastical courts.   The *Decretum Gratiani* provided the Church with a magisterial compilation of ecclesiastical legislation up to the middle of the twelfth century — a summary of the *ius antiquum* — and as such it was to remain the basis of the study of canon law for centuries. All subsequent canonists were to build on the foundations laid by Gratian.   His book appeared just at the right time and it marked a turning point in the history of canon law — 'd'un coup, il remplaçait une bibliothèque'.[5]   The existence of a universally

---

[4] S. Kuttner, 'Liber Canonicus. A Note on Dictatus Papae c. 17', in *Studi Gregoriani,* Rome, 1947, vol. 2, pp. 387-389.

[5] G. Le Bras, *Institutions ecclésiastiques de la Chrétienté mediévale: Préliminaires et Ière Partie,* Paris, 1959, pp. 50-55.   For a full and well-documented discussion of Gratian and the importance of his *Decretum,* as well as of canonistic scholarship in the Middle Ages, see W. Ullmann, *Law and Politics in the Middle Ages,* London, 1975, pp. 117-189.   Cf. also

recognised collection of the important legal texts from the past cleared the way for the full development of ecclesiastical legislation which took place during the late twelfth and the thirteenth centuries.

The canonists who followed Gratian in the second half of the twelfth century took his collection as their basic text on Church law. They were known as the Decretists and they produced an abundance of glosses and commentaries on the *Decretum*. The marginal or interlinear gloss was gradually developed into a systematic *Summa* or ordered commentary. The glossators of the *Decretum* were numerous and there were outstanding jurists among them. Rolandus Bandinelli had been a pupil of Gratian and had produced a *Summa* on the *Decretum* before he became Pope Alexander III in 1159. Another distinguished Decretist, Albert of Beneventum, became Pope Gregory VIII in 1187. Other influential commentators on the *Decretum* were Paucapalea, Rufinus (d. 1203), John of Faenza (d. 1220) and Stephen of Tournai (1128-1203). There were many others.

> Perhaps the greatest of all these twelfth century Decretists was Huguccio, Bishop of Pisa, whose able *Summa* on the *Decretum*, written c. 1190, reviewed in the light of the author's own searching intelligence, the substantial achievement of the preceding half-century of canonistic scholarship.[6]

Huguccio lectured at Bologna and had among his pupils the brilliant young Roman, Lothar of Segni who, in 1198, was to become Pope Innocent III. Huguccio's influence on Lothar of Segni was to be important for the whole Church, and it has been argued that the papal legislation introduced by Innocent III was simply the putting into practice of the canonical theory of his teacher, Huguccio.[7]

During the reign of Innocent III and his immediate successors the centralising activity of the papacy was at its height. The central government of the Church was gaining more control over the direction of the local Churches. An ever-increasing

S. Chodorow, *Christian Political Theory and Church Politics in the Mid-Twelfth Century: The Ecclesiology of Gratian's Decretum*, California, 1972; J. Rambaud, 'Le Legs de l'Ancien Droit: Gratien', in *L'Age Classique*, Paris, 1965, pp. 49-129.

[6] Brian Tierney, *Foundations of the Conciliar Theory*, Cambridge, 1955, p. 15.

[7] M. Maccarone, *Chiesa e stato nella dottrina di papa Innocenzo III*, Rome, 1940, p. 68.

number of local disputes were being referred to the Holy See for settlement and the papacy was intervening more and more frequently in ecclesiastical appointments throughout the whole of Christendom. The central authority of the pope was invoked to provide rulings on the law of the Church. Recourse to the papal curia became the order of the day and the idea of the pope as 'universal ordinary' became a practical reality. This increase of appeals to Rome consolidated the judicial supremacy of the pope. There was also the growing practice of appointing judge-delegates a procedure by which a local judge received delegated papal authority to deal with the case on the spot in first instance. This practice had already become common in the twelfth century, it increased in the thirteenth and contributed to the growing centralisation. [8] The juridical character of this period in the Church is reflected too in the number of lawyers who became pope in the century between the accession of Alexander III in 1159 and the death of Innocent IV in 1254. Alexander III, Gregory VIII, Innocent III and Innocent IV reigned for more than fifty of these years. While Gregory IX, who reigned for fourteen years, had been trained at Bologna. His interest in canon law is clearly shown in the promulgation of the *Liber Extra*. This ascendency of the canonists did not escape criticism and there were many complaints about the immersion of Churchmen in legal business.

c) *The Decretals of Pope Gregory IX*

This growing centralization and the practical realisation of the doctrine of the plenitude of papal power was marked by an increased flow of papal rescripts and decretals from the Roman Curia. It was through decretal legislation that the popes were able to exercise their authority throughout the whole Church. Cases referred to the papal court led to an abundance of papal decisions on a great variety of questions and although these decretals were usually answering specific cases they were generally held to be valid for the whole Church. That this was a legitime method of papal legislation was taken for granted by most Christians. [9] The binding force of papal rescripts had, of course, been traditional for centuries. What was new and the object of severe criticism was the increase

---

[8] A. Morey, *Bartholomew of Exeter, Bishop and Canonist*, Cambridge, 1937, chapter IV.

[9] Cf. *Decretum*, DD, 19-20; C. 25.

in the volume of this sort of legislation and its greatly enlarged scope. It now included all kinds of detailed matters of procedure and legal interpretation covering the whole field of law and morals, and it influenced the daily lives of all Christians.

It was during the long reign of Alexander III (1159-1181) that papal decretals began to multiply dramatically. He issued so many decretal letters that Stephen of Tournai referred to them as an 'impenetrable forest'. To England alone he dispatched about 360. [10] Then there was the Third Lateran Council of 1179 which enacted legislation for the universal Church. Innocent III (1198-1216) was another prolific legislator and at the end of his reign the Fourth Lateran Council enacted a further large body of important legislation for the whole Church. The steady expansion of decretal legislation was continued by the succeeding thirteenth-century popes, as a glance at the *Liber Extra* and the *Liber Sextus* will clearly show.

All this led to an important development in the study of canon law. It was now no longer sufficient to have a mastery of the *Decretum* of Gratian. One had also to try to keep abreast of the latest decretal legislation. Moreover, the papal decretals not only added to the legislation, they also clarified, modified or abrogated laws of the past. They contained a *ius novum* which was quite distinct from the *ius vetus* of the *Decretum*, and this new law stood in need of codification and commentary. So decretals were collected and classified and a school of decretalist glossators or commentators grew up alongside that of the decretists and they perfected the glossatorial technique. The result was that by the early years of the thirteenth century there were in circulation a large number of private compilations of recent papal decretals. The best known of these are the *Quinque Compilationes Antiquae* which were compiled between 1188, when Bernard of Pavia produced his very influential *Compilatio Prima* (or *Breviarium Extravagantium*), and 1226, when the Bolognese professor, Tancred, published the *Compilatio Quinta* for Honorius III. A large number of other collections have survived from this period. The multiplicity and variety of these collections tended to lead to confusion and uncertainty about the law. It was to clear up this confusion that Pope Gregory IX in 1230 commissioned Raymond of Peñafort, who had been a lecturer in law at Bologna before he be-

---

[10] Cf. C. Duggan, *Twelfth-Century Decretal Collections*, London, 1963, p. 144.

came a Dominican, to make an official and authoritative collection of all the important papal and conciliar legislation that
had been either omitted by Gratian or issued since his time.
This collection and selection — modelled on the *Quinque Compilationes Antiquae* — was published in 1234 and recommended
by Gregory IX to the lawyers of Bologna and Paris. It became
known as the *Liber Extra* since it contained the law not included in, or *outside*, the *Decretum*. This official papal codification immediately became the subject of gloss and commentary by the decretalists. All previous collections were rendered
obsolete. Interpreting and expounding the law contained in
the Gregorian Collection was to be the main occupation of canonists for the rest of the century. The same thing happened
to further decretals as they appeared. Innocent IV, who produced a commentary on the Gregorian Decretals while he was
pope, also published a collection of his own decretals which
were commented on by other canonists including Cardinal Hostiensis. Then in 1298, Boniface VIII promulgated an official
collection of all the legislation since 1234. This *Liber Sextus*
in turn became the object of gloss and commentary.

A new phase had thus begun in canonistic studies. The
decretalists became an important and influential body in the
Church.

> The rise to importance of decretal collections coincided with
> the scientific evolution of canon law, and both factors were
> interlocking elements, of a single whole. The individual de-
> cretals provided the principal instrument whereby the papacy
> controlled the development of doctrinal, moral, jurisdictional
> and administrative policies, while the decretal collections pro-
> vided a continuously revised corpus of law both for legal
> administration and academic instruction. [11]

One of the earliest of these commentators on the Gregorian
Decretal Collection was Henry of Segusia who was lecturing on
these decretals in the fourth decade of the thirteenth-century
at the University of Paris. It was in Paris in the thirties that
he began his large exposition of canon law that we know as
the *Summa Aurea* and which was to become one of the most
influential canonical text-books of the period. It was also in
Paris that he began his voluminous commentary on the Gregorian
Decretals, though he did not complete this until the last few

---

[11] C. Duggan, 'Decretals,' *New Catholic Encyclopedia*, 1967, vol. 4: 708-9.

years of his life. Another important decretalist who appears
to have studied at Bologna at the same time as Henry of Segusia
was Sinibald Fieschi. He continued at Bologna as a lecturer
in canon law before being made a cardinal and papal legate
in Italy. He became Pope Innocent IV in 1241. 'The works
of the mid-thirteenth century Decretalists, especially of the two
greatest, Sinibald Fieschi (Innocent IV), and Hostiensis (Henricus de Segusio, Cardinal-bishop of Ostia), were perhaps the
supreme achievements of medieval canonistic science.' [12]

2. *Views of Canonists and Popes on the Role of Law*

There was then in existence a large and rapidly developing
corpus of canonical legislation in the thirteenth century. What,
it may be asked, did men think was the function of this large
body of law? To provide an accurate and fully documented
answer to such a question would, of course, involve a detailed
study of all the principal canonical writings of the period and
this cannot be attempted in these pages. It does, however,
seem useful at this point to consider briefly the views of a
few of the more influential medieval canonists on the role of
law in the Church. This, it is hoped, will provide some indication of medieval thought on the matter under discussion.
It will also help the more detailed study of Hostiensis that is
to follow by showing the kind of tradition that he in fact inherited.

a) *Gratian and the Decretists*

Gratian is the obvious canonist to begin with, although he
has very little to say on the subject in his short treatise on
the sources of law at the beginning of the *Decretum*. [13] Most
of his theory of law he seems to have taken from Isidore of
Seville rather than from Roman law and in this he is at one
with the general medieval tradition of the Church. For Gratian
the function of law appears to have been primarily moralistic.
That is to say, it was the law's task to prescribe what had to
be done, forbid what is evil and permit what is licit. [14] In doing
this the law would provide a clear guide to the Christian for

---

[12] B. Tierney, *Foundations of the Conciliar Theory*, Cambridge, 1955,
p. 17.

[13] *Distinctiones* 1-20.

[14] D. 3,3 *dict. post*: 'precipere quod necesse est fieri, prohibere quod
malum est fieri, permittere vel licita'.

his daily life. The very word 'canon', explains Gratian, is simply
the Greek for 'regula', and it is called a 'regula' 'because it leads
in the right direction and does not lead astray. Others say it is
called a "regula" because it rules or provides the norm for right
living'.[15] The function of the law, then, was to act as a guide
towards Christian perfection.

A similar approach to law is shown in the writings of the
commentators on the *Decretum*, the decretists of the twelfth
century. Rolandus Bandinelli produced a commentary on the
Decretum some ten years before he became pope in 1159.[16] In
the preface to this *Stroma Rolandi* the function of canon law
is touched upon though not explicitly discussed. It is clear,
however, that Magister Rolandus thought that canon law was
there to provide the faithful with instruction. Through its four-
fold role of counselling and permitting, forbidding and com-
manding, it provides the means by which Christians are led to
perfection. Its function is to command what has to be done,
forbid what is to be avoided, grant leave for those things that
may be done and provide exhortation and counsel concerning
the most perfect conduct. In short, it should provide a guide
towards the Christian ideal, the 'excellentissima'.[17]

Another early commentary on the *Decretum* was the *Summa*
by Paucapalea who had also been one of Gratian's pupils at
Bologna. In his introduction Paucapalea is mainly concerned
with the origins of Church legislation, but he makes a few observations about the function of canon law in general. The
primary aim of the law is to prohibit what is evil and command
what is good. It is according to the natural law, he continues,
that each man should be forbidden to do to another what he
does not want done to himself; and that he should be ordered
to do for another what he would like to see done for himself.[18]
Paucapalea goes on, however, to give a very clerical slant to
the function of canon law. It is concerned, he says, with clarifying the hierarchical structure of the Church — 'ecclesiastici
ordines' and 'ecclesiasticae dignitates'. It is the role of canon
law to make clear the duties of ecclesiastical ministers and show

---

[15] D. 3,1-2.

[16] Cf. J. F. von Schulte, *Die Geschichte der Quellen*, vol. I, 114-118;
S. Kuttner, *Repertorium der Kanonistik*, 127-129.

[17] *Die Summa magistri Rolandi*, edited by F. Thaner, Innsbruck,
1874, p. 3.

[18] *Die Summa des Paucapalea*, edited by J. F. von Schulte, Giessen,
1890, p. 3.

how they ought to live.[19] This would seem a rather narrow view of the role of canon law. Its function is clear enough, though very restricted. It has to clarify the rights and duties of ecclesiastics and regulate the procedure for ecclesiastical trials. As will be seen shortly, this is not out of harmony with the lawbook that Paucapalea was about to comment on in detail, the *Decretum* of Gratian.

A somewhat different emphasis is given by Archbishop Rufinus, another early and influential decretist, who produced his *Summa* in the late fifties of the twelfth century.[20] Rufinus sees the role of canon law as that of recalling fallen man to the practice of righteousness. He observes that all men consider with admiration how 'the ranks and classes within the Church harmoniously differ and harmonise amidst differences under such strict justice and upright discipline'.[21] Before the fall man had the support of two great qualities — 'rectitudine iustitie et scientie claritate'. But these were severely damaged by original sin.[22] The aim of the natural law and of the *ius gentium*, Rufinus continues, was to provide man with a way of life that would mark him off from the animal world and allow him to live in peace and harmony with his fellow-men. Therefore sound laws were established by men to control man's savage tendencies and help him to live an honourable life and live in peace and harmony. These human laws were not sufficient. So God gave men the Ten Commandments. But even this was not enough. So God sent his Son to provide man with that new law that we call the gospel.

> Denique cum auctore Deo ecclesia cresceret gradusque in ea disponerentur et ordines et tam in eis discernendis quam in litibus inter ecclesiasticas personas provenientibus sedendis evangelium sufficere non videretur, tam ab apostolis quam ab eorum vicariis nec non ceteris ecclesiae ministris multa sunt addita, que, licet multimode in specie appellentur, uno tamen generali vocabulo nuncupantur: quod est canones.[23]

From this it seems clear that Rufinus looked upon canon law as a means of providing order and harmony within the Church

---

[19] *Ibid.*
[20] Cf. H. Singer (Editor), *Die Summa Magistri Rufini zum Decretum Gratiani*, Paderborn, 1902, pp. cxv-cxviii; S. Kuttner, *Repertorium*, p. 132.
[21] *Die Summa Magistri Rufini*, edited by H. Singer, Praefatio, p. 3.
[22] *Ibid.*, p. 4.
[23] *Ibid.*, pp. 4-5.

as well as of carrying out that function of moral reform which he considered to be the function of all law.

b) *The Popes*

More light can be gained about what medieval canonists thought canon law was for from the *prooemia* to the official collections of papal decretals that were issued at that time. In all of these the reforming role of law is heavily emphasised. One is reminded of the statement by Ivo of Chartres, more than a century earlier, in the famous prologue to his own canonical collection: 'Cogunt enim multas inveniri medicinas multorum experimenta morborum'. [24]

Pope Honorius III, in his short preface to the *Compilatio Quinta* in 1226, mentions the need for a variety of remedies if justice is to be protected. New laws and new decisions, he observes, are necessary 'ut singulis morbis, competentibus remediis deputatis, ius suum cuique salubriter tribuatur'. [25]

Eight years later, when Pope Gregory IX issued the first official collection of papal decretals that claimed to be complete and exclusive, he forbade any further collections to be produced without the authority of the Holy See. In his preface commending this collection to the masters and scholars at Bologna he underlines the need for law in the Church. The King of heaven, he notes, has ordained that his subjects should live virtuous, peaceful and honourable lives, but the unbridled passions and cupidity of men have made this extremely difficult. To maintain concord, therefore, it is necessary that the law should ensure the reign of justice and rid the community of the abuses that have crept in. 'Ideoque lex proditur, ut appetitus noxius sub iuris regula limitetur, per quam genus humanum, ut honeste vivat, alterum non laedat, ius suum unicuique tribuat informatur'. [26] The function of law, then, according to Gregory IX would seem to be primarily that of moral reform within the Church and of instruction in the ways of justice.

This same approach was adopted at the end of the century by Boniface VIII in his preface to the *Liber Sextus*. His aim was to ensure the peace and harmony of the faithful. He had spent sleepless nights, he informs the reader, in anxious thought about how he could remove scandals from the Church and sup-

---

[24] Migne, *P. L.*, vol. 161, col. 50.

[25] A. Friedberg, *Quinque Compilationes Antiquae*, Lipsiae, 1882, p. 151.

[26] A. Friedberg, *Corpus Iuris Canonici*, Lipsiae, 1879, vol. II, pp. 1-2.

press the abuses that had arisen within the Christian community. He thought that this task would be made somewhat easier if there were greater clarity and certainty about Church legislation. So he decided to supplement the Gregorian Decretals with a new and authoritative collection of the papal legislation that had been promulgated since 1234. The new collection was to be known as the *Liber Sextus* since it was to be used in conjunction with the five books of the Gregorian Decretals. In these decretals it is again the reforming function of the law that is put in the first place, though its role in securing peace and settling litigation is also mentioned. [27]

And finally, to mention the last official collection of papal decretals that is contained in the *Corpus Iuris Canonici*, a similar concern for moral reform is shown by John XXII in his preface to the *Clementinae* of 1317. It is here stated quite explicitly that the aim of the collection was to clear up doubts in forensic matters and to reform the morals of both clergy and people. And the image of the gardener wielding his hoc is used to illustrate the preoccupations of church legislators at this period. [28]

To sum up the results of the inquiry so far, it can be said that medieval canonists put forward a variety of functions for the law to perform within the Christian community. It was to be a means for securing order, peace and harmony within the Church. It was to be an instrument of moral reform and provide instruction for the faithful, protecting them from harm as well as guiding them towards Christian perfection. Professor Le Bras described its role in these words:

> Le droit canon est au service des bonnes moeurs. Il a pour fonction d'assurer la pureté de l'Eglise, la rectitude de la Chrétienté, le salut de chaque chrétien. [29]

Moreover, the law clarified the hierarchical structure of the Church and delineated the rights and duties of ecclesiastical officials. And, of course, it prescribed the procedure for ecclesiastical trials. Each of these functions will be examined later in greater detail.

---

[27] *Corpus Iuris Canonici*, (edited by A. Friedberg), vol. II pp. 933-936.
[28] *Ibid.*, pp. 1129-1130.
[29] G. Le Bras, *Institutions ecclésiastiques de la Chrétienté médiévale*, vol. I, p. 109.

3. *The Practical Concerns of Medieval Canon Law*

So far the development of canonical collections has been outlined and the views of medieval canonists on the function of this legislation have been briefly considered. But this is only one aspect of the picture, the theoretical aspect. What of the actual practice? What in fact were the main legal problems dealt with by this large body of law and how in practice did the law try to solve them? To be able to discuss such questions and discern the main emphases of medieval canonical legislation a clear picture of the actual contents of the main collections is required. Consequently it has been thought useful to provide here an outline of the structure and contents of the *Decretum* and of the Gregorian Decretal Collection. This is intended to give a bird's eye view, so to speak, of the whole corpus of Church legislation in the mid-thirteenth century and provide the necessary background for the understanding of the work of one of the greatest commentators on this legislation, Cardinal Hostiensis.

Gratian's compilation is divided into three parts. Part One, consisting of 101 *distinctiones*, begins with a short section on the nature of law and papal legislation and goes on to deal with the clerical ministry in the Church — the rights and the duties of clerics and the qualities required of candidates for ordination. It also contains legislation on ordination, the different grades in the ministry and the qualities required in the bishop. It has often been pointed out that this part of the *Decretum* contains an extended commentary on the *regula apostoli*, those directions on the qualities required of the Christian minister that are given in the Pauline letters to Titus ad Timothy. It is here that we have a particularly clear example of canon law and moral theology merging into each other since it was felt that the moral state of the Christian community would be greatly influenced by the moral qualities of the clergy. Their teaching and example would be decisive factors in the general state of Christendom. Part Two of the *Decretum* consists of 36 *causae* which are in turn divided into *quaestiones*. These contain the legislation on ecclesiastical administration in general, — ecclesiastical trials, episcopal jurisdiction, religious, simony, heresy, excommunication and so on. This part also contains lengthy treatises on matrimony (*causae* 27-36) and the sacrament of penance (*causa* 33, *quaestio* 3 which is divided into 7 *distinctiones*). Here Gratian raises a great variety of problems and proposes solutions by citing authorities in the form of patristic texts, conciliar canons and papal decretals. These *canones* are to be carefully distinguished from Gratian's own comments which are usually referred to as the *dicta Gratiani*. Part Three consists of five *distinctiones* which deal with the Eucharistic sacrifice and sacrament and the rest of the sacraments. [30]

The structure of the Gregorian Decretals, compiled by Raymond of Peñafort, is modelled on that of Bernard of Pavia's *Compilatio Prima* and is divided into five books (*judex, judicium, clerus, connubia* and *crimen*) which are arranged in *tituli* and *capita*. Each *titulus* contains the relevant canons or decretals, the *capita*, in chronological order according to the date of promulgation. Book One deals with ecclesiastical judges and their jurisdiction, Book Two with procedural law, Book Three with clerics and religious, Book Four with marriage, and Book Five with crimes and penalties and criminal procedure. [31]

A study of the list of contents of these collections will give some idea of what canon law was doing in the thirteenth century. The main preoccupations stand out fairly clearly. A very large proportion of the legislation is concerned with clerics and with the hierarchical structure of the Church and there is a preponderance of legislation dealing with Church organization. This is only to be expected since it was a period during which the powers of the papal monarchy were rapidly being clarified and consolidated. In the eyes of some historians the stress on organization and on politics had grown to such an extent that it obscured the spiritual purpose of the Church.

> The genuine fervour, writes Professor Barraclough (describing the conditions of the Church in 1216), 'which had possessed reforming circles at the turn of the eleventh and twelfth centuries, had given way to a preoccupation with organization. The desire among reformers like Humbert, Damian and Hildebrand to shake the Church free in order to enable it to pursue its spiritual mission had degenerated into the pursuit of independence for its own sake, generally interpreted as a sovereign papal state. In theory, the church was still conceived of, in Hugh of St Victor's words, as "the multitude of the faithful, the whole community of Christians". In fact, the development of the papal monarchy, with its centre in the curia, had in practice substituted for the church in the wider sense a narrower hierarchical church, the clerical order in

---

[30] Cf. A. van Hove, *Prolegomena*, pp. 339-348.
[31] Cf. A. van Hove, *Prolegomena*, pp. 357-361.

its ascending ranks, jealous of its privileges and insistent
on its rights; and the ideal and the privileged institution
confronted one another at an ever-widening distance. These
were the dichotomies which the self-confident advance of the
papacy had created. [32]

Ideas about law cannot, of course, be fully appreciated
apart from the context of the society for which the law was
intended and it has been pointed out that

> much of the thirteenth-century thought about papal power
> in temporal affairs was only meaningful on the assumption
> that there existed a common international society of which
> the pope was the head. The papal political logic developed
> from this premise and it was only within the framework of
> the idea of Christendom that it acquired much of its ra-
> tionality. [33]

In medieval society it was taken for granted that the spiritual
and temporal powers were two separate powers which had to
cooperate harmoniously for the well-being of the whole of Christendom. It was also generally believed that the spiritual power
was in some sense superior to the temporal, though this did
not necessarily imply that the pope was absolutely supreme
and the emperor no more than his assistant in temporal affairs.
None of the popes was the absolute hierocrat that some historians have tried to make out. [34] The real situation often lacks
complete clarity and logical coherence and it does not promote
understanding if men are forced into pre-conceived moulds as
'monists' or 'dualists'. The truth is often more complex than
this. [35] Undoubtedly the conflict between the pope as temporal
ruler in Italy and the emperor which raged during much of
the century between 1150 and 1250 was the cause of much
canonical legislation. The clarification of the relations between

---

[32] Geoffrey Barraclough, *The Medieval Papacy*, London, 1968, p. 117.
[33] J. A. Watt, 'The Theory of Papal Monarchy in the 13th Century'
Traditio, 1964, p. 180.
[34] Cf. W. Ullmann, *The Growth of Papal Government in the Middle
Ages*, London, 1955. W. Ullmann, *Medieval Papalism. The Political
Theories of the Medieval Canonists*, London, 1949.
[35] Cf. A. Stickler, 'Concerning the Political Theories of the Medieval
Canonists', *Traditio*, 7 (1949-1951), pp. 450-463; J. A. Watt, 'The Theory of
Papal Monarchy', *Traditio* 20 (1964), pp. 179-317; B. Tierney, 'Papal Political
Theory in the Thirteenth Century', *Mediaeval Studies*, XXVII (1965),
pp. 227-245.

the spiritual and temporal powers was certainly a classical subject of debate among canonists at this time.[36] It would, however, be inaccurate to label the canonists as extreme papalists since while it is true that they attributed some sort of superiority to the spiritual power in Christendom, they also accepted the distinction of powers and stressed elements that tended to limit papal competence in the government of the Church. They showed a real interest in constructing defences against the abuse of papal power and some of the most influential held realistic views on the joint interests of both powers.[37]

Another feature of this legislation which catches the eye of the modern reader is the apparent confusion between canon law and moral theology.

> Pendant un millénaire, comments Professor Le Bras, morale et droit tendent à se confondre dans la discipline de l'Eglise. Legislation, collections, enseignement attestent cette intimité: beaucoup de lois se bornent à formuler les règles de conduite, les collections font large place aux fragments éthiques.[38]

In fact it was not until the fourteenth century that moral theology came to be treated as a distinct theological discipline. For Peter Lombard and St Thomas Aquinas moral theology and dogmatic theology were but two aspects of a single theological discipline, though many questions which today would be regarded as belonging to moral theology were then dealt with by the canonist. This is particularly true of the sacraments of penance and marriage. Canonists played an active part in formulating a theology of penance and editing manuals for the use of confessors. Indeed one of the best known of these handbooks was produced by the compiler of the Gregorian Decretals, Raymond of Peñafort.[39]

---

[36] Cf. G. Le Bras, 'Canon Law', *The Legacy of the Middle Ages*, Oxford, 1926, p. 336.

[37] Cf. J. A. Watt, 'The Theory of Papal Monarchy' *op. cit.* and B. Tierney, 'Papal Political Theory in the Thirteenth Century', *op. cit.*

[38] G. Le Bras, *Institutions Ecclésiastiques de la Chrétienté Médiévale*, *Histoire de l'Eglise* (Fliche et Martin), vol. 12, Part I, pp. 109-110.

[39] Cf. L. Vereeke, 'Moral Theology, History of', *New Catholic Encyclopedia*, 1967, vol. 9: 1119-20. O. Lottin, *Psychologie et morale aux XIIe et XIIIe siècles*, vols. 1-6, Louvain-Gembloux, 1942-1960. Pierre Michaud-Quantin, *Sommes de Casuistique et manuels de confession au Moyen Age*, (XII-XVI siècles). Analecta Medievalia Namurcensia, 13. Louvain, 1962 (especially for Raymond of Peñafort). F. Broomfield (Editor), *Thomae de*

Both the *Decretum* and the Gregorian Decretals contain many laws which are really moral rules of conduct. A very large section of Part One of the *Decretum*, for example, can be looked upon as a guide for the moral life of the priest and the bishop and the same is true of much of Book Three of the Gregorian Decretals. The legislation on marriage in both collections has much to say about the moral duties within the family. This same concern for morality is also particularly evident in the legislation on the sacrament of penance,[40] and in the lengthy treatment of simony in the Decretals where no less than 46 chapters are devoted to the topic.[41] In fact moral concern pervades the whole legislation which in general set out to provide a detailed moral guide for the Christian. It aim was to lead man to God and do everything possible to keep him from sin. This was quite explicitly stated, of course, by those canonists and compilers whose prefaces have been considered earlier in this chapter. It seems to have been the general view and Le Bras sums up the situation as follows:

> A quoi tendent préceptes et interdits? Au salut de chaque chrétien. Si l'Eglise et la Chrétienté en tirent profit et gloire, c'est pourtant le bien spirituel de leur membres, leur avenir éternel par leur moralité temporelle que papes et docteurs ont en vue dans la sanction de la bonne foi et de la vérité, de la justice et de l'equité, de la paix et de la charité ... Pour soutenir la vertu, le droit dispose de moyens préventifs, subsidiaires et répressifs. Il évite mainte occasion de chute, par toutes les barrières qu'il pose dans la vie sociale et les menaces propres à empecher le délit.[42]

He could also conclude a discussion on medieval canon law with these words:

> It is indeed the highest moral tradition of the West and of the Mediterranean peoples which has been gathered up and handed down to us in the classic law of the Church.[43]

Chobham Summa Confessorum, Analecta Mediaevalia Namurcensia, vol. 25, Louvain, 1968.

[40] C. 33, q. 3 and X. 5,38 (De poenitentiis et remissionibus).
[41] X. 5,3 (De simonia).
[42] G. Le Bras, *Institutions Ecclésiastiques, op. cit.*, p. 109-110.
[43] G. Le Bras, 'Canon Law' in *The Legacy of the Middle Ages*, p. 361.

CHAPTER THREE

THE GENERAL APPROACH OF HOSTIENSIS

1. *His Attitude to His Readers*

Several times in the *Summa* Hostiensis states why he is publishing his lectures on the *Tituli* of the Decretals. He says he is writing 'for the instruction of ordinary priests'.[1] He shows too considerable respect for his readers. In the long instruction that he provides for confessors in Book Five, for example, he declares that it is far from his intention to tyrannize in any way over the minds of his readers or compel them to follow the interpretations that he puts forward:

> Non tamen intelligas quod omnia haec superiora et inferiora semper ad unguem servanda sint. Sed discretus sacerdos secundum quod qualitas personae et verborum exiget, eliget quod sibi necessarium videbitur vel utile.[2]

At the beginning of the *Summa* he writes in the same vein. In composing his book, he tells the reader, he has paid careful attention to the writings of other canonists, examining the glosses they have written and the useful distinctions they have made, and stating what he himself thinks is the correct view.[3] In doing so, however, he does not wish to appear to be forcing his own views on others. Each reader should weigh the evidence on each point and then make up his own mind:

> Ego vero per dictum meum nemini legem impono; nec opinionem aliorum renuo vel abscondo, imo ipsas diligenter recito et in lucem produco. Tu ergo perlectis et intellectis iuribus et rationibus quibus unaquaeque fulcitur opinio amplectere quam malueris, et elige cui dicas: tu mihi sola places.[4]

---

[1] *Summa Aurea*, V, De poenitentiis et remissionibus, n. 62: 'ad instructionem simplicium sacerdotum'.
[2] *Ibid.*
[3] *Summa Aurea*, I, Prooemium, n. 1.
[4] *Ibid.*

5

Hard work too will be required of the student if he wishes to become a competent jurist. And Hostiensis quotes a popular verse:

> Si quis forte cupit iurisconsultus haberi,
> Continuet studium, velit quocumque doceri;
> Invigilet, nec vincat eum tortura laboris;
> Fortior insurgat cunctisque recentior horis.
> Nam labor improbus omnia vincit. [5]

It is also part of the student's task to approach his study in a questioning frame of mind, examining carefully the evidence for the positions put forward by the writers he is study-in. 'Studiosus vero debet dubitare de singulis'. [6] This calls for a sense of responsibility. It does not mean that the student may allow himself to be carried away by unfounded criticisms or judgements that cannot be supported by the necessary evidence. This is a frequent failing, observes Hostiensis, and there are many ways in which a student can be misled into forming rash conclusions. Here he gives a list of ten snares that lie in the path of the searcher after truth. These are worth mentioning not simply on account of their intrinsic value but also because of the light they throw on the mind of Hostiensis. [7]

First of all, one should take care not to pass judgement on anything before one has fully understood the matter at issue. Secondly, one should not find fault with a work before one has examined it thoroughly and read it over several times. Thirdly, one should be on one's guard against corruptions in the manuscript. The omission of a 'non', for example, can make a great difference and yet a scriptor can quite easily make such a slip. [8] This applies even to copies of papal decretals and the reader is warned against forgeries and defective manuscripts.

Fourthly, one should refrain from condemning waspishly the teaching of others out of ill-will. This only takes away a man's good name and causes trouble. Fifthly, one should be careful not to suppress mention of those views of other doctors which differ from one's own. If there is a variety of opinions and the names of their authors should be known and declared. They should not be passed over in silence, 'scribimus

---

5 *Summa*, I, Prooemium, n. 1.
6 *Summa*, I, Prooemium, n. 2.
7 *Summa*, I, Prooemium, n. 2.
8 *Summa*, I, Prooemium, n. 2.

enim, sicut et legimus aliqua ne ignoremus, aliqua ne negligamus, aliqua ut repudiemus'. [9] Sixthly, one must weigh carefully both the intention of the writer and the context of his remarks, the circumstances with which he is dealing and also the particular style of the document that is being considered. Seventhly, one must take care not to rely on one's judgment to such an extent that the truth gets obscured. Eighthly, one should not condemn ancient opinions indiscriminately simply because they are not in harmony with the 'ius novum'. Ninthly, when there is need to cut away superfluous growths one must be careful not to remove at the same time what is in fact essential. Here Hostiensis adds that autobiographical touch already referred to about his inability to be brief without tending to become obscure. [10] Tenthly, beware of sticking rigidly to the literal meaning of words when in fact it is the mind of the writer and the truth that matter. These are the ten ways of avoiding rash judgments that Hostiensis recommends to the young law-student, and he backs them up by frequent reference to the *Decretum* of Gratian.

Hostiensis warns the reader that he will find some innovations in the *Summa*. This, however, should in no way alarm him since, as Julian puts it, 'no law has come to the Roman republic sufficient in itself right from the start. Because of the variety and inventiveless of nature there are many laws which stand in need of correction'. [11] It is for this reason, he continues, that while maintaining all due respect for our forefathers, it is permissible to correct their statements should these run counter to the truth. Here he refers to the following passage, which was attributed to St Augustine in the *Decretum*:

> We should not treat the discussions of men — even of praise-worthy Catholics — as if they were canonical scripture; with due respect to these authors, if with the help of God we, or anyone else, come across anythings that runs counter to the truth, then this should be condemned and rejected. I shall deal with the writings of others in just the same way as I would like my readers to deal with mine. [12]

---

[9] *Summa*, I, Prooemium, n. 2.

[10] *Summa Aurea*, I, *Prooemium*, n. 2.

[11] *Summa Aurea*, I, *Prooemium*, n. 1: 'nullum ius ab initio sufficiens emanavit in rempublicam; sed a naturae varietate et eius machinatione multa egent correctione'.

[12] *Decretum*, D. 9, c. 10. (St. Augustine, *Ep. ad Fortunatum*, 148, 4, 15. ML. 33, 628).

Hostiensis clearly intends to follow the example of St Augustine
in this matter, declaring that he expects to receive the same
treatment from those who come after him.

2. *His Method in Argumentation*

a) *The Use of Scriptural and Theological Arguments*

Hostiensis was primarily a canonist but his interests were
by no means confined to the field of law. He consistently maintained that religious principles derived from theology should
permeate Christian legislation and the interpretation of all law,
including the civil law. This is clear from the importance he
attached to the notions of canonical equity, the natural law,
good faith, *periculum animae*, and so on.[13] As will be seen
when his views on the nature of canon law are considered in
greater detail, Hostiensis held that there was a close bond between canon law and theology and his commentaries reflect the
great renaissance in theology that had taken place between 1150
and 1250. According to Professor Le Bras, 'Henri est un type
de juriste parfait, à la fois canoniste et romaniste, théologien
et humaniste'.[14]

This interest in and concern for theological principles show
themselves in the method he uses in argumentation which casts
some light on his view of canon law and the role of the canon
lawyer within the Christian community. A clear example of
this theological approach can be seen in Book One of the *Summa*
where he is discussing bigamy as an impediment to sacred orders. Bigamy, of course, in this context does not mean the
crime of attempting to have two wives at the same time which
the word has come to mean in modern speech. In the Middle
Ages the word was used to describe the status of a widower
who had remarried quite legitimately. It was bigamy in this
sense that was held to be an impediment to sacred orders. This
was considered not only an impediment but one which, based
as it was on the teaching of St Paul in his letter to Timothy,
was regarded by medieval writers as practically incapable of
dispensation.[15] But why, it may be asked, was ordination re-

---

[13] Cf. C. Lefebvre, 'Hostiensis', in *DDC*, V, 1222.

[14] C. Le Bras, 'Théologie et droit romain dans l'oeuvre d'Henri de
Suse', in *Etudes Historiques à la memoire de Noel Didier*, Grenoble, 1960,
pp. 195-204.

[15] For a detailed discussion of the whole question of bigamy as an
impediment, see S. Kuttner, 'Pope Lucius III and the Bigamous Archbishop

fused to the bigamist since presumably the second marriage
had been entered into legitimately in the eyes of the Church?
Hostiensis agrees that there is quite clearly no sin involved in
marrying a second time, yet he maintained, in line with the
general tradition of the Fathers, that the law forbidding ordination to the bigamist was both wise and just. He did not think
it was fitting that a man who had married twice, and so 'divided
his flesh,' should stand in the place of Christ and minister
to his Church. There is, he argues, a 'defectus sacramenti' here,
and he refers to the classical text of St Augustine on the matter.
'Prohibetur ergo bigamus non propter peccatum, sed propter
normam sacramenti amissam; non ad vitae meritum, sed ad
ordinationis signaculum. [16] He then goes on, quoting Tancred,
to argue from theological symbolism: the union of the faithful
with God in faith; the union of human nature with God; the
unity of Christ and the Church. The bigamist, it is argued,
can no longer symbolise this unity and therefore it is not fitting
that he should be admitted to sacred orders.

      Whatever one may thinks of this approach to the problem,
— which was, of course, the traditional and patristic one, —
it does provide an instructive example of how a canonist of
the calibre of Hostiensis can put forward mystical and theological arguments to support the law. He sees the law on
bigamy not simply as part of an arbitrary structure, but as the
expression of theological truth. And this is an important aspect
of his whole approach to the law of the Church. It may also
be mentioned at this point that his treatment of bigamy illustrates another characteristic of the *Summa* and of the *Lectura*.
This is the practice of backing up every statement he makes
with references to ecclesiastical authorities and to other canonists. In the short passage about bigamy he refers to the
Decretum, to Tancred, Huguccio, Raymond, Goffredus and Pope
Innocent. This extremely thorough cross-reference system was
common to all medieval canonists and they provide constant
and copious documentation throughout their commentaries. The
commentaries of Hostiensis are full of such references; he quotes
frequently from the writings of his predecessors and from contemporary canonists and Roman Lawyers, at times citing lengthy
passages practically verbatim. [17] Nothing shows more clearly

---

of Palermo', *Medieval Studies Presented to Aubrey Gwynn, S. J.*, Dublin,
1961, pp. 409-453.
    [16] *Summa*, I, De bigamis non ordinandis, n. 5.
    [17] Cf. the description of the *Summa* already given in Chapter One;

than this regular series of references how widely read and how firmly rooted he was in the whole canonistic tradition.

Another example of his concern for theological interests in arguing a case is provided by his treatment of tithes.[18] This is one of the most elaborate attempt to prove a point to be found in the *Summa*. The problem concerned the obligation of the individual Christian to pay tithes to the Church. Hostiensis stresses that this law *de decimis et primitiis* imposes a strict obligation on the faithful. He goes on to ask if custom can release a man from this obligation. His answer is in the negative but it is his method of proving his point that is of particular interest to us here. He begins his argument by giving some views of theologians who taught that custom could modify the obligation. Even such a distinguished canonist as Raymond was hesitant about settling the question definitively though he counselled that the tithes should be paid or commuted to alms by the authority of the bishop. Hostiensis, however, argues that integral payment is a serious obligation and he proceeds to prove his point by a threefold argument — from the Bible, from the authority of the Fathers, and thirdly from Roman and canon law.[19] He then goes on to quote examples from Genesis, Exodus and Deuteronomy, which he follows by a number of New Testament texts which he considers support his point of view. And if some teachers want to take these texts in any other sense they will meet with disagreement in the Fathers of the Church. Hostiensis draws attention to the distinction between *primitiae* and *decimae* and he argues that while it may be possible to interpret somewhat freely the laws about *primitiae*, this is not the case with the laws on *decimae*. He then quotes from Ambrose, Gregory the Great, Augustine and Jerome to confirm his argument.[20] He then appeals to Raymond and to those who agree with him to listen to the divine law and the four principal doctors of the Church, rather than to others who would put a false interpretation on these laws. Hostiensis main-

---

see also C. Lefebvre, 'Hostiensis', *DDC*, V, 1216, 1221-22. J. F. von Schulte, *Die Geschichte der Quellen und Literatur des canonischen Rechts*, vol. II, p. 126, note 24, (This provides a list of the canonists and legists that are quoted by Hostiensis). H. Kantorowicz, 'Die Allegationen im spätern Mittelalter', in *Archiv für Urkundenforschungen*, 13 (1933), pp. 15-29, where useful hints are given on how to verify these medieval references.

[18] *Summa*, III, De decimis et primitiis.
[19] *Summa*, III, De decimis et primitiis, n. 16.
[20] *Summa*, III, *ibid*.

tains that there is no doubt whatever in this matter. The canonical legislation, he argues, also supports this interpretation, as does the authority of the general councils. The penalty of excommunication has been used to compel payment and such a severe penalty implies a very serious obligation.

This is not the place to criticise the value of the arguments that Hostiensis uses to prove this particular point. The argumentation is mentioned at this point as but another illustration of his general approach to the law and his constant effort to support it with scriptural and theological arguments. It clearly shows that he did not regard the law as standing separately and independently on its own. It had to maintain a close connection with the scriptural revelation and the Christian tradition as this is revealed in the writings of the Fathers of the Church.

b) *The Concern for Morality*

Another characteristic of his canonical commentary that should be touched upon here is the great concern he shows for moral considerations. The *Summa Aurea* clearly illustrates that apparent confusion between canon law and moral theology in the Middle Ages which has already been discussed in Chapter Two. At the very beginning of the *Summa* he states quite explicitly that canon law may be included under the philosophical heading of ethics because it has to concern itself with moral considerations — 'quia tractat de moribus, sicut et ceteri libri iuris'. [21] More will be said about this later but a few examples will illustrate this aspect of his general method and throw some more light on how he viewed the role of the canon lawyer in the Church.

A particularly clear illustration of this aspect of his work is provided in his lengthy treatment of vows in Book Three of the *Summa*. [22] Here it is made quite clear that Hostiensis accepted it as part of his role as a canonist to discuss in detail when a vow would be binding in conscience and how serious such an obligation would be. In doing this he was, of course, simply following in the footsteps of all his predecessors since the vow had been the object of much recent legislation and a traditional topic for canonistic commentary. [23] He provides the

---

[21] *Summa*, I, Prooemium, n. 18.
[22] *Summa*, III, De voto et voti redemptione.
[23] Part Two of the *Decretum* contains four *quaestiones* on the subject

reader with a list of situations and circumstances where one
would be excused from observing a vow, discusses what sort of
matters can form the object of vows and who may not take
vows, and refers quite frequently to the sanction of mortal sin. [24]
The discussion is in fact what would nowadays be thought of
as a short treatise in moral theology where the author is writing
as a moral adviser or spiritual director and giving advice on
different courses of action that may be considered morally sound.
Part of the discussion can, of course, be considered as appro-
priate to the canonist as, for instance, the treatment of the
nature of the vow and the power of the pope to dispense from
vows in virtue of his *plenitudo potestatis*. But much of Hostiensis's treatment of the theme here is in effect a list of cases
of conscience. [25]

This moralising approach is also shown in the short sermon
that Hostiensis delivers on the danger of contacts with women
when he is dealing with consanguinity in Book IV. [26] It appears
too in the doubts he expresses about the desirability of wives
being permitted to take the crusading vow because their chas-
tity might be in danger on the long journey! [27] Another clear
instance of this approach is to be found in his treatment of
the misdemeanors of bishops in Book Five where he provides
superiors with what can best be described as a practical guide
for the examination of their conscience. [28] But the clearest example of all where Hostiensis can be seen playing the role of
the moral theologian is his long treatise on the sacrament of
penance in Book Five of the *Summa*. [29] This extends to about
thirty folio pages and constitutes what must have been an im-

---

(C. 17) and there are eleven *capita* in the *titulus*, *De voto et voti redemptione* of the Gregorian Decretals (X, III, 34, 1-11). J. A. Brundage, in
the carefully documented study that has already been referred to, has
shown that there was a long development in the canonistic doctrine on
vows between Gratian and Hostiensis who in fact put the finishing
touches to a comprehensive and coherent juridical theory in the matter.
Cf. J. A. Brundage, 'The Votive Obligations of Crusaders. The Development
of a Canonistic Doctrine', *Traditio*, 24 (1968), pp. 77-118.

[24] Hostiensis quite regularly refers to mortal sin as a sanction in
canon law. Cf. also *Summa*, I, *De sacra unctione*, n. 6-7; and *Summa*, III,
De praebendis et dignitatibus, n. 6.

[25] *Summa*, III, De voto et voti redemptione, n. 16.

[26] *Summa*, IV, De eo qui cognovit consanguineam uxoris suae, n. 1.
('ni fugias tactus, vix evitabitur actus'!).

[27] *Summa*, III, De voto, n. 9.

[28] *Summa*, V, De excessibus praelatorum et subditorum.

[29] *Summa*, V, De poenitentiis et remissionibus.

portant and influential treatise in moral theology. It is really
a manual for confessors rather than a strictly canonical treatise
and in it Hostiensis declares quite explicitly that he is writing
for the instruction of simple priests to help them in the con-
fessional. [30] He was attempting to provide a practical guide
for active priests and this meant a combination of moral theology with canon law. Indeed he was doing much the same
thing as Genicot and other recent moralists have been doing,
that is to say, providing authoritative spiritual guidance to young
priests which would help them to guide the consciences of the
faithful in confession. There are many examples of this approach throughout his writing.

Very often, of course, Hostiensis simply comments on the
positive legislation and refrains from philosophising or theo-
logising about it. The student had to know the law and Hostiensis tried to provide an elucidation and interpretation of
the actual text. This was obviously his principal task as a
commentator on the law but, as the examples just cited clearly
demonstrate, his vision extended beyond the narrow confines
of the legal text and embraced the whole Christian approach
to life. He stressed the moral character of canon law as a
support for and enforcement of the spiritual and moral values
of the Christian.

3. *The Relationship between Canon Law and Theology*

In his introduction to the *Summa Aurea* Hostiensis discusses
briefly the nature of law in general and of canon law in particular. He rapidly traces the genesis of law from Adam and
the natural law, through the Old Testament period with its
Mosaic Law, right down to the time of Christ and beyond, with
its specific Christian law. The natural law, he notes, is founded
on the precept: 'What you wish done for yourself, do the same
for me; do not do to me what you do not wish to be done to
yourself'. [31] From this basic precept it also follows that no one
should be allowed to grow rich at another's expense. On such
natural and rational foundations as this are constructed the
laws about marriage and all other human laws which are reasonably promulgated. It should, therefore, be possible to give
a rational and natural explanation of these laws. With the

---

[30] *Summa*, V, *ibid.*, n. 62.
[31] *Summa*, I, Prooemium, n. 5: 'Quod tibi vis fieri, mihi fac; quod
non tibi, noli'.

growth of the human race and the division into different na-
tions — with the wars, captivity, and mutual treaties that followed — there arose the need for some kind of international
law, the *ius gentium*. Later still, on account of the degenerate
state of humanity and its failure to observe the natural law,
the people had to be given yet another law. Therefore the
Mosaic Law was promulgated. [32] Hostiensis then mentions the
various developments of Roman Law from the Twelve Tables
down to the imperial codification of Justinian and the Digest.
With the coming of Christ, however, there dawned the era of
grace and the law of the Gospel, the apostolic law and the
teaching of the Fathers of the Church. A new body of law thus
came into being which was to govern the lives of clerics in
particular and by which the spiritual and the temporal were
to be guided and protected. This developed out of a combination of Roman Law and the teaching of the Fathers, the councils
and the popes; and all this was finally incorporated in the *Liber
Decretorum.*

There are then, according to Hostiensis, three kinds of science or wisdom in this matter. There is the 'sapientia civilis'
which deals with the natural law, the *ius gentium* and the civil
law. Then there is 'sapientia theologica' which concerns itself
with the Old Testament, the Gospel and the teaching of the
Fathers. Finally, there is canon law which embraces all laws
both human and divine. [33] Therefore a perfect knowledge of
canon law cannot be obtained without knowledge of these other
laws as well. At this point Hostiensis goes on to extol the
importance of canon law, arguing that it is a sort of queen
among the sciences. [34] It is true that civil law claims this precedence and despises the other branches of learning, but this is,
of course, an erroneous opinion.

> Sed canonica videtur praecellere; nam si hoc bene sciatur per
> eam tam spiritualia quam temporalia regi possunt. Ideo debet
> ab omnibus recipi et teneri... et aliis scientiis praeponenda
> est ... et omnes eius authoritate duci debent non sensu proprio. [35]

---

[32] *Summa*, I, *ibid.*, n. 6.
[33] *Summa*, I, Prooemium, n. 11: 'imo et omne ius comprehendit sive
sit divinum sive humanum, publicum vel privatum'.
[34] *Summa*, I, *ibid.*: 'Est igitur haec nostra scientia non pure theologica
sive civilis, sed utrique participans nomen proprium sortita, canonica
vocatur ... Et haec nostra lex sive scientia vere potest scientiarum scientia
nuncupari'.
[35] *Summa, ibid.*

Even the Emperor acknowledges this by the fact that the *leges* imitate the canons and by his declaring that in all things he wishes to follow the laws of the Church.   Moreover, argues Hostiensis, it can even be shown by the natural light of reason that canon law is nobler than all other branches of learning and should enjoy precedence.   Man is composed of body and spirit.   Now the human combination of these two aspects is nobler than either aspect taken individually.   Is not this the reason for the Apostle's declaration: 'Are you unaware that you will be the judges of angels?' (1 Cor. 6:3).   A fortiori, then, will you be the judge over matters that are purely carnal or temporal?   This view is further supported because the Son of God has so greatly honoured mankind by uniting the divinity to humanity.   Clearly, then, canon law is superior to the other sciences because theology deals with the purely spiritual while civil science is concerned with the purely temporal, but canon law is concerned with both spiritual and temporal.   Moreover, all would agree that the mule is superior to both the horse and the donkey since it combines the virtues of both.   It is clear too that theology may be compared to the horse and civil wisdom to the donkey.   Hence this is a further proof that canon law is nobler than these other sciences!

> Quidquid autem dicatur, haec est veritas quod distinctae sunt iurisdictiones quamvis una maior sit reliqua, et quilibet secundum legem suam iudicabit.   Sed utraque tamen ecclesiasticos canones sequi debet. [36]

This is undoubtedly an exaggerated claim for canon law. Was it meant to be taken seriously by the reader?   Professor Ullmann in his discussion of medieval papalism takes it very seriously indeed.   'We need not ask ourselves', he writes, 'whether this particular example would have enriched Ihering's *Ernst und Scherz in der Jurisprudenz*, but Hostiensis puts the following question with all the zeal and fervour of which he is capable.'   And Ullmann goes on to give an account of the question about the superiority of the mule over the horse and the donkey. [37]   Professor Ullmann clearly takes this as a fully serious claim by Hostiensis in his 'demonstration' that canon law is superior to every other branch of learning.   Hostiensis may indeed have put his question 'with all the zeal and fervour of

---

[36] *Summa, ibid.*, n. 12.
[37] Walter Ullmann: *Medieval Papalism*, London, 1948, pp. 30-31.

which he is capable', but there is little in the text to prove such
a claim or even to support it. The author of the *Summa Aurea*
appears to be a reasonable and balanced jurist, a man of exceptional intelligence and ability. The *Summa* itself is a collection of lecture notes for students. It seems therefore more
reasonable to think that Hostiensis had his tongue in his cheek
when he was making these exaggerated claims for his own subject. Such claims are generally good for a laugh, as any teacher
knows, and they are not meant to be taken too seriously.

Professor Kuttner is nearer the truth when he remarks that
a sense of humour should not be excluded when criticising this
use by Hostiensis of the quotation from St Paul, and his comparison of canon law with the 'species mulina'.[38] And there
are other passages in the writing of Hostiensis which show that
this exaggerated claim for canon law at the beginning of the
Summa is nothing more than a piece of comic rhetoric. 'A fundamental text', writes Kuttner, 'in which Hostiensis casts aside
all dialectic artifice and with fervour expounds his belief in
the dignity of theology and the two laws is his *Lectura*, I,14,14,
tit. De aetate et qualitate ordinandorum, c. cum sit ars artium,
nn. 2-7'.[39] This text is unfortunately passed over in silence by
Professor Ullmann in his criticism of Hostiensis that has just
been cited, yet it is a passage that deserves careful examination

---

[38] That Hostiensis was not devoid of a sense of humour becomes
clear in a number of passage in the *Summa*. For instance, in his
discussion *de praebendis et dignitatibus*, in Book Three (n. 6, et qualiter),
he cites the example of a Roman canon who nominated his donkey for
a canonry in the diocese. The donkey had, argued the canon, served
the chapter faithfully for more than thirty years and because of such
long service was worthier than all the other nominees, — 'et sic fuerunt
confusi alii nominatores', comments Hostiensis! Another example of
this humorous approach can probably be detected in his discussion of
the canonical position of a public harlot who has taken the vow to go
on crusade. Should she be allowed to keep the vow and go on crusade
or should she be compelled to redeem her vow by making a monetary
contribution? This gives rise to a real dilemma which will permit
neither solution. If she were allowed to carry out her vow and go on
crusade then there is the serious risk that she will be followed by a
host of warriors for the wrong reason — 'nihil amore vehementius', as
Hostiensis notes. On the other hand, how could she be permitted to
redeem her vow with money that comes from such an immoral source
as prostitution? Was this story meant to be taken as a serious canonical
problem? It seems unlikely. (Cf. *Summa*, III, De Voto, quoted by
J. A. Brundage, in *Traditio*, 24 (1968), pp. 113-4).

[39] S. Kuttner, *Harmony from Dissonance. An Interpretation of Medieval Canon Law*, Pennsylvania, 1960, p. 63, note 36.

in any attempt to assess Hostiensis's considered views on the relationship between theology and canon law. The passage occurs in Book One of his *Commentaria* where Hostiensis is commenting on a decree of the Fourth Lateran Council — 'Quum sit ars artium' — which is an instruction on the careful preparation and training that should precede ordination to the priesthood. He starts off by mentioning how it is a common practice for the proponents of the various sciences to make exaggerated claims for their own subject. Some assert that dialectics is the most important while others claim grammar to be supreme since it is the foundation of all the other sciences. Neither of these positions can be accepted, argue the Roman lawyers, because in the structure of the civil law there is to be found that wonderful sense of purpose which can be seen in no other art. And so it goes on.

> In this way each extols the value of his own science, like a gardener commending the leeks from his garden. The truth of the matter, however, is that the art of arts is the divine law from which neither human nor canon law is to be excluded. [40]

Hostiensis here acknowledges the importance of the civil law while stressing that at the same time it must remain in harmony with the canon law of the Church and provide support for Christian morality. He then adds the following passage which is as clear an expression as one could hope for of how he thought canon law stood in relation to theology:

> Therefore you may say that these two laws form a whole with theology, and all are necessary for the holy Church of God. The difference between them is this: civil law deals mainly with the organization of temporal matters, which are necessary for the Church of God as the body is for the soul. Theology, however, deals primarily with the soul. Canon law deals now with one of these spheres and now with another, instructing the Church's ministers in many matters that the others leave obscure. Let us therefore put it this way. In the government of the holy Church of God theology holds the place of the head, civil law has that of the foot. Canon law, however, since it has to do at times with the head and at times with the foot, takes the place of the hand. [41]

---

[40] *Commentaria*, I, 14 (de aetate et qualitate ordinandorum), 14, n. 2.
[41] *Commentaria*, I, 14, 14, n. 6.

He goes on to quote the passage from St Paul's First Letter
to the Corinthians to the effect that one part of the body cannot
say to another that it has no need of it. All must work together
for the good of the whole. He points out that while the *regimen
animarum* must certainly be considered the *ars artium*, the other
arts and sciences have their importance and deserve respect.
Here it is perfectly clear that Hostiensis regarded theology as
the guiding influence behind all the other sciences. The im-
agery that he uses in the passage just cited to describe the
unity and the hierarchy of the sciences points unmistakably to
the superiority of theology. As Professor Le Bras asks, with
reference to this text, 'Saurait-on mieux marquer la subordina-
tion du droit à la théologie et du droit romain au droit canon?'[42]
Hostiensis is teaching that it is for theology to interpret the
lex divina while canon law has to be guided by the spiritual
principles laid down by theology. This is in complete harmony
with his whole approach to the interpretation of canon law,
as will be seen later in greater detail.

Hostiensis was an authority on Roman law as well as on
canon law and throughout the *Summa* he makes great use of
Roman legislation and Roman commentaries. It was not for
nothing that he was known as 'monarcha utriusque iuris'. Many
of his definitions in the *Summa* are taken straight from Roman
law and his commentary on each *titulus* is usually introduced
by a Roman law definition. He also drew widely from Roman
law expositions of topics that were either neglected in the Decretals or not so fully treated there. Instances of this are to
be found in his treatment of adoption, of dowries, contracts
and so on.[43] As has already been shown in the detailed description of the *Summa* in Chapter One, Roman law influenced the
whole conception of Hostiensis's work and he quotes large passages almost verbatim from the *Summa Codicis* of Azo. Indeed
one of the great merits of his work was, as Mgr. Lefebvre has
demonstrated, the synthesis it provided of both Roman and
canon law.[44]

He did, however, clearly distinguish canon law from civil
law and, as been seen in the passage from the *Commentaria*
that has just been discussed, he maintained the superiority of

---

[42] G. Le Bras, 'Théologie et droit romain dans l'oeuvre d'Henri de
Suse', in *Etudes Historiques à la mémoire de Noel Didier*, Grenoble,
1960, pp. 195-204.

[43] Gabriel Le Bras, *op. cit.*, in note 42.

[44] C. Lefebvre, 'Hostiensis', *DDC*, V, 1218.

canon law, indicating that in cases of conflict the civil law should yield to the law of the Church. This is typical of his general approach in the *Summa*. In his discussion of usury, for example, he observes that in such matters it is the wish of the emperor that the civil law should be guided not only by the teaching of the four General Councils but also generally by canon law, and he refers back to what he had written about this in his introduction. [45] Indeed, he maintains that this is obvious since the lower law cannot derogate from the superior law. [46] Another example of the sort of conflict that can arise between the laws is to be found in his discussion of the legislation on the marriage of slaves. [47] However, the superiority of canon law must not be pressed too far. As has been already noted, Hostiensis maintained that there were two *fora* — the ecclesiastical and the civil — which were distinct and independent:

> Whatever is to be said, this is the truth. There are distinct spheres of jurisdiction although one is superior to the other, and each will give judgment according to his own law. Both spheres, however, must observe the ecclesiastical canons. [48]

He also taught that 'si canon contradicat legi, cuilibet standum est in foro suo'. [49] The two *fora* were quite distinct, but what Hostiensis stressed very strongly was that both of them were bound to remain faithful to the Christian principles which were central to Christianity. [50]

Hostiensis also maintained that canon law was in general more humane than the civil law. As an example of this he contrasts the severe civil legislation on illegitimate children with the milder canonical legislation, noting that one of the reasons for this more mild approach is the closer link between canon

---

[45] *Summa*, V, De usuris, n. 7; and I, Prooemium, n. 12.

[46] *Summa*, V, De usuris, n. 7: 'siquidem quod lex minoris non derogat legi superioris'.

[47] *Summa*, IV, De coniugio servorum, n. 1.

[48] *Summa*, I, Prooemium, n. 12.

[49] *Commentaria*, V, 33, 2.

[50] On the relationship between the two laws, see A. Rivero Damas, *Pensamiento Politico de Hostiensis*, Zürich, 1964, pp. 42-50; P. Legendre, *La Pénétration du droit romain dans le droit canonique classique*, Paris, 1964; P. Legendre, 'Le droit romain, modèle et language. De la signification de l'Utrumque Ius ', *Etudes d'histoire du droit dediées à Gabriel Le Bras*, Paris, 1965, pp. 913-930; S. Kuttner, 'Some Considerations on the Role of Secular Law and Institutions in the History of Canon Law', *Scritti in Onore di Luigi Sturzo*, Bologna, 1953, vol. II.

law and the natural law. [51]   He reverts to this difference between
the *leges* and the canons frequently in the *Summa*, observing
that the canons are protected by milder sanctions than the civil
laws. [52]

He acknowledged too the distinction between divine law and
canon law. They were by no means identical. He observes, for
example, that certain people may be forbidden to contract marriage by canon law even though there is no prohibition by divine
law, and he refers to the decretal of Innocent III on the degrees
of consanguinity within which marriage is forbidden by divine
law. [53]   And in his whole discussion of consanguinity and affinity
he distinguishes clearly between what is of divine law and what
is of purely canonical institution. And, of course, if an impediment is simply a canonical institution then it can be dispensed.
He makes a similar distinction between canon law and the
natural law. [54]   There are, it is true, a number of statements in
which Hostiensis appears to identify canon law with divine law:
'ius canonicum est divinum', [55] 'de canonica vero lege planum
est quod divina est'. [56]   However, he also on occasion refers to
civil law as divine — 'civilis enim divina est quia imperatores
ad actiones divinitus pervenerunt' [57] — and so, as Rivera Damas
has shown, he does not seem to have used the term 'divine law'
consistently in a strict sense since he applies it to such diverse
objects. [58]

Did Hostiensis share the fairly common medieval view that
the sacred canons were in some way inspired by the Holy Spirit?
He has little to say about this aspect in the *Summa*, but there
is at least one passage from which it would appear that he
accepted the common view. It is to be found in Book Five
in the treatise *de poenitentiis et remissionibus*, where he declares that a bishop who does not obey the canons should be
removed from his diocese: 'Qui enim nescit obedire canonibus
non est dignus altaribus ministrare, *nam canones instinctu Spi-
ritus Sancti facti sunt*'. This suggests some kind of inspiration

---

[51] *Summa*, IV, Qui filii sint legitimi, n. 6.
[52] See, for example, *Summa*, V, De poenis raptorum corporum, n. 1;
Summa, IV, Rerum amotorum, n. 7.
[53] *Summa*, IV, De consanguinitate.
[54] *Ibid.*, n. 17.
[55] *Commentaria*, II, 24, 30.
[56] *Commentaria*, I, 14, 14, n. 6.
[57] *Ibid.*
[58] See A. Rivero Damas, *Pensamiento Politico de Hostiensis*, pp. 37-42.

for canon law but what exactly is meant is not at all clear. It is something quite different from scriptural inspiration since, as has just been seen, Hostiensis also maintains that there is a distinction between canon law and divine law and that those laws of the church which are purely human can be changed according to circumstances. The point is not unimportant but further discussion of it can be postponed until the whole notion of canon law as a guide to Christian living is examined in detail.

4. *Hostiensis on the Role of Law in General*

This investigation is primarily an attempt to discover what Cardinal Hostiensis took to be the function of canon law in the Church. Unfortunately, however, there was no *titulus, De functione iuris canonici* or any equivalent contained in the decretal collections on which he was commenting, and so there is no one section in the *Summa Aurea* which would provide a complete and systematic treatment of this particular problem. One has, therefore, to piece together scattered remarks and observations from different parts of his writing. The dangers inherent in such an attempt are obvious. The modern interpreter runs the risk of allowing his own assumptions and prejudices to influence his interpretation and even his selection of texts, and of attributing views and emphases to the medieval writer which he did not in fact hold. It has been remarked by a recent historian that 'Hostiensis has been down the centuries a conspicuous victim of biased reading, and those who have searched his words for a point of view they wished to find there have rarely been unsuccessful'.[59] To avoid this danger the modern interpreter must be on his guard against treating and individual writer in isolation from his contemporaries and from the tradition that both he and his contemporaries inherited from their own immediate past. The work of Hostiensis has to be interpreted in the light of the legal tradition that he was heir to, and against the general pattern of medieval society as a whole. It is for this reason that a description of the state of medieval canon law was given in Chapter Two. The writing of Hostiensis has constantly to be seen against this background.

---

[59] J. A. Watt, 'The Theory of Papal Monarchy in the Thirteenth Century', *Traditio*, 20 (1964), p. 185. Professor Stickler made the same point in a review of W. Ullmann's *Medieval Papalism* in *Traditio*, 7 (1949-51), pp. 450-463.

What then has Hostiensis to say about the role of canon law in the Church? Towards the beginning of the *Summa* he describes how the *Liber Decretorum* was compiled from the teaching of the Fathers and from the laws in order to provide some help for the secular clergy in particular, 'qua utrumque sibi commissum scilicet spirituale et temporale posset regere, defendere et tueri'. [60] The foundation and raison d'être of this canon law are to be found, he maintains, in the Catholic faith itself and the whole point of papal decretals can be summed up as follows: 'ut inter iustum et iniustum, aequum et iniquum, sciamus discernere et ut honeste vivamus, alterum non laedamus, suum cuique tribuamus'. [61] There is, however, one place in the *Summa* where Hostiensis deals formally — albeit with extreme brevity — with this question about the role of law. The passage occurs towards the beginning of the *Summa* in his treatment of written constitutions and it provides a short but clear account of what he thought was the role of law. The passage is particularly important for this investigation and merits special attention because it provides a framework — given by Hostiensis himself — for the detailed investigation that is to follow, and it should help to reduce the danger of producing a purely subjective interpretation of his thought.

The question Hostiensis here proposes is this: what are the reasons that lie behind the promulgation of legal constitutions? — 'Quae est causa constitutionem promulgandi?' [62] His answer is that there are indeed many reasons to justify the promulgation of laws but that he will mention seven in particular at this point. The first reason he adduces is the need to provide some kind of security and stability by exercising legal control over the harmful passions of men, — 'Prima causa est ut appetitus noxius sub regula limitetur', — and he refers to the preface to the Gregorian Decretals where Gregory IX declares: 'Ideoque lex proditur ut appetitus noxius sub iuris regula limitetur, per quam genus humanum ut honeste vivat, alterum non laedat, ius suum unicuique tribuat, informatur'. [63] The peaceful existence of men depends, then, on law and order being maintained in society.

Secondly, laws are promulgated in order to protect innocent

---

[60] *Summa*, I, Prooemium.
[61] *Ibid.*
[62] *Summa*, I, De constitutionibus, n. 10.
[63] *Gregorian Decretals*, Prooemium.

people from the excesses of criminals. — ' Secunda, ut humana coerceatur audacia, tutaque sit inter improbos innocentia'. Here Hostiensis refers to the *Decretum* of Gratian for confirmation: 'Factae autem sunt leges ut earum metu humana coerceatur audacia, tutaque sit inter improbos innocentia, et in ipsis improbis formidato supplicio refrenetur nocendi facultas'. [64] This implies that the law should provide a clear delineation of rights and duties. It implies too, of course, that penalties have to be enacted against those who fail to respect these rights or fulfil these duties. The third reason for law is to ensure that compassion is shown by society to those who are the victims of oppression — 'Tertia, ut oppressis compatiatur'. Professor Le Bras has observed that the protection of the oppressed was an idea 'sedulously fostered by the canonists' of the Middle Ages. [65]

Another reason for law is the need to provide for due process in the courts, and this is the fourth reason put forward by Hostiensis — 'Quarta, ut mota negotia terminentur'. This he supports with references to Roman Law and to the treatment he gives later on in Book Two to the *Titulus, De dolo et contumacia*. All this has to do with the legal protection of rights. There has to be clear legislation to ensure the fair completion of legal proceedings and avert the danger of fraudulent delays and so on. Laws are required to make sure that justice is done in the courts, that unnecessary delays are avoided, that deceitful practices are not introduced, and that the parties are not overburdened with undue expense and other injustices. — 'ne partes ultra modum graventur laboribus et expensis'. The fifth οαиσα is closely related to the fourth, — 'Quinta, ut occurratur laboribus partium et expensis'. Here he refers again to his commentary on the *titulus, De dolo et contumacia*, in which he discusses a number of fraudulent practices. The law grants court action in favour of those who have suffered from such practices. He cites too the same decretal of Innocent III that he had just referred to and which decreed that anyone bringing an *exceptio* which cannot be substantiated has to pay the extra expenses of the other party. [66] This is put forward as an example of how the law tries to provide remedies and relief against unfair activity in the courts.

---

[64] D. 4, c. 1.
[65] G. Le Bras, 'Canon Law', *The Legacy of the Middle Ages*, p. 321.
[66] X, II, 14, 5 (finem litibus).

Sixthly, the law should prevent discord as far as this is possible and provide remedies against trickery and fraud, — 'Sexta, ut discordia evitetur, et fraudibus occurratur'. He adds a reference to his treatment of elections and to instructions given by Innocent III on election procedure. Failure to observe such regulations can invalidate the election.[67] He refers too to another decretal of Innocent III which limits the power of a litigant to cite the accused to a distant court.[68]

Lastly, Hostiensis mentions the role of law as a deterrent from crime and an encouragement towards virtue. The fear of punishment should deter evil men from wrong-doing and compel them to lead a good life, while the hope of reward should encourage good people to live even better lives: 'Septima, ut metu poenae mali boni, et boni meliores spe praemiorum fiant'.

Hostiensis at once goes on to consider very briefly the advantages that derive from written laws or constitutions, and he enumerates four such advantages. The laws positively permit certain courses of action while they punish others and they command some actions while forbidding others:

> Quattuor ex verbis virtutes collige legis: Permittit, punit, imperat atque vetat.[69]

He does not enlarge on this but simply indicates a few examples of these qualities in the law while referring the reader either to the *Decretum* or to his own more detailed treatment later in the *Summa*. He adds that a fifth advantage should he noticed — 'quod dubia solvit' — and he mentions as an example of this the laws on prescription. Such laws provide a certain stability and recognised order in society and they exist 'ne dominia rerum sint in incertum'.[70] Some would maintain that there is a sixth advantage that deserves mention, namely, that the laws at times positively recommend certain courses of action. Counsels are proposed but no one is obliged to follow them unless he freely undertakes to do so. Hostiensis mentions a number of examples of this aspect of the law but he does not number counselling as a separate quality since he regards it as included under the first of the four he has

---

[67] X, I, 6, 42 (quia propter).
[68] X, I, 3, 19 (nonnulli).
[69] *Summa*, I, De constitutionibus, n. 11.
[70] Cf. *Summa*, I, De rescriptis et eorum interpretationibus, n. 9.

already discussed. If the law counsels a particular course of action then it certainly also permits it.

This is what Hostiensis has to say about the role of law in general in his short, formal treatise on law at the beginning of the *Summa*. That he thought all this should apply to canon law is clearly demonstrated by his constant reference to the law of the *Decretum* and the Decretals for support. Throughout the *Summa Aurea*, of course, he makes a number of observations on the variety of roles that the law is called upon to play in the community. It is time now to move on and gather together these observations and examine them carefully. By doing this systematically one can hope to arrive at a fairly clear and complete picture of how Hostiensis viewed canon law and its function in the Christian community. And this is the main question that is here being considered. He has indicated that laws are promulgated to restrain violence, to safeguard the rights of innocent people, to provide sympathy for the oppressed, to ensure just dealings in the courts and fairness in business contracts, to see that equitable remuneration is given for services rendered, to avoid discord and protect against fraud, and finally, to encourage virtue through the hope of reward and restrain vice through the fear of punishment. These seven headings do not, of course, exhaust the function of law for Hostiensis and he indicates others in the course of his writing. But these headings provide a helpful pattern and will be used to give direction and shape to the rest of this investigation.

Chapter Four

CANON LAW AND THE PROMOTION OF ORDER AND HARMONY

1. *Security against Fraudulence*

Pope Gregory IX, in his preface to the *Decretales*, observes that the *Rex Pacificus* ordained that men should live peaceful and honourable lives but that the unbridled passions of mankind tend to make this extremely difficult. To maintain concord, therefore, it is necessary that laws be drawn up to ensure the reign of justice and protect the community against disrupting influences. 'Ideoque lex proditur ut appetitus noxius sub iuris regula limitetur'.[1] As has already been seen, Hostiensis refers to this preface in his brief discussion of the role of law and quotes part of it as his first reason for law — 'Prima causa est ut appetitus noxius sub regula limitetur'.[2] The sixth reason that he gives is the prevention of discord and protection against fraudulence, — 'Sexta, ut discordia evitetur, et fraudibus occurratur'.[3] These aspects of the law are closely connected with each other and so they will be treated together in this chapter, which is an attempt to show how in actual practice, according to Hostiensis, these functions were carried out by the law of the Church. Such functions are not, of course, peculiar to canon law. They must form part of the role of law in any society. But how in fact did canon law make provision for security against violence and fraudulence and promote stability and concord within the Christian community?

Throughout the *Summa Aurea* Hostiensis returns again and again to the law's constant preoccupation with the need to provide protection against violence, trickery and fraud of all kinds. The law exists, he frequently asserts, to prevent innocent people being tricked into false positions and to provide them with

---

[1] *Decretales*, Prooemium.
[2] *Summa Aurea*, I, De Constitutionibus, n. 10.
[3] *Ibid.*

remedies when they have been made the victims of deceit, — 'quia deceptis et non decipientibus iura subveniunt'.[4] If, for instance, a bishop fraudulently deprives the cathedral chapter of its rights in the granting of benefices then his action is invalid by law and the canons may proceed with the election even although the normal statutary time-limit may have expired', — 'quia sicut praelato non debet dolus proprius prodesse, sic neque canonicis debet obesse ... nec debet quis alieno odio praegravari',[5] and he underlines the point that the law is out to provide protection against fraud. When clerics are given leave to be absent from their churches care must be taken that the cult is not neglected by their absence, and he draws attention to a number of safeguards that ought to be observed in this matter.[6] Contractual agreements are to be held as invalid and therefore not binding if they are made 'in fraudem legis'.[7] Examples could easily be multiplied from the *Summa*. Moreover, the large body of legislation governing the making of bequests has been drawn up as a protection against deceit and fraudulence. It is for this reason that minors, madmen and prodigals are forbidden by law to make such bequests. And if deceit is used to extract such gifts provision is made for their revocation in certain circumstances, — 'item propter fraudem suscipientium, ut si monachi alliciendo laicum tonsuraverunt, ut eius bona percipiant'.[8] Similarly the legal formalities that surround the making of last wills and testaments are another necessary safeguard against lies, deceit and fraud.[9] Much too of the marriage legislation is a deliberate attempt to guard against collusion and lies which would undermine the stability of the marriage bond, — "for there is a great variety of fraudulent behaviour in this matter"[10].

Many more texts could be adduced from the *Summa* on this same point, but these will suffice to illustrate how Hostiensis stressed this particular function of canon law. The provision of security against fraud is a regular theme running through

---

[4] *Summa*, III, De fideiussoribus, n. 3.
[5] *Summa*, III, De concessione praebendae et eccl. non vacantis, n. 3.
[6] *Summa*, I, De clericis non residentibus, n. 3.
[7] *Summa*, III, De pignoribus, n. 4.
[8] *Summa*, III, De donationibus, n. 8.
[9] *Summa*, III, De testamentis et ultimis voluntatibus, n. 5.
[10] *Summa*, IV, De frigidis et maleficiatis et de impotentia coeundi, n. 12. Cf. also IV, De matrimoniis, n. 11; IV, De eo qui cognovit consanguineam uxoris suae, n. 4.

the whole of his commentary. It is worth remarking that in a number of the instances cited he freely quotes principles from Roman Law. This was a common practice with the medieval canonists who looked upon Roman law as a valuable auxiliary to canon law, provided there was no conflict between the two. If there were any conflict, then, as has already been noted, it was the canon law that prevailed in ecclesiastical courts.

2. *Promotion of Harmony through the Juridical Order*

It was also the view of Hostiensis that those 'harmful passions' mentioned by Gregory IX would to some extent be kept under control and concord achieved through careful legal provision for stability and security in the community. One of the most effective means of doing this according to the canonists was to clarify areas of power and responsibility and define carefully different spheres of competence. Hostiensis, along with the rest of medieval canonists, regarded this as one of the principle functions of the canonist in the Church.

> The maintenance of orderly life in the Church — nothing less — was the real task that the canonists faced in dealing with the flood of litigation, usually petty in itself, concerning the authority of ecclesiastical corporations and the rights of their various members, as a recent historian of the period has observed. [11]

The Church of Christ is, of course, a mysterious and complex reality. It is more than a merely human institution; it is the People of God, the Mystical Body of Christ, the community of all the faithful drawn together by the Spirit of God. But as it is a visibly organised human society it does have an institutional aspect. Stability and concord will, therefore, to a great extent depend on the smooth running of the organisation. And the smooth running of the organisation will in turn depend on the existence of a recognised body of clear legal rules ordering and delimiting the various spheres of authority and responsibility and the acceptance of these regulations as binding by the members of the Church.

Otherwise there will be chaos rather than unity and stabil-

---

[11] B. Tierney, *Foundations of the Conciliar Theory*, Cambridge, 1955, p. 104.

ity, constant friction rather than concord. It is this realisation
that lies behind the concern of medieval canonists for organisation and the canonical definition of areas of jurisdiction within
the Church. It was the canonists of the twelfth and thirteenth
centuries who developed this organisational aspect of the Church
and it is in their writings rather than in the systematic expositions of the theologians that the ecclesiology of the period is
to be found. The *De Regimine Christiano* of James of Viterbo
is said to be the first formal and systematic treatise on the
Church to be written by a theologian, and this did not appear
until the beginning of the fourteenth century.[12] Before that
time it is in canonistic commentaries on the ecclesiastical hierarchy that the clearest expression of the nature of the visible
Church is to be found. Ecclesiastical jurisprudence is, of course,
and always has been concerned with the practical application
of Christian principles to the government of the Church. As
has been shown earlier, canonists in the thirteenth century were
at the height of their power and prestige. The way had been
well prepared for them in advance.

> The *Decretum* of Gratian reproduced a compendium of texts
> which represented the organizational and institutional aspects
> of Christian tradition. The *Decretales* represented the most
> recent implementation of that tradition by the papacy. Canonist
> commentary on this *Corpus Iuris Canonici* was a major in-
> tellectual effort to sustain a critical examination and achieve
> a reasoned solution of the manifold problems of ecclesiastical
> government.[13]

   In recent years there has been a growing desire among
Catholic writers to see canon law as an expression of theology
and particularly of ecclesiology. The structure of the Church,
they maintain, should reflect the theology of the Church and
the laws which establish and protect these structures ought to
be a faithful expression of dogmatic theology. These laws should
be, and should be seen to be, dogmatic theology in the concrete, theology in action, applied doctrine. Similarly with the
ecclesiastical legislation about the sacraments. This should be

---

[12] Cf. P. Glorieux, 'James of Viterbo', *New Catholic Encyclopedia*,
New York, 1967, vol. 7, p. 813.
   H. X. Arquillière, *Le plus ancien traité de l'Eglise: Jacques de Viterbo
De Regimine Christiano*, Paris, 1926.
   [13] J. A. Watt, *The Theory of Papal Monarchy in the Thirteenth Century*,
London, 1965, p. vii.

a faithful expression of the practical conclusions that are to be drawn from sacramental theology. In such matters, it is thought, the role of canon law should be to formulate in clear and practical terms the Church's dogmatic tradition. And the bond between canon law and theology should be clearly visible. For too long, it is argued, canon law has been studied as a purely legal system parallel to the common or the civil law. This is now regarded as an unhappy development which should be altered, because it has tended to effect a divorce, or at least a separation, between theology and law.

What, it may be asked, has Cardinal Hostiensis to contribute to this approach to the law of the Church? What light does he throw on this notion of law as theology in the concrete, as the faithful expression of dogmatic theology? He does not, of course, explicitly discuss this particular question, and one has to read between the lines of his commentary to discover what sort of answer he might have given to the problem formulated in this way. It would, however, be a mistake to conclude from this that he has no contribution to make to the discussion. As has already been shown in a previous chapter, Hostiensis did have a high regard for theology and he maintained that religious principles derived from theology should permeate Christian legislation. He often supports the law with theological arguments and there is much in his whole approach that is in harmony with this idea of canon law as a practical expression of theology. Professor Le Bras considers that Hostiensis did in fact make an important contribution to theology, and that he did so by clarifying and adding precision to ecclesiastical structures and by his teaching on the sacraments. 'Les décrétales lui offraient l'occasion d'une ecclésiologie: en fait, il a perfectionné la connaissance de la structure juridique, sans apporter de nouvelles pierres'. [14] To provide clear directives for the smooth running of the ecclesiastical organisation in the interests of stability and concord was acknowledged by him as one of the primary functions of canon law. This is clearly shown by his repeated assertions that juridical structures existed to ensure stability and harmony and by the care he took to demonstrate that this function was performed by the canonical directives for the Church as a whole and for the subordinate sections within the Church. If peace and harmony are to prevail

[14] G. Le Bras, 'Théologie et droit romain dans l'oeuvre d'Henri de Suse', Etudes historiques à la mémoire de Noel Didier, Paris, 1960, p. 200.

in the community and discord be avoided or dispelled then control by the law is absolutely necessary in his view, and he
returns to the theme time and again throughout the *Summa*.
Some examples will illustrate the point.

Towards the end of Book One of the *Summa* Hostiensis
provides a commentary on the *Titulus, De maioritate et obedientia*. He takes it for granted that there has to be a clear
differentiation in rank and authority among the ministers of
the Church, just as the angels and archangels in heaven form
an ordered hierarchy. This existing Church hierarchy is basic
to his discussion. He quite naturally accepted the whole medieval structure of society together with its feudal relationships
and it is within this context that his writing has to be considered. He is a man of his time and medieval society as a
whole made much of rank and dignity. [15] So did the medieval
Church. The archbishop is superior to the bishop, the legate
greater than the primate, the pope above the legate. This *ordo
ecclesiasticus* has to be respected if harmony is to prevail in
the community. [16] One of the functions of canon law, therefore,
is to protect concord within this orderly structure of society
where peace and harmony will be fostered by a clear and accepted order of precedence. So Hostiensis goes on to discuss
in detail the precise nature of the mutual concord that should
exist and how this should be worked out in the practical details
of life. Clearly defined norms both for rank and for the duty
of obedience are to be decided upon and adhered to by those
under authority and those who exercise authority, — 'a quibus
ultra formam dictam aliquid exigendum non est'. [17] This is the
point of the detailed regulations about the extent and limits
of the duty of obedience and the consequences of acting *ultra
vires*. From this whole discussion it is evident that for Hostiensis
clearly defined structures were a necessary means for preserving
harmony in the community.

Another example of this same concern can be seen in his
treatment of the truce. He repeatedly points out that the 'au-
thoritas iuris' must be respected and that all must be careful
to observe the 'ordinem iuris' if they wish to remain within
the bounds of justice. The truce is a legally binding agreement
which is intended to provide security for those who make it.

---

[15] *Summa*, I, De maioritate et obedientia, n. 1.
[16] *Ibid*.
[17] *Ibid*., n. 5.

The overriding consideration should be the preservation of harmony. [18] The same preoccupation can be seen in Book Three when the subject of discussion is legacies and bequests and the obligations that arise from these. What is the function of all these detailed regulations? They have been drawn up to provide clarity and security in human transactions and contracts. It should be made clear, for example, just when and how a gift may be irrevocable; obligations attached to accepting a gift are to be clearly stated, and so on. And all this should be protected by the law. [19] Again, in his discussion of the immunity of the Church the same concern is shown. The laws too have been promulgated to keep the peace and provide stability — 'Stabilis igitur debet esse libertas' — and he points out, quoting freely from Roman sources, that since in law 'favores ampliantur et odia restringuntur, omnis res libera presumitur; ... ergo nisi res probetur serva, hodie presumitur libera'. [20] Clarity is needed about what precisely is protected by this immunity and what sort of immunity is involved. Many similar examples can be found in Book Four in the legal regulations that surround the marriage contract. Here again the idea of procuring peace and harmony continually reappears. [21] The long list of conditions governing betrothal and similar contracts has this same end in view. They are thought necessary to provide security and stability in such contracts. [22]

A final example may be taken from the treatment of Jews and Saracens and their slaves in Book Five of the *Summa*. Here it is clear that Hostiensis accepts the harsh contemporary views about the Jews, about their crime of rejecting Christ and dishonouring God by false worship and so on. But in spite of these views he still argues that the Jewish observance of the sabbath is to be respected, or at least tolerated by Christians as well as their property, their synagogues and their customs. He notes that while Roman law obliged the Jews to adopt Roman marriage rites the decretals allow them to marry according to their own customs. The reason for this tolerance is not quite ecumenical. It is simply to keep the peace and maintain the rule of justice. 'Nec debent Christiani in eos

---

[18] *Summa*, I, De treuga et pace, n. 1.
[19] *Summa*, III, De donationibus.
[20] *Summa*, III, De immunitate ecclesiae, n. 4.
[21] *Summa*, IV, De desponsatione impuberum, n. 12.
[22] *Summa*, IV, De conditionibus appositis in desponsatione vel aliis contractibus, n. 4.

sevire etsi scoeleribus teneantur; ideo enim iudicialis vigor
in medio positum est ne quisquam audeat sumere ultionem';
and he adds, 'si ergo iudex non sit in medio ad arma et rixas
poterit perveniri'. [23] Moreover, since this peacekeeping role is
so important Hostiensis draws attention to the fact that on
occasion the law itself can be modified in the interests of peace:
'Verum est quod prohibentur sponsalia contrahi ante puberta-
tem ... nisi iusta causa instet, puta bonum pacis. Unde versus:
ut pax servetur moderamen iuris habetur', and he quotes the
Decretum to bear him out. [24]

3. *The Primacy of the Pope*

a) *The Supremacy of the Spiritual Power*

It is, then, clear that for Hostiensis the maintenance of
peace and stability was an important function of the law. It is
also apparent from his discussion of *De maioritate et obedientia*
that the recognition and acceptance of clearly defined structures
of authority would do much to promote harmony in the Church.
But what was the nature of this juridical structure that he
regarded as so important? As has been noticed earlier, canon
law and the canonists played an important part in the consoli-
dation of papal power throughout the whole Church, in which
many of them occupied leading positions of power and influence.
It is time now to examine the contribution that Hostiensis
made to this development.

> Indeed, within the Church the jurisdictional primacy of the
> Roman bishop was most authoritatively defined by the canon
> lawyers. By their leadership and loyalty, as well as through
> the ideological weapons which they forged for the papal
> armoury, the canonists more than anyone else brought the
> papacy to the preeminence which it had throughout the thir-
> teenth century, with regard both to the Church and to the
> secular world. [25]

The author of the *Summa Aurea* was without doubt a strenuous and untiring advocate of the sovereignty of the pope. Clear
assertions of papal supremacy appear again and again through-

---

[23] *Summa*, V, De iudaeis, sarracenis et eorum servis, nn. 3-4.
[24] *Summa*, IV, De desponsatione impuberum, n. 9.
[25] R. L. Benson, *The Bishop-Elect. A Study in Medieval Ecclesiastical
Office*, Princeton, N. Y., 1968, p. 19.

out his commentary. What is not so clear is whether he deserved the reputation of being a fanatical curialist and extreme papalist that he has gained among some later historians. The direct quotations from the *Summa* that have been given above show the importance that Hostiensis attached to the clear definition of the various areas of power and responsibility within the Church. In this whole matter the authority of the pope is of first importance. His position has to be clearly defined and protected by the law. Throughout his writing Hostiensis shows great reverence and respect for the pope. For him the pope is the Vicar of Christ and the divinely appointed spiritual head of the whole of Christendom whose supremacy should be acknowledged by all Christians. What better guarantee of unity and stability within the Christian community could there be than respect for and obedience to the one Vicar of Christ? It is for this reason that Hostiensis, both in the *Summa* and in the *Apparatus*, pays so much attention to the position and power of the pope. What he has to say on this subject is not to be found conveniently collected in one place but is scattered here and there throughout his commentaries. In these scattered comments, however, he approaches papal authority from many different angles and, according to one recent historian, has provided 'the most complete analysis of papal power up to his time'.[26] As a canonistic commentator he did much to clarify the nature of papal authority both within the Church and in its relation to the temporal rulers in Christendom. This is most clearly evident in his discussions of the *plenitudo potestatis* which he regards as an essential foundation for the unity and stability of the *Respublica Christiana*.

Plenitudo potestatis could, of course, carry a variety of meanings but in the context of the papacy it was used to express the supremacy of the pope within the ecclesiastical hierarchy and, through an extension of this, to denote his position as supreme spiritual head of Christian society as a whole. In the interests of unity and concord this position of the pope had to be clearly defined and protected by the law and in this Hostiensis made an important and influential contribution in

---

[26] J. A. Watt, *The Theory of Papal Monarchy in the 13th Century*, London, 1965, p. 107. On the unifying force of papal authority, see Professor Ullman's lecture, *The Medieval Papacy, St Thomas and Beyond*, London, 1960, p. 2: 'What actually made medieval Christendom one entity, one unit, one body, was the indisputable fact of the papacy acting as the organ of unity'.

his canonistic commentaries. Three aspects of his contribution
will be considered in this chapter. First of all, he argued strenuously for the primacy of the pope and the general supremacy
of the spiritual power. But he also maintained that there was
a distinction of powers and that the temporal authority could
claim autonomy in its own sphere, acknowledging that the emperor too possessed a *plenitudo potestatis* in temporal matters.
These two powers had, however, to cooperate with each other
if there were to be a stability and concord within Christendom.
Each of these aspects calls for a closer investigation.

The term *plenitudo potestatis* had a long history in papal
documents before the thirteenth century and can be traced back
to the pontificate of Pope Leo I in the fifth century. [27] Gratian
used the term to describe the fullness of papal power in relation to that of the other bishops in the Church. [28] This was
commented on and enlarged by the early decretists so that by
the end of the twelfth century the term had come to mean the
pope's supreme legislative authority and his supreme appellate
jurisdiction.

> In the former case, *plenitudo potestatis* was postulated in the
> language of Roman law, either directly quoted or in language
> reminiscent of it. For the *lex animata* had been substituted
> the *canon vivus*, with all canon law in *pectore suo*, whose will
> likewise had the force of law, who was, too, *legibus solutus*.
> In the second case, *plenitudo potestatis* was associated with
> a second term, now too in regular canonist usage, *papa est
> iudex ordinarius omnium*. [29]

Pope Innocent III used the term frequently to describe his supremacy of power and jurisdiction. Hostiensis developed the
concept and gave it greater precision.

The theological foundation for his argumentation was the
pope's position as successor of St Peter and Vicar of Christ
on earth. It was the teaching of both canonists and theologians
that St Peter had been constituted Christ's vicar on earth with
the primacy of power in the Church and that this position had
been passed on to his successors in the Roman see. St Thomas

---

[27] Cf. J. A. Watt, 'The Use of the Term "Plenitudo Potestatis" by
Hostiensis', in *Proceedings of the Second International Congress of
Medieval Canon Law*, Vatican City, 1965, pp. 161-187.
[28] C. 9, q. 3, dict. pr. (quoted by Watt, *op. cit.*, p. 164).
[29] J. A. Watt, *op. cit.*, p. 165.

Aquinas, for example, taught that the primacy of Peter was instituted to safeguard order and unity in the Church:

> Soli (Petro) promisit: Tibi dabo claves regni coelorum, ut ostenderetur potestas clavium per eum ad alios derivanda, ad conservandam Ecclesiae unitatem.[30] And again, Quamvis apostolis data sit communiter potestas ligandi et solvendi, tamen ut in hac potestate ordo aliquis significaretur, primo soli Petro data est, ut ostendatur quod ab ipso in alios debeat ista potestas descendere, propter quod etiam dixit ei singulariter: Confirma fratres tuos; pasce oves meas.[31]

This was also the teaching of St. Bonaventure: 'Ab ipso (Summo Pontifice) manat in omnes inferiores per universam Ecclesiam omnis auctoritas'.[32] It was this commonly accepted teaching on the pope as the Vicar of Christ with plenitude of power that Hostiensis took over and developed. A clear statement of his position is presented in his discussion of the power of legates in Book One of the *Summa*:

> Plenusque vicarius extat: quamvis enim quilibet episcopus dici possit vicarius Iesu Christi... est tamen particularis; sed Papa est vicarius GENERALIS, unde omnia gerit de omnibus prout placet, iudicat et disponit,... Plenus: id est, habens plenitudinem potestatis, ad quam vocatus est, alii vero in partem sollicitudinis.[33]

This same theme can be seen running all through the *Summa Aurea*, and further texts will be cited shortly. Although his treatment of the question was in harmony with the traditional teaching, it was not simply the handing on of other men's views.

---

[30] *Summa Contra Gentes*, I, IV, cap. 76, n. 4. For this and the two following references I am indebted to the article by Pio Fedele, 'Primato Pontificio ed Episcopato con Particolare Riferimento alla Dottrina dell'Ostiense', in *Studia Gratiana*, XIV (1967), p. 352.

[31] *In IV Sent.*, d. XXIV, q. III, a. 2, ad 1.

[32] *Quare Fratres Minores Praedicent*, tom. VII.

[33] *Summa*, I, De officio legati, n. 3. The same teaching was given in the *Apparatus*, as the following quotation will show: 'scilicet, in te, ut sic urbs ista altera Hierusalem intelligatur, et effusione tui sanguinis, qui primus meus vicarius es in terris, fundetur, firmetur et consecretur hic locus quem elegi mihi, ut sic ecclesia sit caput et domina et princeps omnium ecclesiarum, non ab homine sed a me recipiens plenitudinem potestatis'. *Apparatus*, IV, 17, 3, s.v. *crucifigi* (quoted by Watt, *op. cit.*, p. 186).

7

He had, as Dr Watt points out, his own contribution to make
to the discussion.

> Hostiensis' view of the *plenitudo potestatis*, however, is of more
> significance than as merely an ample and rhetorical restatement
> of an already existing position. It was he, it seems, who was
> the first to introduce a new clarification of the concept by
> introducing a distinction between two sorts of power exercised
> by the pope. There was his ordinary power *"potestas ordinaria"*
> or *"ordinata"* when by virtue of his *plenitudo officii,* he acted
> according to the law already established. There was also his
> absolute power, *"potestas absoluta",* when by virtue of his
> *plenitudo potestatis,* he passed over or transcended existing
> law. [34]

It was this fullness of power — this 'absolute power' — that
enabled the pope to take decisive action even outside the ordinary course of law whenever he judged that the general good
of the Church demanded such action. This was the power that
enabled the pope to grant dispensations from or supply for
inadequacies in the existing law. It was a discretionary power
to be used in exceptional cases when the need arose. Hostiensis
did, however, argue that this discretionary power had to be
used to support the structure of the Church as a whole. It could
not be used legitimately to undermine the general welfare of
the Church. But he considered it a necessary safeguard against
all kinds of legal formalism that might obstruct the real good
of Christendom. And, as he himself remarks, it proved at times
to be an extremely useful power, — 'per hanc viam provisionis
multa expediuntur in curia de plenitudine potestatis quam am-
plexamur totis affectibus, cum perniciosa vel inutilis subtilitas
obviat veritati'. [35]

A few examples from the *Summa* will illustrate this power
that Hostiensis attributed to the pope and show why he thought
it a valuable means of providing for the stability and unity
of Christendom. In Book Five when he is discussing who may
be liable to an accusation before the courts he states that anyone
is open to such a charge but he draws attention to a few ex-
ceptions:

---

[34] J. A. Watt, "The Use of the Term 'Plenitudo Potestatis' by Hostiensis",
op. cit., p. 167.

[35] *Apparatus,* V, 1, 22, s.v. *ipsum providimus* (quoted by Watt,
op. cit., p. 186).

Regulariter igitur verum est quod potest quilibet accusari, fallit tamen in casibus. Primo excipiuntur quaedam personae in perpetuum propter summae dignitatis honorem, et quia solutae sunt legibus, ut Papa et Imperator qui super se iudicem non habent ... Sed dic quod Imperator *ratione peccati* accusari potest coram Papa cui omnes reges et principes peccatores subditi sunt ... Papa ergo tamquam superior omnes iudicat et ipse a nemine iudicatur ... [36].

This passage refers the reader to the treatment in Book Four of the question of legitimization, and since this is one of the most important discussions to be found in the *Summa* of the relationship between the pope and the emperor it is worth examining in some detail. The legitimization of illegitimate children was a matter that closely concerned the temporal power since it affected heredity and succession, and it had for a long time been a source of conflict between the Church and temporal rulers. The famous decretal, *Per venerabilem* of Innocent III, had dealt with this issue and kept it before the eyes of the canonists whose commentaries show a variety of opinions on the subject. Hostiensis maintains that since legitimization is so closely connected to the sacrament of marriage it must be regarded as an ecclesiastical matter which as such pertains to the competence of the spiritual head of Christendom. Some canonists argued that since there was a recognised distinction of jurisdictions the most suitable solution to the problem would be to allow the temporal ruler to legitimize 'quo ad temporalia' and the spiritual ruler 'quo ad spiritualia'. 'Non ergo Papa debet intromittere se de legitimatione facienda quo ad temporalem hereditatem, sed debet hoc dimittere Imperatori,' they proposed. [37] Hostiensis emphatically rejects this solution. 'Sed contra, quia Papa etiam de temporalibus se potest et debet intromittere'. He then cites different views on the relationship between the spiritual and the temporal powers, those of Huguccio, who took a moderate line and favoured what has since been called a fully 'dualist' approach, and those of Alanus and Tancred, who defended papal superiority in both spheres. Hostiensis then gives his own view of the matter, accepting Huguccio's statement of the principle that the two powers are distinct and that both the pope and the emperor receive their authority from God; but he goes on at once to assert the supe-

---

[36] *Summa*, V, De accusationibus, n. 7.
[37] *Summa*, IV, Qui filii sint legitimi, nn. 9-11.

riority of the spiritual power: 'Ego iurisdictiones distinctas assero, et utramque a Deo processisse, ... tamen quanto altera magis Deo appropinquatur, tanto maior est, ergo sacerdotium maius est'. He then proceeds to 'prove' this superiority by means of somewhat far-fetched comparisons. He distinguishes the authority of the bishop from the power of the temporal ruler by observing that the bishop is anointed on the head whereas the king is anointed on the arm. This is the case, he argues, because 'episcopus est vicarius capitis nostri, id est Christi, et ut ostendatur quanta sit differentia inter auctoritatem pontificis et principis potestatem'. He goes on to the sun and the moon as instructive symbols of the spiritual and the temporal power: just as the moon is dependent on the sun so also is the temporal power dependent on the spiritual, 'unde et lex secularis debet servire canonice'. He continues the argument by introducing some strange mathematical comparisons in the same vein to prove his point, which is that the spiritual jurisdiction which Christ left to his Church is obviously superior to any purely temporal jurisdiction. Legitimization is a *causa matrimonialis,* and as such it belongs to the spiritual court of the Church and not to the jurisdiction of temporal rulers. All this Hostiensis puts forward not simply as his own personal view but as the correct interpretation of the law. He admits that the civilians disagree with him on this, 'sed de rigore iuris, et ratione naturali non dubito sic tenendum'. Nor has he any doubts about the general superiority of the spiritual jurisdiction, — 'et de hac maioritate quis sani capitis dubitabit?' What, one may ask, lay behind this rather exaggerated defence of the superiority of the spiritual authority? It was concern for the unity of Christendom. The Church of Christ forms one body and therefore it can have only one head on earth, namely his Vicar, the pope. Can one body have two heads? This point is made by Hostiensis in this same discussion of legitimization: 'Ergo quo ad maioritatem unum caput est tantum, scilicet Papa, unus debet tantum esse caput nostrum, dominus spiritualium et temporalium, quia ipsius est orbis et plenitudo eius'. This may appear to be as extreme a claim for papal supremacy as one could hope to find anywhere, and if it alone is taken as representing Hostiensis' complete view of the problem then it is not surprising to find him labelled as an extreme papalist. But this has to be balanced against other equally clear statements in his writing if a fair assessment of his position is to be made.

Before passing on to these qualifications that have to be made, however, another clear example of Hostiensis' defence of papal primacy should be considered. This is to be found in his treatment of tithes in Book Three of the *Summa*. [38] The problem under discussion is this: Can a layman be allowed to receive tithes that are due to the Church? Some argue that not even the pope may permit this since it is by divine and not merely human law that tithes are to be paid to the Church. 'Quomodo ergo potest Papa contravenire?' they ask, and reply quite firmly that he cannot. Hostiensis refuses to accept this opinion. He argues that the pope does have the power to grant such privileges to laymen and that in the past popes have in fact used this power.

> Dicas ergo quod aliqua sunt praecepta in quibus non servatur aliqua privata utilitas, sive temporalis, nisi praeiudicium alterius committat aliquis, ut in furto, et ideo talia sine peccato non possunt omitti quo ad affirmativa vel committi quo ad prohibitoria, et in talibus Papa nullam potestatem habet, et sic intelligenda sunt iura de quibus opposui. [39]

So there is some limitation to the papal power; he may not cause or permit such a 'praeiudicium alterius'. He continues:

> Aliqua vero sunt in quibus versatur privata sive temporalis utilitas ut in decimis, primitiis, oblationibus, et similibus, per quae nemini paratur praeiudicium, imo nisi reddantur peccatum est, et cum temporalitas ad ecclesiam spectet et Deum cuius vicarius universalis est Papa potest in his statuere, et de his disponere sicut placet. Et cio oino cuiusque luluria potest concedere laico quod decimas alicuius loci percipiat.

He immediately adds, however, that the pope should have a good reason for granting such a permission, — 'sed non debet hoc facere nisi ex causa, puta favore fidei'. He asserts too that no one else apart from the pope has such power over tithes, not even bishops. The pope alone in his capacity as God's 'vicarius universalis' is possessed of such power.

Such passages as these — and many similar texts could be quoted from the *Summa* — show clearly how forcefully Hostiensis argued for the supremacy of the Roman pontiff. But it is also clear that in spite of the exaggerated language

---

[38] *Summa*, III, De decimis et primitiis.
[39] *Summa*, III, De decimis et primitiis, n. 13.

in which from time to time he indulged he did not regard this *plenitudo potestatis* as entirely unrestricted or unconditional. It remained in his view a power for intervention *in exceptional cases*, a prerogative that should not be used excessively but only with great caution and for serious reasons when the good of the Church or the requirements of justice demanded it. He did not consider it an entirely unlimited power since, as he repeatedly observed, it had to be used in harmony with the Catholic faith and within the limits of the divine law. As he declared in his treatment of the papal power of dispensation,

> Hoc solum tene quod in omnibus potest dispensare dummodo non sit contra fidem, et dummodo per dispensationem suam evidenter non nutriatur mortale peccatum, nec inducat subversionem fidei, nec periculum animarum. Nam in talibus nullam habet contra Deum penitus potestatem. [40]

This is a point that he reiterates throughout the *Summa*. He argues, for example, that whereas the spiritual marriage between a bishop and the universal Church is indissoluble, that which exists between him and a particular diocese can be dissolved by the pope if he wishes to transfer the bishop to another diocese. Why, then, is there this difference between the spiritual marriage and 'matrimonium carnale', which cannot be so dissolved? Because, says Hostiensis, in the case of carnal marriage it is laid down in the Scriptures that man cannot put asunder what God has joined together, 'et Papa contra verbum Domini dispensare non potest'. [41]

In his treatment of the possibility of obtaining dispensations from vows he cites a number of opinions on the subject including that of Huguccio who held that not even the pope could grant such dispensations 'quia redditio voti est de iure naturali sive divino, et ideo contra hoc non potest Papa venire'. Hostiensis does not agree with this and after presenting some other views he expresses his own opinion as follows:

> Quarti dicunt et verius, et hoc omnino teneas, quod Papa de plenitudine potestatis in omni voto dispensare potest, quod ab initio voluntarium fuit; peccat si sine causa dispensat; nec ei obediendum est si manifeste liqueat quod fit contra dominorum domini voluntatem, alias ei obediendum est. [42]

---

[40] *Apparatus*, III, 8, 4 s.v. dispensare (quoted by Watt, *op. cit.*, p. 168, n. 39).

[41] *Summa*, I, De electione et electi potestate, n. 25.

[42] *Summa*, III, De voto et voti redemptione, n. 16.

While Hostiensis taught with great clarity that the pope could not be put on trial or judged before any human tribunal, he also maintained that the pope remains morally responsible to God and will be answerable before his tribunal if he acts sinfully or arbitrarily or without real justification. This can be seen in the passages that have already been quoted and it crops up frequently in others. 'Peccat si sine causa dispensat' is a thought that Hostiensis often expresses. Moreover, while maintaining that the pope is not strictly and legally bound by ecclesiastical laws — *princeps solutus est legibus* — nevertheless he still thinks that he ought to live according to them: 'licet enim ab observatione canonum sit solutus, *decet tamen* quod secundum eos vivat, suis privilegiis semper salvis'. [43]

b) *The Distinction between Spiritual and Temporal Jurisdictions.*

From all that has already been said it will be clear that Hostiensis thought that stability and harmony depended upon the recognition of an established legal order in Christendom. He maintained too that this order consisted of both spiritual and temporal authorities. But how did he think that these distinct jurisdictions should be related to each other and harmonised according to canon law? Was the pope to be regarded as the supreme and absolute ruler of Christendom, equally competent in both spiritual and temporal affairs? This is not the place to examine in detail or try to evalue the various theories that have been proposed by later historians about medieval papalism. The subject of Church and State relations in the Middle Ages is both complex and controversial and a detailed study of it is obviously outside the scope of this investigation into the role of law. It cannot, however, be passed over in complete silence because the conflict between *regnum* and *sacerdotium* did in fact exert considerable influence on the development of canon law. What follows is simply an attempt to show that Hostiensis regarded the law on this matter as an important factor in promoting unity, stability and concord within the Christian community. [44]

---

[43] *Summa,* I, De tempore ordinationum et qualitate ordinandorum, n. 3.

[44] This part is particularly indebted to the following studies by recent historians:

W. Ullmann, *Medieval Papalism,* London, 1949; A. Stickler, 'Concerning the Political Theories of the Medieval Canonists', *Traditio,* 7 (1949-51), pp. 450-463, (this is a detailed and critical review of Ullmann's *Medieval*

The medieval canonists in general have been accused of constructing a legal system which placed the pope as supreme monarch and independent head of the whole of Christendom with absolute power in both the spiritual and temporal spheres. Hostiensis in particular has frequently been portrayed as an extreme papalist, a canonist who exploited all the resources of the law to support an absolute papal theocracy or world dominion where the pope stood in the place of God, while all temporal rulers were regarded as no more than mere servants of the spiritual power of the papacy. There are certainly many texts in his writing which can be used to corroborate this accusation. A number of the passages considered in this chapter lie open to this interpretation. The discussion of the powers of legitimization is a case in point and one that is frequently quoted. It is, however, questionable whether such texts, taken in isolation from the rest of his writing, truly represent his all-round view of the matter.

He regularly taught that canon law recognised a distinction of powers and two separate spheres of jurisdiction. He expressly stated, for example, that the emperor held a *plenitudo potestatis* in temporal affairs, — a sphere in which he had more power than the pope. Nor did he consider that the pope had any right arbitrarily to usurp this temporal power. A few examples from the *Summa* will illustrate this point.

When discussing the immunity of the Church he explains that while it is the pope who has the juridical competence to deal with *negotia ecclesiastica*, this is not the case with feudal matters which are not ecclesiastical and therefore *not normally* any concern of the pope. The pope, he asserts, 'non habet iudicare de feudo, nisi ratione pacti vel consuetudinis, vel privilegii'. A little further on he adds,

> Iterum cognitio feudi non ad ecclesiam pertinet, sed ad dominum feudi; et quo ad talia, nil ad Papam de feudo nisi

Papalism); B. Tierney, 'Some Recent Works on the Political Theories of the Medieval Canonists', in *Traditio*, 10 (1954), pp. 594-625; J.A. Watt, 'The Theory of Papal Monarchy in the Thirteenth Century', *Traditio*, 20 (1964), pp. 179-317 (This has also been published separately as a book under the same title, London, 1965); B. Tierney, 'Papal Political Theory in the Thirteenth Century', in *Medieval Studies*, XXVII (1965), pp. 227-245. J.A. Cantini has tried to demonstrate the *dualist* approach of Pope Innocent IV in 'De autonomia judicis saecularis et de Romani pontificis plenitudine potestatis in temporalibus secundum Innocentium IV', *Salesianum*, 23 (1961), pp. 407-80.

ratione violentiae, vel negligentiae vel peccati; sic loquuntur iura, supra alleg. de foro competenti. Et est ratio, quia in his non privilegiavit princeps ecclesiam, ergo nec Papa debet ei iniuriari nec forte posset sua constitutione. [45]

On the other hand, neither the emperor nor any other temporal ruler has authority over ecclesiastical affairs. These are the pope's responsibility and it is for him as 'totius mundi princeps' to decide 'quae ad Dei cultum, vel fidem Christianorum, vel ad stabilitatem procuranda fuerint'. [46] This same respect for the rights of temporal rulers in feudal matters is shown also in Book Two of the *Summa* in the discussion of appeals. Feudal problems are not normally ecclesiastical matters and if there is an appeal against a bishop in his capacity as a temporal prince holding authority under the local temporal ruler, then such an appeal is to go to the temporal ruler and not to the metropolitan, 'sed ad dominum temporalem a quo tenetur feudum est merito appellandum; nam ad proximum superiorem appellandum est; ... ibi non negamus quin praecellat Imperator in temporalibus'. [47] Earlier in this section he had reiterated his teaching that there were two distinct jurisdictions, and at the end of the discussion he explicitly recognises the 'princeps' as being 'solutus legibus' and that he too was possessed of a 'plenitudo potestatis', 'contra quam non intendimus disputare, verumtamen ut iura et ius suum servet cuilibet decet ipsum'. [48] Again, when discussing ecclesiastical legislation concerning accomodation to be let to university students, Hostiensis acknowledges that there are people over whom the pope does not have jurisdiction, — 'secus de aliis in quibus Papa iurisdictionem non habet'. [49] He even states that there may be occasions when the pope may submit to the judgement of the emperor. 'Sed et Papa aliquando se submittit iudicio imperatoris, quia quamvis minor sit est tamen receptum quod imperio minoris iudicis se submittere possit'. [50]

In the *Prooemium* to the *Summa* he asserts quite clearly the distinction of powers: 'quidquid autem dicatur, haec est

---

[45] *Summa*, III, De immunitate ecclesiae, coemiterii et rerum ad eas pertinentium, n. 13.

[46] *Summa*, III, De immunitate ecclesiae, n. 12.

[47] *Summa*, II, De appellationibus, n. 4.

[48] *Ibid.*

[49] *Summa*, III, De locato et conducto, n. 7.

[50] *Summa*, V, De accusationibus, n. 7.

veritas quod distinctae sunt iurisdictiones, quamvis una maior
sit reliqua, et quilibet secundum legem suam iudicabit'. [51]   And
when discussing who has the power to promulgate laws he observes that it is for the pope to do so in all spiritual and ecclesiastical matters while the emperor has this power with regard
to temporal affairs. [52]   Even in his well-known discussion of the
power to legitimize, which contains those exaggerated similes
illustrating the supremacy of the pope, he includes, as has been
seen, an acknowledgement of the distinction of powers: 'Ego
iurisdictiones distinctas assero et utramque a Deo processisse'. [53]

There does, therefore, seem to be a lack of consistency in
the teaching of Hostiensis on this matter.   By a careful selection of texts from the *Summa* he can be shown to be either a
'dualist' or an extreme papalist.   Professor Stickler and Dr Watt
have shown that a similar ambiguity is to be found in the *Apparatus.*

> Thus Hostiensis stands clearly for the independence of the
> pope, also in matters secular; but with equal clearness he
> upholds the dualism of powers and the bestowal of the tem-
> poral authority on the emperor by God himself.   It is there-
> fore difficult to see why he is constantly being quoted as an
> advocate of *unlimited* papal power'. [54]

Difficult as it may be to harmonise theoretically this real
distinction of jurisdictions with a papal supremacy that can at
times intervene in temporal matters, it is none the less clear
that this is what Hostiensis taught and he made frequent reference to canonical authority to show that the law of the Church
did recognise and protect two distinct spheres of competence.
But perhaps this inconsistency in theory was overcome in actual
practice.   The canonists in general, and Hostiensis in particular,
were men of action and closely involved in the practical politics
of their time.   In such circumstances a certain papal pre-emi-
nence was thought to be a necessary safeguard for justice and
unity in exceptional cases while it was not thought to be part
of the usual procedure.

> Normally speaking, the *temporalia* were under the charge
> of the emperor, who held his *principatus* from God *immediate,*

---

[51] *Summa,* Prooemium.
[52] *Summa,* I, De constitutionibus, n.
[53] *Summa,* IV, Qui filii sint legitimi, n. 10.
[54] A. Stickler, "Concerning the Political Theories of the Medieval
Canonists", *op. cit.,* pp. 459-60.

had supreme legislative authority, was *legibus solutus* and even was *vicarius Dei in temporalibus*. In short, his was a plenitude of power in relation to the temporal order, and in the ordinary working of that order, papal authority had no part. [55]

It was only in exceptional circumstances that the law of the Church allowed the pope to intervene in the temporal sphere for the common good of Christendom. Papal power *in temporalibus* was therefore a discretionary power to be used only when the ordinary legal system broke down in some way or other. But this was considered a necessary safeguard within Christendom against the abuse of power by temporary rulers or their negligence in the provision of justice. According to Hostiensis, canon law tried to ensure that the salvation of souls should not be endangered by incompetent or evil temporal rulers, and one of the ways it did this was by recognising a discretionary papal power of intervention in special circumstances.

> Loss of salvation is of course the ultimate sanction in the logic of Christianity, and for Hostiensis, it was this consideration which must always dominate papal thinking about the exercise of the absolute power. The whole body of law and procedure had been established in the past to guarantee 'to each his own', and to maintain *iustitia*. Law and due legal process were the technical means by which the *ordo ecclesiasticus* was preserved from disruption. The *plenitudo potestatis*, as the absolute power, was to be used to ensure that legal organization continued to perform its function. If therefore that organization was defective in any way, the *plenitudo potestatis* was there to remove the obstacle that was impeding justice. When the pope was "debitor iusticiae in omnibus", the absolute power was a recognized way by which he fulfilled his function. [56]

Hostiensis did, however, insist that the two powers, though quite distinct, ought to work together harmoniously for the general good of Christendom. Stability and concord within the Christian community depended on such cooperation. 'Una enim potestas alia semper eget, et ideo tenentur se ad invicem adiuva-

---

[55] J. A. Watt, 'The Use of the Term *Plenitudo Potestatis* by Hostiensis', p. 170.

[56] *Ibid.*, p. 174.

re'. [57]   Bishops and princes were, therefore, expected to assist
each other towards the general good of all.

That this was the traditional canonistic teaching is shown
by the constant corroboration that Hostiensis produces from
the *Decretum* and the *Decretales* for his statements.   He fully
acknowledged that the secular power had its own sphere which
was not to be confused with that of the spiritual authority in
the Church.   At times these spheres overlapped and it was then
that the secular power was expected to come to the assistance
of the ecclesiastical order if required to do so.   The clearest
case where such cooperation was both necessary and very common was, of course, in the suppression of heresy.   Hostiensis
deals with this in Book Five of the *Summa* but his teaching
on this point will be examined in detail later when the deterrent
and reforming functions of the law are being considered.

c) *Papal Primacy and the Bishops*

Hostiensis' firm defence of the primacy of the pope that
has been discussed in the preceding pages may have given the
impression that he was a solid supporter of the papal centralization of Church government that had been gaining ground
rapidly throughout the thirteenth century.   This seems to be
the case, but qualifications have to be made because Hostiensis
did not favour arbitrary or despotic government.   He also insisted on the due observance of the whole juridical structure.
Hence his lengthy commentary on the detailed legislation concerning the various areas of responsibility within the Church.
A glance at the *Tituli* contained in Book One of the *Decretales*
reveals how important this was held to be in canon law: *De
electione et electi potestate, de officio archidiaconi, de officio
et potestate iudicis delegati, de officio legati, de officio ordinarii,* and so on.   A more detailed discussion of the rights and
duties of these subordinate officials will be presented in the
next chapter, but the *Tituli* themselves give an indication of
how the law tried to provide for stability and harmony by
clear legislation on the juridical structure within the Church.
Hostiensis continually advocated the proper observance of these
structures: as he himself put it in a passage that has already
been quoted.

> Ad hoc enim dispensationis provisio gradus diversos et ordines
> constituit esse distinctos ut dum minores maioribus reveren-

---

[57] *Apparatus,* I, 31, 1 s.v. *fuerit.*

tiam exhiberent et potiores minoribus dilectionem impenderent, vera fieret concordia ex universitate contentione. Quia nec ecclesia aliter subsistere poterat nisi eam huius differentiam magnus ordo servaret. [58]

Throughout his commentary he shows great respect for the bishops of the Church and in Book One when he is commenting on posts of responsibility within the Church he is careful to bring out how the law defines and protects the competence of the local ordinary. Others may not presume to usurp this competence. He begins his discussion on the duties of the archdeacon, for example, by counselling him to show reverence and respect to all bishops since every bishop is to be regarded as the 'vicarius Christi'. [59] Certain powers, such as that of solemn excommunication, are reserved to the bishop, and others are forbidden to interfere in his diocese, — 'non licet episcopo falcem suae jurisdictionis ponere in messem alienam, ordinando vel iudicando subditos alienos'. [60] There are too a number of customs and regulations whose function it would seem to be to maintain due reverence for the bishop. Hostiensis mentions, for instance, the custom which forbids an inferior prelate to give the blessing if a bishop happens to be present, stating that this is to foster reverence for the episcopal dignity. [61]

Mgr Lefebvre has drawn attention to the accusation made against Hostiensis by Baldus that he tended to exaggerate the powers of the bishops and he thinks that a tendency can be seen in this direction, particularly in the episcopal power of dispensing which Hostiensis seems to have interpreted rather generously. [62] Hostiensis was, however, very clear that the bishops were fully dependent on the pope in the exercise of their power. That the bishops were called by the pope 'in partem sollicitudinis' was the common teaching of canonists and theologians in the thirteenth century. Hostiensis accepted this teaching and expounded it frequently and with great clarity. All ecclesiastical dignities derive from the pope, 'nam ab illo omnis dignitas ecclesiastica originem sumit'. [63]

A clear impression of what this papal supremacy meant in

---

[58] *Summa*, I, De maioritate et obedientia, n. 1.
[59] *Summa*, I, De officio archidiaconi, n. 3.
[60] *Summa*, I, De clericis peregrinis, n. 2.
[61] *Summa*, I, De officio archipresbyteri, n. 4.
[62] Cf. C. Lefebvre, 'Hostiensis', *DDC*, V, col. 1226.
[63] *Summa*, I, De sacra unctione, n. 8.

the practical daily life of the Church can be gained by a study
of the lengthy list of *causae maiores* which were reserved by law
to the Apostolic See. These are discussed by Hostiensis in detail
in his treatment of the duties of legates in Book One of the
Summa. [64] He notes that there are eleven such reserved cases
enumerated in a mnemonic verse commonly used by lawyers:

> Restituit papa, solus disponit et ipse
> Dividit ac unit, eximit atque probat.
> Articulos solvit, synodum facit generalem,
> Transfert et mutat, appellat nullus ab ipso.

Raymond of Peñafort in his *Summa* enlarged this to cover
twenty-four reserved *causae,* but Hostiensis goes even further
and expands the list to more than sixty such cases which take
in a vast field of administrative, legislative and judicial matters.
The list in itself is a vivid illustration of the growth of centralisation in the Church and Hostiensis' commentary on it is
a *locus classicus* for his defence of the plenitude of papal power
in the Church. He reiterates the common teaching that all
authority in the Church derives from Rome, 'ab ecclesia Romana omnis dignitas originem sumpsit'. By his plenitude of power
the pope can supply for defects in the observance of the law
and convalidate invalid transactions, 'nam secundum ipsam potest de iure supra ius dispensare'. He himself is not bound
by the law, 'legi nec subiacet ulli, quia princeps solutus est
legibus, ... hoc ideo quia nulli subest, nec ab alio iudicatur; ... decet tamen ipsum iura servare'. Papal supremacy over all the
other bishops is brought out particularly clearly later in this
discussion of the duty of legate, in a passage that has already
been mentioned. The pope is called the *Summus Pontifex* because 'summa sede sedet; in illa videlicet quam Dominus sibi
in personam Petri specialiter eligit'. Although every bishop is
in fact the *vicarius Christi,* 'sed Papa est vicarius generalis,
unde omnia gerit de omnibus prout placet, iudicat et disponit'.
The pope too is *plenus vicarius*:

> id est, habens plenitudinem potestatis, ad quam vocatus est,
> alii vero in partem sollicitudinis, ... Ideo breviter dic, quod
> dummodo contra fidem non veniat, in omnibus et per omnia
> potest facere et dicere quicquid placet ... Licet autem hoc
> possit, caveat quod non peccet. [65]

---

[64] *Summa,* I, De officio legati.
[65] *Summa,* I, De officio legati, n. 6.

This passage clearly illustrates how firmly Hostiensis defended the full supremacy of the pope. Moreover, the passage contains many references to the *Decretum* and is a good example of how careful he generally was to support his statements with references to the traditional law of the Church. This is typical of all his writing. He claimed to be expounding the existing law of the Church and not simply presenting his own personal opinions. He goes on in this passage to warn legates against attempting to usurp these powers that are reserved by law to the pope.

Another development in the medieval Church which strengthened the centralising power of the papacy and tended to weaken the authority of local bishops was the rapid increase in the number of cases that were brought directly to the papal court. Growing recognition of the pope as the universal ordinary for the whole Church consolidated the judicial supremacy of the papacy. Hostiensis accepted this development. In his exposition of the law on appeals he observes that in the normal course of events these ought to be made *gradatim*, that is to say, through the regular hierarchy of jurisdictions. This is the case in Roman law and it is also the usual procedure in canon law. But in ecclesiastical cases the pope occupies a particularly privileged position 'quia ordinarius est cunctorum'.[66]

As has been seen, the *Summa Aurea* provides abundant evidence that Hostiensis fully accepted and handed on the current canonistic teaching that the bishops derived their authority from the pope who called them 'in partem sollicitudinis'. The pope was considered by him to be the centre of unity in the Church and he had been granted all the power that was needed to maintain this unity. Professor Tierney, in his study of the canonistic foundations of the conciliar theory, has drawn attention to the fact that Hostiensis, a cardinal himself when he composed the *Apparatus*, was a strong defender of the dignity and prestige of the cardinals.[67] Hostiensis certainly did maintain that the college of cardinals should share with the pope the 'sollicitudinem pro statu ecclesie generalis'.[68] He held that they should be consulted by the pope and allowed to assist him in the exercise of his *plenitudo potestatis*. Professor Tierney

---

[66] *Summa*, II, De appellationibus, n. 4.

[67] B. Tierney, *Foundations of the Conciliar Theory*, Cambridge, 1955, p. 151.

[68] *Apparatus*, I, 5, 4 s.v. *ecclesie generali*.

appears, however, to have gone beyond the evidence of his
texts when he argues that Hostiensis was in effect substituting
for the monarchy of a single pope 'the rule of a self-perpetuating
oligarchy in whom all rights of government over the Church
were vested by a direct act of the divine will'. [69]   The passages
that have been quoted in this chapter show that Hostiensis did
not propound such a view in the *Summa Aurea*.   The author
of the *Summa* does not reveal conciliarist tendencies.   His emphasis, as has been seen, is repeatedly on the unique authority
of the pope.   Had he changed his mind by the time he came
to complete the *Apparatus* when he himself was a member of
the college of cardinals?   Dr Watt maintains that the *Apparatus*
does not reveal such a change of view.   While Hostiensis did
maintain that the cardinals should be consulted by the pope and
should share with him in his exercise of the plenitude of power,
he did not put this forward as a legal obligation for the pope.

> It was *fitting* that the cardinal should be included in the
> expression of that power, but the pope was not bound to
> include them.   'There are those', said Hostiensis, 'who say
> that the pope cannot make any precept without the advice
> and consent of his brothers.   Others hold the contrary.   But
> whatever is said, this I can confess without trouble: that in
> the pope alone resides the plenitude of power'. [70]

---

[69] B. Tierney, *op. cit.*, p. 151.

[70] J. A. Watt, 'The Use of the Term *Plenitudo Potestatis* by Hostiensis',
in *Proceedings of the Second International Congress of Medieval Canon
Law*, Rome, 1965, p. 169.   The passage cited from Hostiensis is taken from
Apparatus, III, 4, 2, s.v. *in synodo*.   Dr. Watt adds the following footnote,
in which he gives the text adduced by Tierney: ' "multo fortius ergo *decet*
papam consilium fratrum suorum requirere ... ut non solum papa sed
et cardinales includerentur etiam in expressione plenitudine potestatis"
(*App.* IV, 17, 13 s.v. *fratres nostri*).   It is a misreading of this passage
to interpret it as meaning that the *plenitudo potestatis* is legally entrusted
to the pope and cardinals together.   Hostiensis write "decet" not "debet".
His view was that while the pope alone had been granted the *plenitudo
potestatis*, it should be exercised with the advice of his cardinals.'   On
this same point see also J. A. Watt, 'The Constitutional Law of the College
of Cardinals: Hostiensis to Joannes Andreae', *Mediaeval Studies*, 33 (1971),
pp. 127-157.   Professor Tierney has defended his interpretation in 'Hostiensis and Collegiality', *Proceedings of the Fourth International Congress
of Medieval Canon Law*, Rome, 1976, pp. 401-409.   However, the arguments
he puts forward do not seem to me to prove more than that it was
fitting or expedient that the pope should consult the cardinals about
important matters.   He has not shown that Hostiensis maintained that
the pope was under a legal obligation to consult.

4. *Legal Protection for Ecclesiastical Interests and Institutions*

It was, then, the function of canon law to promote stability and concord by clearly delineating areas of competence and responsibility within the Church and within the whole of Christendom. It was also part of the law's function, thought Hostiensis, to protect the institution of the Church from suffering harm of any description. Ecclesiastical interests, both spiritual and material, stood in need of positive legal protection against undue interference by the temporal authorities and irresponsibility or negligence on the part of churchmen themselves. Hostiensis considered this an important element in the interpretation of the law and he constantly draws attention to it throughout the *Summa*. One of the primary aims of the canonists during the Investiture Controversy had been to free the Church from lay control and protect its spiritual interests. This remained a canonical concern and was frequently adverted to. This, as Hostiensis observes, had been the mind of the legislator in drawing up a number of laws, — 'quae vult quod vitetur dissensionis materia et ne patiantur ecclesiae detrimenta'.[71] Even unnecessary expenditure is to be avoided. What will be to the greater advantage of the Church is the deciding factor for him and he frequently refers to the 'utilitas ecclesiae' as the motive behind his legal interpretation. And by 'ecclesia' he means both the universal Church and the local church, the diocese and even the parish.

The long treatise on elections in Book One contains many references to the need to protect the Church from harm which may result either from outside interference or from negligence.[72] Again, a number of examples will illustrate the point. There is the threat of legal sanctions against anyone 'qui ultra sex menses per suam negligentiam teneret ecclesiam viduatam'.[73] He suggests that it will normally be better to elect a member of the local chapter to rule a church rather than an outsider, 'quia illi qui sunt de collegio melius et fidelius procurent utilitatem ecclesiae quam extranei'.[74] It is also important to take decisive action to avert any danger that may be threatening the church. This can even be at times a valid justification for modifying some

---

[71] *Summa*, I, De electione et electi potestate, n. 2.
[72] Cf. R.L. Benson, *The Bishop-Elect. A Study in Medieval Ecclesiastical Office.* Princeton University Press, 1968.
[73] *Summa*, I, De electione, n. 10.
[74] *Summa*, I, De electione et electi potestate, n. 10.

of the procedural regulations for elections. If, for instance, in
particular circumstances danger were to threaten the church
if an election were delayed to complete the time specified, then
the chapter should proceed with the election and ensure the
safety of the church. [75]

In his treatment of the possibility of renouncing personal
rights, Hostiensis draws attention to a number of rights that
cannot legally be renounced. The aim of such restrictions is
to protect the interests of the church. Hence church property
cannot be renounced or alienated 'nisi in casu concesso et modo
debito'. [76] Nor can the immunity granted to the Church by law
be renounced by an individual, not even by the bishop, because
this exists for the general welfare of the Church as a whole. [77]
It was a general canonical tradition that the 'status generalis
ecclesiae' must be considered normative in all legislation and
in dispensations. [78] There was a clear legal tradition whose aim
was to protect the Church against irresponsible alienations and
other actions by individuals which would endanger the general
welfare of the Church. Personal rights, on the other hand, may
normally be renounced by the individual concerned, but even
here certain qualifications have to be made. Such rights can be
renounced only so long as their renunciation does not affect
the good of the Church, — 'In quantum tangit privatam utilitatem renuntiari potest'. In the case of bishops, for example, the
good of the local church must be taken into consideration as
well as the personal wishes of the individual bishop. Hostiensis
does not think he is really free to be guided by purely selfish
motives :

> Est enim causa consideranda et specialiter si praelatus ... re-
> nuntiari velit ... quia praelatura non datur alicui propter ipsum
> solum, sed propter alios, non ut praesit sed ut prosit; 1. q. 1
> ecce cum honoris, 8. q. 1 qui episcopatum. Debet enim praelatus
> se servum facere ut plures lucrifaciat ... et plus ceteris labo-
> rare, 28. q. 1 iam nunc. [79]

A bishop should, therefore, have very good reason for resigning
from his diocese, and Hostiensis provides a list of the sort of

---

[75] *Ibid.*, n. 11.

[76] *Summa,* I, De renuntiatione, n. 2.

[77] *Ibid.*

[78] Cf. J. C. Hackett, ' "State of the Church": A concept of the Medieval
Canonists', *Jurist,* 23 (1963), pp. 259-290.

[79] *Summa,* I, De renuntiatione, n. 6.

reasons that would justify such action. But the good of the Church must be preferred to private convenience.

A very large part of the law which Hostiensis was expounding was concerned with clerics. Much of Book One of the *Decretales* deals with the appointment, the rights and the duties of ecclesiastical administrators. The same is true of Part Two of the *Decretum*. While Part One of the *Decretum* and Book Three of the *Decretales* are principally taken up with the mode of life that clerics ought to follow. Ecclesiastical interests, both spiritual and temporal, were regarded as a clerical prerogative in which the laity had no part, — except, of course, when they were asked to provide material assistance and protection. Hostiensis fully accepted this clericalist tradition. Clerics alone were considered the 'ministri iuris canonici' and laymen were thought unsuitable, — 'laicus autem idoneus non est in ecclesiasticis'. [80] Nor apparently would he have advocated too much consultation of the laity in Church affairs,, 'nec enim sequendus est populus, sed docendus'! [81]

A common theme, therefore, in the *Summa* is the concern of canon law to protect and enhance the dignity and the rights and privileges of the *ordo clericalis*. Bishops and priests, for example, should not normally take part in legal proceedings 'ne vilescat eorum dignitas'. If they do get involved in a lawsuit then they ought to employ the services of a lay advocate, 'Est enim opprobrium clericis si velint se peritos forensium ostendere'. [83] Such legislation aims at protecting the *dignitas* and *reverentia* of the clergy, but it also has in view the spiritual good of the Church. It aims at preserving the Church from harm or neglect. In the passage just referred to Hostiensis goes on to argue that it is not simply to protect their dignity that clerics are advised against going in for litigation, but also because doing so would prevent them from carrying out their spiritual duties to the faithful, 'cum status ecclesiae ex hoc laedatur, et divinum officium retardetur'. [83] Similarly, the general 'utilitas ecclesiae' demands that religious should concern themselves with spiritual matters and not get involved in temporal affairs. If they have such business to transact they ought to employ an agent, since they themselves ought to be 'in ecclesiis et circa

---

[80] *Summa*, I, De officio et potestate iudicis delegati, n. 3.
[81] *Summa*, I, De electione et electi potestate, n. 28.
[82] *Summa*, I, De postulando, n. 7.
[83] *Summa*, I, De postulando, n. 7.

spiritualia et orationes intenti'.[84]   This function of the law in
promoting spiritual values is an important one for Hostiensis
and more will be said about it later.   The Church too must be
protected against suffering harm through the misconduct of
individual clerics.[85]   There is also the considerable body of
legislation against simony which, while safeguarding the sacred
nature of the sacraments and trying to prevent their being made
a source of material profit, also aimed at protecting the Church
against avarice and venality in her ministers.   This interest of
the law in ensuring that a worthy clergy was formed to carry
out the spiritual mission of the Church is manifest too in the
detailed legislation on the qualities of candidates for Holy Orders.
The dignity of the *ordo clericalis* had to be upheld and the
Church preserved from unworthy ministers.   This is clearly the
point, for example, of a number of the *Tituli* in Book One of
the *Decretales*: *De servis non ordinandis, de corpore vitiatis ordinandis vel non, de bigamis non ordinandis, de tempore ordinationum et qualitate ordinandorum, de scrutinio in ordine fa-
ciendo, de aetate et qualitate et ordine praeficiendorum*, and
so on.   A large part of the *Summa Aurea*, is taken up with
such matters where the law can be seen in its role of guardian
of the institutions of the Church.

Similar motivation lies behind the legislation governing beneficed clerics.   Hostiensis makes it plain that he thought the
purpose of this legislation was to protect the interests of the
Church in general.   If beneficed clerics refuse to reside in their
benefices then they ought to be deposed because the Church
ought not to be left 'servitoribus destituta'.   'Ad hoc enim sunt
constituta beneficia, ut servitium inde fiat; unde ipse non debet
recipere qui non servit'.[86]   He is opposed to any kind of formalism or pretence in this matter, and he castigates what he
calls the 'perverse custom' of some churches 'quae reputant
canonicos residentes ex quo praesentes sunt, licet non intrent ecclesiam'.[87]   Such practices he regards as intolerable.   Another
point that Hostiensis frequently makes is that clerics should not
be regarded as owners of church property, 'non sunt domini sed
procuratores', and their duty is to administer prudently the

---

[84] *Summa*, I, De Syndico, n. 9.
[85] *Summa*, I, De integrum restitutione, n. 9.
[86] *Summa*, III, De clericis non residentibus in ecclesia vel praebenda,
nn. 1-2.
[87] *Ibid.*

property that does not belong to them but to the Church. Hence the large body of legislation to ensure that they do not abuse their position and squander what has been given to them in trust for the Church.[88] A bishop is to be regarded as the administrator of Church property and his administration must always be within the limits of the law. He may not act arbitrarily in such matters but must take the advice of his chapter in a number of cases and obtain the permission of the pope in others. 'Praelatus habet generalem administrationem sed non liberam', and he is warned against causing any harm to the Church.[89] This is the point of the laws on alienation and the like. The general aim is to prevent the Church from suffering harm of any description.[90] For this reason the consent of the chapter is normally required for alienation, which will be allowed only on condition that the Church does not suffer. Incompetent or negligent Church officials should be removed from their posts if they are unable to reform themselves and provide for the good of the Church. This is one of the functions of the legislation on denuntiation, for example.[91]

Many further texts could be cited from the *Summa* to illustrate the same point. It was an important function of the law to protect the material and spiritual interests of the Church. And this fits in with the general theme of this chapter since it is not only individuals who are to be protected from the harmful passions of men but also the institution of the Church in general. 'Ideoque lex proditur ut appetitus noxius sub iuris regula limitetur'.

5. *Directions for the Administration of the Sacraments*

It has been the aim of this chapter to show how canon law, according to Hostiensis, provided for security and stability in the Church both by delineating spheres of authority and responsibility, and by affording legal protection for the spiritual and temporal interests of the Church as an institution. There is, however, one area where the spiritual interests of the Church are particularly involved, and that is the administration of the sacraments. Here more than anywhere else did

---

88 *Summa*, III, De concessione praeb. et eccl., n. 2.
89 *Summa*, I, De transactionibus, n. 2.
90 *Summa*, III, De rebus ecclesiae alienandis vel non, n. 2.
91 *Summa*, V, De denuntiationibus, n. 6.

theologia practica have full scope for development. The doctrine concerning the sacraments is, of course, the concern of
the theologian rather than of the canonist, but because sacramental administration was so closely related to the practical
life of all Christians, in this area above all others the need
for unity and security was considered paramount. The Christian life to a great extent depended on the authentic sacramental tradition being preserved and handed on intact and
this was the practical task entrusted to the clergy. Hence
there were in fact a large number of ecclesiastical regulations
concerning the sacraments and these regulations traditionally
occupied the attention of the canonists. This was the case
in the Middle Ages, and indeed it is still true today since
sacramental legislation takes up a large proportion of the current Code of Canon Law. It will not, therefore, be out of
place to conclude this chapter with a brief examination of
the function of canon law in relation to the administration of
the sacraments.

A glance at the list of the contents of the *Decretum* is
enough to show how much the canonists concerned themselves
with the sacraments. Part One contains a large collection of
patristic texts, conciliar canons and papal decretals on the sacrament of holy orders, and the subject is dealt with from every
angle. In Part Two there is the long treatise on marriage and
the treatise on the sacrament of penance which comprises seven
Distinctions containing 219 chapters. And almost the whole of
Part Three — De Consecratione — is concerned with the Eu-
charist, baptism and confirmation. Indeed marriage and holy
orders had so completely passed into the hands of the canonists
that a number of twelfth-century theologians apparently did
not produce any special treatise on them but simply referred
their students to the *Decretum*. [92] Gratian's collection had in
fact provided the theologians with a mine of information on
sacramental tradition and they borrowed freely from it. [93]

The *Decretales* continued this tradition and there is a great
deal of sacramental legislation gathered together in this collection also, as a look at the *tituli* will show. It is in Hostiensis'
commentary on these *tituli* that his views on this aspect of

---

[92] Cf. A. M. Landgraf, 'Diritto Canonico e Teologia nel Secolo XII', in
Studia Gratiana, I (1953), pp. 371-413.
[93] Cf. J. de Ghellinck, S.J., *Le Mouvement Théologique du XII siècle*,
Brussells, 1948, pp. 416-510.

canon law are to be found. Under the *titulus, De sacra unctione*, in Book One he discusses the distinction between valid
and invalid administration. 'Quid si contra formam ecclesiae
ordinetur quis?' Hostiensis replies that it will depend on what
has been omitted from the rite and he goes on to distinguish
between *substantialia* and *sollemnia*. If what was omitted belongs to the *substantialia*, then the sacrament has not in fact
been conferred. [94] Parts of the sacramental rite, he explains,
are required for the validity of the sacrament while others have
been introduced 'ob honestatem sacramentorum'; 'hoc enim ho-
nestatis est non necessitatis'. [95]

His commentary on the following *titulus, De sacramentis
non iterandis*, contains a discussion on the nature and number
of the sacraments as well as how these may be divided. He
considers who may confer and who may be the recipient of
the sacrament of baptism, observing that all must be done 'iuxta
morem ecclesiasticum quem Apostolica Sedes observat', and in
accordance with the canons. [96] He then provides some practical
directions about what should be done if any of the ceremonies
happen to be omitted. After discussing which sacraments may
be repeated and which may not, he concludes with a brief treatment of the effects of the sacraments, noting that these will
depend on the heart and conscience of the recipient. He points
out too that the sacraments may not be denied to anyone on
account of sins which are not publicly known, 'nam propter
occulta non possunt alicui sacramenta negari'. Throughout the
whole passage he refers frequently to Part Three of the *Decretum*
and to the discussions of other canonists.

Another clear example of his interest in sacramental administration is to be found in his commentary on a group of *tituli*
at the end of Book Three: *De consecratione ecclesiae, De bap-
tismo et eius effectu, De custodia eucharistiae*, and so on. Here
he explicitly states that he intends to follow the order of the
Decretum in the five *Distinctiones, De consecratione*. Again, he
combines discussion of the nature and the theology of the sacraments with practical directions for their administration. He
observes that a number of customs have developed around the
sacraments in the course of time. These, he says, although

---

[94] *Summa*, I, De sacra unctione, n. 4.
[95] *Summa*, I, *ibid.*, n. 6.
[96] *Summa*, I, De sacramentis non iterandis, n. 10.

not belonging to the essentials of the sacraments, have been introduced to ensure reverence in their administration and should be respected. The eucharistic fast is an example of such a custom [97] and he refers to the following passage from the *Decretum*: 'quod a patribus nostris propensiori cura novimus esse servatum, a nobis quoque volumus custodiri' (D. 75,4). There are other particular regulations and customs that have been introduced 'ut ecclesia magis revereatur.' [98] Similarly, the additions that have been made to the Mass should be revered as coming from a holy tradition: 'sed ea credimus ab Apostolis et sanctis patribus fuisse adiecta'. [99] The tradition must always be respected. Mass, for instance, can be celebrated only by 'presbytero rite ordinato secundum traditionem ecclesiasticam', [100] and, as has been seen throughout this discussion on the sacraments, Hostiensis frequently adverts to the importance of tradition. The theological tradition has to be preserved. In another part of the *Summa* he stresses the importance in theology of safeguarding the traditional teaching of the Church. The teacher is to hand on what he has been taught:

> quod de theologia potissime intelligendum est et servandum, quia ibi contra dicta sanctorum patrum non est dicendum, nisi auctoritate Papae fieret in quibusdam, quia et si Papa contra fidem scribere vellet non crederem ei. In aliis autem scientiis possumus dicere contra maiores. [101]

Reference has already been made to the long treatise in Book Five on the sacrament of penance. [102] This is one of the clearest instances where Hostiensis appears as moralist and sacramental theologian combined. He provides a fairly complete manual for confessors in which he discusses the nature of the sacrament as well as providing detailed practical directions on how it should be administered.

Perhaps one of the best illustrations of the role of canon law in promoting stability and security in the community and protecting Church institutions is to be seen in the large body of canonical legislation surrounding the sacrament of matrimony.

---

[97] *Summa*, III, De consecratione ecclesiae vel altaris, n. 13.
[98] *Summa*, III, De consecratione ecclesiae vel altaris, n. 6.
[99] *Summa*, ibid., n. 17.
[100] *Summa*, III, De consecratione ecclesiae vel altaris, n. 12.
[101] *Summa*, V, De magistris et ne aliquod exigatur pro licentia docendi, n. 2.
[102] *Summa*, V, De poenitentiis et remissionibus.

Precisely because it was a sacrament, marriage was regarded as within the province of canon law rather than that of civil law. [103] Because of this the Church claimed competence over all allied matters as well, such as impediments, legitimacy, dowries and so on. Hence the lengthy treatise on matrimony in Part Two of the *Decretum* and the compilation of a complete book of decretals on the same subject in the *Decretales* of Gregory IX (Book IV). In the early Middle Ages matrimonial law had tended to vary considerably because of the multiplicity of rites and customs that surrounded it in different parts of Christendom. Roman law, with its stress on the contractual element of consent, Jewish traditions, which emphasised the importance of *copula carnis*, and the various national customs all had some influence on the law of the Church and even led to differences of practice in the ecclesiastical courts. Towards the end of the twelfth century, however, Alexander III settled the long-standing conflict about whether copula or consent constituted the essence of marriage, — coming down on the side of the consensual theory of Lombard and the Paris theologians rather than that of the Bolognese canonists, — and the way was clear for a unified legislation. By the mid-thirteenth century canon law had succeeded in producing a great measure of certainty and uniformity in the matter.

Hostiensis' commentary shows how he thought this legislation provided for security and stability and protected the institution of marriage. He discusses at some length the nature of the sacrament of matrimony and teaches with firmness and clarity the by then accepted view that consent alone makes the marriage valid and complete. [104] He does add, though, that *carnis copula* gives a certain firmness to the marriage bond through signifying the union between Christ and his Church, and so it is the *matrimonium consummatum* that is absolutely indissoluble. [105] Because of its sacramental nature and the indissolubility of the bond, Hostiensis repeatedly affirms that the institution of marriage is protected by the law of the Church and favoured by legal presumptions. Hence the accepted canonical principle, 'in dubio semper est pro matrimonio iudicandum', [106] which he repeats again and again. He goes through

---

[103] *Summa*, IV, De matrimoniis, n. 7.
[104] Cf. *Summa*, IV, De matrimoniis, n. 10.
[105] Cf. *Summa*, IV, De matrimoniis, n. 1.
[106] *Summa*, IV, De sponsalibus et matrimoniis, n. 7.

the matrimonial legislation and makes it clear that part of its function is to guard against deceit and collusion that would tend to undermine the stability of marriage or give rise to injustice. If the bond is not firmly protected by law, then 'quilibet posset illudere matrimonio iam contracto, et dicere: ludens feci'. Another reason he adduces is its value in controlling the passions of youth: 'imo et in hoc iuveniles calores bonum est coarctare'. And, of course, there is the need to keep the peace and remove sources of discord: 'unde etsi in totum discordias fugare, seu pacificare non possumus, tamen prout possibile refrenamus'. [107]

What, it may be asked, is the canon lawyer doing in these incursions into sacramental theology? He seems to be demonstrating in actual fact, though perhaps he does not theorise about it, that there is and must be a close connection between canon law and theology. Just as he is insistent on basing the authority of the pope on theological and scriptural foundations, so also he is careful to knit the sacramental practice of the Church to the theology that lies behind it. By offering a clear and authoritative presentation of the traditional teaching on the sacraments he is doing much to preserve and protect the Church's dogmatic tradition in this matter. He is also supplying the priest with a reliable and practical guide to help him in his pastoral mission. Hostiensis expressly states several times that his purpose in composing the *Summa* is to offer such guidance to priests, — 'ad instructionem simplicium sacerdotum'. [108] By providing clarity and precision about the Church's sacramental tradition in such a practical way for active priests in their apostolate the canonist would seem to be exemplifying theology in action, *theologia practica*.

Summary

It may be useful at this point briefly to summarise the results of the investigation so far. Hostiensis stated at the outset of the *Summa* that it was the function of canon law to make provision for security against violence and fraud and promote stability and concord within the Christian community. Together with the popes and canonists of the period he viewed canon law as an instrument for order, peace and harmony within

---

[107] *Summa*, IV, De desponsatione impuberum, n. 12.
[108] *Summa*, V, De poenitentiis et remissionibus, n. 62.

the Church. Examination of the *Summa Aurea* has shown how in practice he thought the law performed these functions. In a variety of ways it protected innocent people from falling victims to trickery and deceit, and by delineating areas of responsibility it tried to promote stability and concord. It was for the law to clarify the juridical structure of the Church and provide protection against disruption of the *ordo ecclesiasticus.*

Of primary importance in this hierarchical structure were the position and power of the pope. The *Summa Aurea* reveals Hostiensis as a loyal and enthusiastic 'papalist' who took great pains to clarify and defend the plenitude of papal power. This he did in the interests of unity and concord. The Church, he argued, is one body and therefore it can only have one head on earth, the Vicar of Christ. He bases his arguments here on the scriptural foundation of Christ's promise to Peter and stresses the theological basis for the doctrine of papal supremacy, an illustration of his esteem for theology. As has been shown earlier, Hostiensis did not regard canon law as a self-contained and autonomous discipline. On the contrary, it had to be closely related to theology which he regarded as the superior science. It has been seen too how devotion to the pope at times could carry Hostiensis away on flights of far-fetched rhetoric and lead him into strange exaggerations on the subject of papal plenitude of power. Yet the *Summa* itself also provides the qualifications that have to made to such exaggerated language. Even the rhetoric will not cause too much surprise if the political background is kept in mind and it is remembered that for most of the active life of Hostiensis there was open war between the empire and the papacy. One of Henry of Susa's first experiences as a bishop would have been to witness the solemn deposition of Frederick II at Lyons in 1245. Against such a background it is perhaps a greater cause for suprise that an archbishop should assert so clearly his acceptance of the distinction of jurisdictions and even grant a *plenitudo potestatis in temporalibus* to the emperor.

Lastly, the role of canon law in providing protection for the institutional Church has been considered and attention has been drawn to its concern for sacramental theology, with its provision for the preservation of the theological tradition in this matter. The detailed examination of the *Summa* does seem to indicate that Hostiensis was a man of his time and a canonist who fits into the main stream of the medieval canonistic thinking that was briefly examined in Chapter Two.

CHAPTER FIVE

DELINEATION OF RIGHTS AND DUTIES & LEGAL PROTECTION THROUGH DUE PROCESS

To keep in check the bold recklessness of mankind and protect innocent and upright men from the excesses of criminals is the second function of law that is mentioned in Hostiensis' list. But only by making clear the rights that are to be so protected and attaching sanctions to the infringement of these can law perform this task effectively. It is therefore implied in this second function that the law must provide a clear delineation of the rights and duties that are to be legally secured, and enact penalties to be incurred by any who fail to respect these rights or fulfil these duties. The fear of punishment is to deter evil men from inflicting injury on others and violating their recognised rights. In particular need of legal protection of this kind, thought Hostiensis, were those unfortunates who were being subjected to cruelty or injustice. He considered that the law should enable society to show compassion to the victims of such oppression. This is the point of his third function: 'tertia, ut oppressis compatiatur'. Since both the second and third functions of law are concerned with the protection of innocent people, they will be treated together in this chapter.

To guarantee protection, however, it is not enough for the law to delineate rights and duties and enact penalties against offenders. It must also make provision for the enforcement of these through a recognised court procedure. As Hostiensis repeatedly affirms throughout the *Summa*, referring to the famous passage from the Digest, 'parum prodest iura habere in civitate nisi sit qui iura reddat'.[1] And so court procedure is the subject of the fourth and fifth functions of law which he goes on to mention, — 'quarta, ut mota negotia terminentur'. That is to say, there is need of clear directives which will ensure

---

[1] *Summa*, I, De postulatione praelatorum, n. 1; and frequently elsewhere in the *Summa*; cf. D. I, 2, 2, 13.

the fair completion of legal proceedings and avert the danger
of fraudulent delays in obtaining judicial settlements. It is for
the law to ensure that justice is done in the courts, that unnecessary delays are avoided, that deceit is excluded and that
the parties are not everwhelmed with unreasonable costs or
other grave inconsciences — 'ne partes ultra graventur laboribus
et expensis'. If, however, such difficulties should arise in the
courts it is for the law to provide legal remedies and relief
for the victims. Hence the fifth function of law: 'quinta, ut
occurratur laboribus partium et expensis'.

It would seem then to follow from all this that Hostiensis
quite clearly considered it the function of the Church's legal
system to clarify the rights and duties of individuals and provide for the enforcement of these through due legal process.
To demonstrate in some detail how, according to the *Summa
Aurea*, canon law carried out these tasks is the main purpose
of this chapter. But Hostiensis also thought that the legal
system he was describing should embody the Christian principles
of justice and equity. These were for him, — as for all medieval canonists, — the basic principles which should govern
all legal activity and determine the interpretation of law. Comments on particular texts must always be read in the light of
these guiding principles. For this reason the study of the delineation of rights and duties and the protection of these by
due process will be prefaced by a consideration of Hostiensis'
views on justice and canonical equity. This chapter will, therefore, examine three questions. First of all, what meaning did
Hostiensis attach to the idea of justice and why did he stress
the importance of equity? Secondly, how in particular does
the *Summa Aurea* illustrate canonical protection for individuals
through the delineation of rights and duties? And lastly, what
provision did canon law make for the enforcement of these by
means of due legal process?

1. *The Primacy of Justice and Equity*

Concern for justice and for the rights of the individual
was a frequent theme in the writing of medieval lawyers and
philosophers. It was firmly rooted in the Roman legal tradition.
The first discussion in the *Institutes* of Justinian concerned 'de
iustitia et iure', where justice is defined as 'constans et perpetua voluntas ius suum cuique tribuens'; [2] and the *Digest* opens

---

[2] *Institutes*, I, 1, 1.

with Ulpian's declaration that the task of the lawyer is the pursuit of justice:

> Iustitiam namque colimus et boni et aequi notitiam profitemur, aequum ab iniquo separantes, licitum ab illicito discernentes, bonos non solum metu poenarum, verum etiam praemiorum quoque exhortatione efficere cupientes.[3]

This tradition was accepted by the medieval lawyers, who taught that the aim of law was to attempt to realise the ideal of justice among men.   This implied respect for what was objectively owing to each person or to the community in general.   'Iuris praecepta sunt haec', continued the first discussion in the *Institutes*, 'honeste vivere, alterum non laedere, suum cuique tribuere'.[4]   Medieval Roman lawyers held that the Roman law, based as it was on the natural law, should be taken as an expression of the divinely conceived harmony of the universe. Professor Ullmann has shown how this ideal was exemplified in the writings of the distinguished Roman lawyer, Lucas de Penna (1320-90).[5]   Law, for lawyers like de Penna, was seen as the realisation of justice.   It was the instrument which transformed the metaphysical idea of justice into a workable reality in the affairs of men.   And Lucas de Penna taught that the Roman law was an embodiment of this ideal of justice, an ideal that should be personified in the ruler and made the fundamental principle of all government.

Similar ideas about justice and law pervade the whole thought of antiquity and the Middle Ages and have frequently been commented on by historians.[6]   Professor Southern, for intance, while describing conditions in the eleventh and twelfth centuries, remarks: 'One common need at this time dominates the whole scene of human government whether secular or spiritual: the need for justice'.[7]   He adds that justice was a word that was often on the lips of that great medieval reformer,

---

[3] *Digest*, I, 1, 1.

[4] *Institutes*, I, 1, 3.

[5] W. Ullmann, *The Medieval Idea of Law*, London, 1946. (In a long introduction to this book, Professor H. D. Hazeltine outlines the medieval idea of justice and law).

[6] Cf. Ullmann, *op. cit.*   Also H. D. Hazeltine, 'Roman and Canon Law in the Middle Ages', in the *Cambridge Medieval History*, vol. V, (1926), pp. 697-764.

[7] R. W. Southern, *The Making of the Middle Ages*, London, 1953, pp. 145-146.

Pope Gregory VII. Indeed, the last words of Hildebrand are familiar to even the most amateur dabbler in medieval history: 'Dilexi iustitiam et odivi iniquitatem, propterea morior in exilio'. It had become traditional too to describe the pope as the 'debitor iustitiae', and the phrase appears regularly in papal letters from the time of Pope Gregory VII onwards.[8] In the following century Gratian taught that all law must be in harmony with justice and that if any laws happened to run counter to the *ius naturale*, which he identified with the divine law, they were to be regarded as 'vana et irrita'.[9] He stressed the ideas of justice and equity, describing the Church as the 'mater iusticiae', which in granting privileges and dispensations, should never do anything that would be out of harmony with these fundamental principles.[10] This was also true of the thirteenth-century papacy.

> There runs through the registers of Innocent III's letters the ever-recurring, insistent theme that it was for the apostolic "sedes iustitiae" to make provision for "uniuscuiusque iura", to have charge of the "communis Christiani populi utilitas".[11]

The same concern for justice has been shown to be a principal theme in the commentary on the *Decretales* published by Pope Innocent IV a few years before the *Summa Aurea* of Hostiensis.

> 'As one works through his lengthy Commentary,' writes Fr Kemp, 'it is quite evident that, fluid though medieval society was in the thirteenth century, it was a society based on the Christian concept of justice, a justice that had to agree not only with reason but with the revelation of Christ, and this justice was described as related to society in terms of "sin", "evil" and offences against the teachings of Christ. Any law

---

[8] Cf. J. A. Watt, *The Theory of Papal Monarchy in the Thirteenth Century*, London, 1965, p. 42.

[9] D. 8, c. 1 dict post; also D. 4, cc. 1-2.

[10] C. 25, q. 1, c. 16 dict post: 'Valet, ergo, ut ex praemissis colligitur, sancta Romana ecclesia quoslibet suis privilegiis munire, et extra generalia decreta quedam speciali beneficio indulgere, *considerata tamen rationis equitate*, ut *que mater iusticiae est* in nullo ab ea dissentire inveniatur'.

[11] Cf. J. A. Watt, *op. cit.*, p. 70; also B. Tierney, *Medieval Poor Law*, California, 1959, p. 5, and *passim*.

without agreement with charity and reason had no validity
at all. [12]

Even the supreme power of the pope had to be used in harmony with reason and revelation and for the general welfare
of Christendom. The pope was not free arbitrarily to violate
the jurisdiction of another who validly and justly exercised his
office. He too had to observe the 'ius vel publica utilitas'.
Referring to the Register of Innocent IV, as well as to his Commentary, Fr Kemp goes on:

> ... the pope is describing a Christian *society of justice* which
> could only be a Christian society of justice if the Christian,
> and those with whom he dealt, were given justice. Therefore
> it is under the heading of *defectus iustitiae* — that deplorable
> situation of unrest in society where a man cannot get justice —
> that the pope insists that he has a clear right to hear a case,
> as the representative of Christ. [13]

For Innocent IV, then, all authority is ultimately to be asso-
ciated with Christ, and he contended that there was only one
justice that all authority, whether civil or ecclesiastical, had to
protect. Otherwise Christian society would perish.

Hostiensis shared these views of his contemporaries on the
supremacy of justice. As has been seen in the last chapter,
one of his reasons for insisting on the special prerogatives of
the papacy was the need to have some means of ensuring that
justice would be done throughout Christendom. There had to
be a court of appeal to which all Christians could bring their
grievances and obtain redress. The papal *plenitudo potestatis*
was looked upon as a safeguard against the negligence and
irresponsibility of spiritual and temporal rulers. Hence the
common view of medieval popes and canonists that the pope
could intervene even in temporal affairs to see that justice was
done. As Innocent III had declared: 'Propter defectum iusticiae
ius reddimus, etiam in temporalibus'. [14]

---

[12] J.A. Kemp, SJ, 'A New Concept of the Christian Commonwealth',
in *Proceedings of the Second International Congress on Medieval Canon
Law*, Rome, 1965, pp. 156-157.

[13] Kemp, *op. cit.*, p. 157.

[14] Cf. J.A. Watt, *The Theory of Papal Monarchy in the Thirteenth
Century*, London, 1965. Here Dr Watt has provided an excellent and
well-documented study of this aspect of the medieval papacy together
with a full bibliography. Confer in particular pp. 48-49; 115-117. On

The whole of the *Summa Aurea* is permeated with this concern for justice. One of the benefits to be derived from the study of canon law, Hostiensis declares in the preface to the *Summa,* is that it enables a man to distinguish between what is just and what is unjust and allows him to render to each man what is his due. He is consistently concerned that justice should always be done, — 'veritas iustitiae, vel bonae vitae, numquam deserenda est'. [15] He insists too that a Christian should, in accordance with the teaching of St Paul, be moved by the love of justice to lead a good life and obey the law rather than by fear of punishment: 'si spiritu ducimini, non estis sub lege; ex quo apparet eum qui sub lege est, id est qui timore poenae non amore iustitiae servit, non ducitur Spiritu Sancto'. [16] The whole aim of law and legal procedure is that justice be maintained, and administered impartially by judges who obey the law, and do not allow themselves to be influenced by wealth or rank or anything else that would lead them to deprive any man of his rights. This duty of the judge will be discussed in greater detail later in this chapter in connection with procedure.

Hostiensis was, however, equally insistent that true justice must always be tempered by compassion and administered in a humane manner. While it is true that a judge is not free to alter at will statutory penalties clearly enacted by the law, he does have greater freedom where no such legal limitations exist, and in these cases Hostiensis urges him always to observe equity and adopt the course that will prove to be more humane in the circumstances.

Ubi vero certa poena statuta non est, vel ex officio mero et puro inquiritur, iudex procedere debet aequitate servata, sem-

---

p. 141 he sums up this approach: 'What received special emphasis was the principle that the pope intervened in temporal affairs to ensure that no individual Christian or people should be denied due measure of justice for lack of recourse to a superior tribunal. The thirteenth-century canonists agreed that redress could be had from the pope either by application to him, or on his initiative, when the normal judicial machinery was obstructed through the negligence or culpability of a secular ruler, or through the vacancy in the office of a secular ruler, or when the matter in question was especially difficult, or existing law the canonist fashioned a distinctively juridical formulation of the papal *cura totius Christianitatis* in a theory of prerogative power, based on the known instances of its exercise.'

[15] *Summa*, I, De renuntiatione, n. 8.
[16] *Summa*, I, De his quae vi metusve causa fiunt, n. 6.

per in humaniorem partem declinando secundum quod personas, loca, causas et tempora viderit postulare. [17]

He should always exercise compassion, even when he has to inflict punishment, — 'condolendo his quos puniet; nam vera iustitia compassionem habet, falsa dedignationem'. [18] The phrase is taken from a passage of Gregory the Great and Hostiensis refers to it repeatedly; the need to temper justice with compassion is a theme that runs through the whole of the *Summa*.

Even in those cases where a definite penalty is enjoined by the law Hostiensis suggests that a judge can often use his discretion to modify the outcome by granting a dispensation or some other sort of relief. [19] The judge should always have regard to the age and condition of the prisoner, and see whether he might adapt the penalty to particular circumstances and according to the degree of guilt of the person convicted. Mitigating circumstances, if there are any, should be seriously taken into consideration. The prisoner too ought to be treated in a humane manner and Hostiensis lists a number of amenities to which he has a right before the trial, such as food, light, clothing and so on. 'Carcer enim ad custodiendum non ad puniendum est inventus', he declares, and draws attention to penalties that may be incurred if these humane regulations are not observed. [20]

A key concept to the thought of Hostiensis in this whole matter of the protection of rights and the administration of justice is the idea of equity. This is constantly stressed by him as the guiding principle which a judge has to keep before his mind at all times. Innumerable examples of his emphasis on the equitable administration of justice are provided by the *Summa*. Rescripts, for instance, should only contain what is in harmony with equity:

> Illud quod consonat iuri et aequitati, maxime quando continet in se iuris determinationes aequaliter et generaliter, puta, vocatis quae fuerint evocandi; ... quae aequalitas servanda est

---

[17] *Summa*, I, De officio ordinarii, n. 4.
[18] Cf. D. 45, c. 15: 'Vera iusticia compassionem habet, falsa dedignationem ... At contra, qui de falsa iusticia superbire solent, ceteros quosque despiciunt, nulla infirmantibus misericordia condescendunt, et quo se peccatores esse non credunt, eo deteriores peccatores fiunt'.
[19] *Summa*, IV, De clandestina desponsatione, n. 12.
[20] *Summa*, V, De accusationibus, nn. 9-12.

regulariter ... Nam summam aequitatem ante oculos debet habere iudex. [21]

In keeping with equity is another factor that Hostiensis often
mentions, namely, the legal understanding that a man can be
required to perform only what he can do without extreme dif-
ficulty or inconvenience, — 'quia illud solum possumus quod
commode possumus'. [22]   Again it is the qualities of mercy and
equity that he stresses when discussing the sort of punishment
that prelates may at times have to administer.

> Praelati igitur caveant ut in poenis, disciplinis et correctionibus
> infligendis, stateram in manu gestent, in utroque penso iusti-
> tiam et misericordiam portent. Et iusto libramine quaedam
> per aequitatem corrigant, quaedam vero per misericordiam
> indulgeant; ... et ex utroque temperamentum faciant ut nec
> vigor iustitiae sit rigidus nec mansuetudo sit dissoluta. [23]

Although this balance between justice and mercy was particularly stressed by Hostiensis it was not peculiar to him.   In fact,
as his references to the *Decretum* clearly demonstrate, the blend-
ing of justice with mercy was a characteristic trait of medieval
canon law and was firmly rooted in the traditional teaching
of the Church.   It had been clearly advocated by Gregory the
Great in his *Moralia*, which had been used by priests as a theological and moral *vade mecum* for centuries. [24]   There can, however, be no doubt that Hostiensis was a particularly forceful
exponent of this approach to law.

High on his list of the qualities required in a candidate
for the episcopate come those of equity and moderation.   Since
he will at times have to administer correction, the bishop should

---

[21] *Summa*, I, De rescriptis et eorum interpretatione, n. 19.

[22] *Ibid.*, n. 33.

[23] *Summa*, I, De tempore ordinationum et qualitate ordinandorum,
n. 27.

[24] Hostiensis here refers to several passages from the *Moralia*: D. 45,
c. 10: 'Omnis qui iuste iudicat, stateram in manu gestat: in utroque penso
iusticiam et misericordiam portat; sed per iusticiam reddit peccatis
sententiam, per misericordiam peccati temperat penam, ut iusto libra-
mine quedam per equitatem corrigat, quedam vero per misericordiam
indulgeat'. Also D. 45, c. 9, where Gregory is advocating that discipline
and mercy must always be combined together and that firmness and
gentleness should never be separated: 'Disciplina vel misericordia multum
destituitur, si una sine altera teneatur ...'. Similar moderation is counselled
by Ivo of Chartres in the very influential *Prologus in Decretum* (P. L.,
161, 47-60).

be a man of discretion and compassion. 'In virga disciplinae sive correctionis attendere debet ut non ex odio sed ex charitate corrigat; ... quia falsa iustitia indignationem habet, vera compassionem'.[25] He should be of a tolerant nature who when he has to punish does so with the desire to heal rather than simply to vent his own anger. This same emphasis on equity appears in the discussion of the bishop's role as judge in his diocese. Again the qualities of humanity and generosity are underlined.[26]

It is also on equitable grounds that special legal remedies have been devised such as *restitutio in integrum*; and supplications to the Roman pontiff;[27] and in arbitration it is again equity that must dictate the outcome, — 'prout aequum fuerit'.[28] The whole point of laying the dispute before a just and reasonable man is to obtain a decision that will be recognised as fair by both parties. Equity is also put forward by Hostiensis as a sound reason for the alienation of church property. It is, for instance, only fair to grant a very long lease of land to those who have in fact cultivated it, or to their families, since the labourer deserves fair remuneration for his work.[29] Debtors too should be treated with fairness and not forced to pay what they do not in fact possess. Nor should they be imprisoned nor excommunicated, nor deprived of their whole livelihood, — 'impossibile iudicis praeceptum non obligat'.[30] J. A. Brundage has drawn attention to another example of humane interpretation of the law by Hostiensis.[31] The problem concerned the wife of a crusader who goes off on crusade and fails to return. Can the wife remarry? Gratian had argued that the death of the first husband must be demonstrated before the wife can contract a second marriage and the early decretists apparently accepted this position also. But the decretalists tended to take a more lenient attitude, as did the *Glossa Ordinaria* on the *Decretales*, holding that reasonable presumption of the death of the first husband was sufficient. It should be noted that

---

[25] *Summa*, I, De tempore ordinationum et qualitate ordinandorum, n. 20.

[26] *Summa*, I, De officio ordinarii.

[27] *Summa*, I, De restitutione in integrum, nn. 9-10.

[28] *Summa*, I, De arbitris, n. 1.

[29] *Summa*, III, De rebus ecclesiae alienandis vel non, n. 3.

[30] *Summa*, III, De cessione bonorum, n. 1.

[31] *Summa*, IV, De sponsa duorum, n. 6. A fully documented discussion of the problem has been provided by J. A. Brundage in 'The Crusader's Wife Revisited', *Studia Gratiana*, XIV (1967), pp. 241-251.

Roman lawyers, such as Accursius, were very strict on the question: no re-marriage if there was any doubt about the death
of the first husband. Hostiensis, in keeping with his emphasis
on equity and benignity, put forward the more lenient approach:

> The principles governing cases of presumed death were further
> spelled out by Hostiensis, who taught that a reasonable pre-
> sumption of the death of the first husband was all that should
> be required in order to make a second marriage possible, and
> that such a presumption was established when it was generally
> believed that the first husband had perished. Although he
> observed that others disagreed with his position, Hostiensis
> concluded that his teaching was the truer one. [32]

Brundage remarks that it was this position of Hostiensis that
became the normative teaching for later medieval canonists with
the single exception of Panormitanus in the 15th century.

Many further instances could be given to show how consistently Hostiensis maintained that a truly humane approach
is to be preferred to intricate legal formalities and subtle eva-
sions. Another clear case is the legislation surrounding wills.
In such matters 'est humanitatis veritas praeferenda'. [33] Even
judges in the civil courts would rightly reject hairsplitting subtleties that defeat the purpose of the law. Hostiensis also holds
that it is a requirement of equity that the bishop receive some
remuneration for all the work that he has to carry out for the
good of the diocese. 'Quis ergo umquam aequitatem prae oculis
habens iudicabit quod sic oneratus nihil emolumenti percipiat'. [34]
Again, although Hostiensis argues forcefully for the strict duty
of paying tithes to the Church, nevertheless he also maintains
that remissions should be made on occasion, and he claims
support from a number of passages in the Decretum. [35] When
there is question of granting a commutation of a vow it is
again equity that should be one of the main criteria in coming
to a decision. [36] Hostiensis repeatedly advises his readers that
difficult circumstances should be taken into consideration when

---

[32] Brundage, op. cit., p. 249.
[33] Summa, III, De testamentis et ultimis voluntatibus, n. 9.
[34] Summa, I, De officio Iudicis ordinarii.
[35] Summa, III, de decimis et primitiis, n. 16.
[36] Summa, III, De voto et voti redemptione, n. 23: 'Sed in redemptione
vel commutatione cuiuslibet voti, tria sunt praecipue attendenda: quid
liceat secundum aequitatem, quid deceat secundum honestatem, quid
expediat secundum utilitatem seu necessitatem'.

the law is to be applied; it must always be interpreted in a fair and humane manner. Hence the poor should not be over-burdened with Church collections and the like. [37] In penances, such as fasting, all the circumstances of the individual must be taken into consideration.

It will by now be clear that Hostiensis regarded it as the function of the law to promote justice and protect the rights of all and that equity was a vitally important element in the interpretation of the law. It will also be plain from the numerous references in the *Summa* that he believed he was expressing the true spirit of ecclesiastical legislation as this was to be found in the writings of the Fathers of the Church and embodied in the *Decretum*. He did not regard himself as a liberal revolutionary, but as a faithful interpreter of the traditional teaching. Yet in fact he did gain the reputation of being unusually concerned about equitable interpretation and particularly opposed to that rigorously juridical approach which seemed to him to be out of harmony with the spirit of the Gospel. A number of writers have drawn attention to the contrast between Hostiensis and Innocent IV in this matter. In doing so they are recalling what seems to have been a long-standing tradition at Bologna. Professor Tierney writes:

> Innocent is usually portrayed, and perhaps with reason, as the very embodiment of that harsh legalism that was to fetter the life of the Church in the later Middle Ages, while Hostiensis was remembered at Bologna as a doctor who loved justice more than the law, and who tempered in a spirit of equity Innocent's harsh decisions. [38]

---

[37] *Summa*, III, De censibus, et exactionibus, et procurationibus, n. 20: 'Sed et miserabiles personae, et pauperes, sicut caeci in collectis gravandi non sunt, cum ipsis potius providendum sit de collectis'.

[38] B. Tierney, *Foundations of the Conciliar Theory*, Cambridge 1955, p. 106. He cites the following sources: M. Sarti, *De Claris Archigymnasii Bononiensis Professoribus*, ed. M. Fattorini (Bononiae, 1888), I, p. 444: '... erat aequitatis magis quam summi iuris amator, sed verear ne iste aequitatis amor in iuris canonici minus laudabilis sit quam in iuris civilis interprete ...'. G. Panciroli, *De Claris Legum Interpretibus* (Venetiis, 1655); 'Aequitatis amator, duras Innocentii opiniones libenter damnat'. Cf. also C. Lefebvre, 'Rigueur et équité chez Innocent IV et Hostiensis', in *Ephemerides Iuris Canonici*, XVII (1961), pp. 200-230; '"Aequitas canonica" et "periculum animae" dans la doctrine de l'Hostiensis', *Ephemerides Iuris Canonici*, VIII (1952) pp. 305-321. For the development of the idea of equity from Gratian to Hostiensis, see the chapter by C. Lefebvre in *L'Age Classique*, pp. 352-362.

Hostiensis consistently argued that excessive rigour should be avoided, and that the law should be applied to particular cases in a spirit of equity. But what precisely did he mean by *aequitas*? The clearest answer to this question in the *Summa Aurea* is to be found in the treatment of dispensations, to which Hostiensis devoted a separate *titulus* towards the end of Book Five. The passage is worth examining in some detail. He points out that there are four things here that should not be confused with each other. 'Hic tamen notandum quod aliud est rigor, aliud ius, aliud aequitas, aliud dispensatio'.[39] A dispensation he defines as 'rigoris iuris per eum ad quem spectat misericors canonice facta relaxatio'. *Rigor iuris* may be either an excessive severity in a written law, whose purpose is to act as a deterrent from evil, or a kind of formalism in interpretation which allows adherence to the strict letter of the law to stand in the way of true justice.

> Rigor est districtio iuris, sive excessus et austeritas iuris scripta aliquoties ad terrorem, secundum quod dicit canon quod non est danda communio etiam in fine vitae his qui defecerunt in accusatione clericorum[40] ... Item quod non oretur pro illo qui presbyterum nominavit tutorem in testamento filio suo.[41] ... Sed iste rigor non est servandus nisi ubi timetur exemplum mali.

Equity stands midway between the dispensation and *rigor iuris*. 'Aequitas vero media est inter rigorem et dispensationem sive misericordiam'. Since true justice is held traditionally to involve the 'ars aequi et boni' then to be genuine it must avoid excessive rigour on the one hand yet remain quite distinct from a dispensation on the other. Hostiensis' definition — which he attributes to St Cyprian — steers a middle course between these two:

> Aequitas est iustitia dulcore misericordiae temperata, vel dic quod aequitas est motus rationabilis regens sententiam et rigorem. Haec enim est aequitas quam iudex qui minister iuris est semper debet habere prae oculis ...; scilicet, sciat bonos remunerare, malos punire, via regia incedens et se rationabiliter regens non declinans ad dexteram vel sinistram.

---

[39] *Summa*, V, De dispensationibus, n. 1.
[40] Reference to C. 2, q. 3, c. 4, which concerns false accusations against bishops, priests and deacons.
[41] Reference to D. 88, c. 14, which is concerned to keep clergy from being drawn away from their duties in the Church.

This definition combines the patristic stress on mercy, which appears frequently in the *Decretum*, [42] with the Roman law concept of justice. It does not confuse equity with mercy. Equity remains true justice, but justice applied to a particular case. It implies, of course, that true justice must always be tempered with Christian mercy. Here Hostiensis can find support not only in the canonical tradition recorded by Gratian, but also in the Roman legal tradition where *ius* is described as 'ars aequi et boni' and the judge is urged to follow 'iustitiae aequitatisque quam stricti iuris rationem'. [43]

He has, however, joined together these two traditions of theologians and of jurists to produce a particularly felicitous combination, in which the requirements of law and order are balanced and controlled by specifically Christian values. The result is, as P. G. Caron has recently demonstrated, a brilliant synthesis of Roman law with canon law which reveals Hostiensis as one of the greatest of medieval jurists. [44]

This study of justice and equity in Hostiensis has been considered a necessary prelude to the more detailed discussion of rights and duties within the community that is to follow. It is for the law, Hostiensis has declared, to keep in check the recklessness of criminals and protect innocent and upright

---

[42] Hostiensis' references reveal the patristic foundations for his emphasis on mercy. Cf. C. 26, q. 7, c. 12: 'Melius est errare in misericordia remittendi quam in severitate ulciscendi'. '... Deinde, etsi erramus modicam penitenciam imponentes, nonne melius est propter misericordiam rationem dare, quam propter crudelitatem? Ubi enim paterfamilias largus est, dispensator non debet esse tenax. Si Deus benignus, ut quid sacerdos eius austerus vult apparere?' (attributed to Chrysostom). Also D. 45, c. 9: 'Disciplina non est servanda sine misericordia, nec misericordia sine disciplina'. 'Disciplina vel misericordia multum destituitur, si una sine altera teneatur. Sed circa subditos inesse debet rectoribus et iuste consulens misericordia, et pie seviens disciplina ...' (from the *Moralia* of Gregory the Great). Also D. 50, c. 14 & c. 28.

[43] C. 3.1.8: Roman imperial legislation enjoined this duty on the judge: 'Placuit in omnibus rebus praecipuam esse iustitiae aequitatisque quam stricti iuris rationem'. Quoted by Carleton Kemp Allen in *Law in the Making*, Oxford, 1964, p. 394.

[44] Cf. P. G. Caron, ' "Aequitas" romana, "Misericordia" patristica ed "Epicheia" Aristotelica nella dottrina Decretalistica del duecento e trecento', in *Studia Gratiana*, XIV (1967), pp. 307-347; p. 316: 'Enrico da Susa — il grande Cardinale Ostiense — nella sua *Summa* che fu detta *Aurea*, porta alla più compiuta espressione la sintesi fra il diritto romano ed il diritto canonico, affermandosi in tal modo come il sommo artefice del *ius commune*, e raggiungendo in tale opera una delle più alte vette del pensiero giuridico'.

men. Hostiensis clearly thought that this could be done only by an assiduous cultivation of justice in the spirit of canonical equity. The discussion of justice has shown that innocence will be effectively protected if there is general respect for the rights of all men; and it is the role of the judge to ensure and enforce this respect. 'Nam iudex debet esse sollicitus ut violentiis hominum resistat; ideo enim iudicialis rigor in medio positus est, ne quis audeat sibi sumere ultionem'.[45] Yet in a Christian society the judge has to carry out this task in keeping with the spiritual values of the Gospel. Hence the importance of canonical equity, 'quam iudex ... *semper* debet habere prae oculis'. The law of the Church can be correctly interpreted only in the light of Christian principles and priorities and the judge must see that these take precedence over all other considerations.[46]

2. *The Delineation of Duties and Rights*

Effective legal protection of the rights of the innocent and the oppressed will be provided if these rights are clearly delineated by the law and legal penalties enacted against their infringement. Rights, however, imply duties, and so it will be helpful if these too are specified. Moreover, since oppression is frequently the result of the abuse of authority as well as being caused by common criminals, legal clarification is needed concerning the extent and limits of the powers granted to those in authority. The exposition in the *Summa Aurea* of what the law in fact does, reveals how in practice such functions were carried out. Three points will be treated here. First of all, what did canon law do about specifying the duties of church officials? Secondly, what was done to clarify the extent and limits of the powers of authority? And lastly, did canon law do much about delineating the rights that were to be protected?

a) *The Duties of Officials*

The *Corpus Iuris Canonici* contains a large volume of legislation on the rights and duties of the clergy. Indeed a glance at the list of contents of the *Decretum* and at the *tituli* of the *Decretales* is sufficient to indicate that this was *the* major con-

---

[45] *Summa*, I, De officio iudicis, n. 1.
[46] C. Lefebvre, 'La doctrine de l'Hostiensis sur la préférence à assurer en droit aux intérêts spirituels', in *Ephemerides Iuris Canonici*, 8 (1952), pp. 24-44.

cern of canon law in the Middle Ages. The last chapter has shown how much attention medieval canon lawyers paid to the position and power of the pope, which they regarded as of central importance for the stability and well-being of the whole Church. They also sought clarity and precision about the powers and responsibilities of other members of the ecclesiastical hierarchy; and a large proportion of their commentaries is concerned with the rights and the duties of all who hold posts of authority in the Church. It is proposed to illustrate how Hostiensis dealt with this aspect of the law by considering a few key examples from the *Summa,* his discussions, namely, of the duties of the local ordinary, the archdeacon, and the beneficed cleric.

Throughout the *Summa* Hostiensis has much to say about the duties of the bishop or archbishop who is in charge of a diocese. Some of these, — those concerning the protection of the Church and the 'debitus status ecclesiae' — have already been discussed in the last chapter and need not be reconsidered here. [47] But what about his duties towards the faithful in general? Here Hostiensis, who had been a bishop himself for almost ten years when he published the *Summa,* is quite lavish in the advice he has to offer. The local ordinary has a special duty of care towards those under his authority and he should provide help and relief for them in so far as he can, — 'Non ergo spoliet illos quibus tenetur paterna provisione consulere'. [48] And he refers to St Augustine's teaching about the bishop having to work for his people, 'quia nomen est operis, non honoris'; his aim should be 'prodesse' rather than 'praeesse'. [49] He should be generous towards those who are in need, 'et alienam inopiam suam credat'. Here again he calls on patristic support from the *Decretum,* referring to Gregory the Great's view that 'sine liberalitate inane portatur nomen episcopi'. [50] He has, of course, the right to ask for financial assistance for the work of the diocese if the church is in debt and his own income is insufficient, but in doing so he should beware of indulging in sheer greed. If a dispute should arise in this matter between himself and his subjects, it should be taken to a higher superior for arbitration. Moreover, he must remember that he may not

---

[47] See above, pp. 113 ff.
[48] *Summa,* I, De officio ordinarii, n. 3.
[49] C. 8, q. 1, c. 11.
[50] D. 86, c. 6.

demand more than the law permits. [51] He has too the duty to
see that the rights of all are safeguarded and that justice is
done at all times, acting himself with strict impartiality according to the law. 'In correctione debet esse benevolus, ... in iudicio
iustus, ... in animadversione misericors'. Nor is the subject obliged to obey a command that is either manifestly unjust or impossible. A primate must bear in mind that he is not entitled
to make laws for his suffragan dioceses without consulting the
bishops and obtaining their consent; he has no jurisdiction over
the subjects of his suffragan bishops. [52]

Hostiensis also mentions here the rights and duties of religious to whom the bishop has entrusted a parish church; the
bishop retains the right to the *cathedraticum*, as well as the
duty of visitation and correction. The law prescribes how the
visitation is to be carried out. In estimating particular rights
and duties in such matters he draws attention to the importance
of local customs which will often clear up doubts that may
arise. [53] He also advises the bishop to make it a general rule
not to try to settle an issue without first taking counsel. There
are, of course, a number of matters where he is bound by law
to consult the chapter — these will be discussed shortly — but
even when he is not so bound he should make a habit of consultation. 'Episcopus vero quia solus est, habet necesse consilium aliorum requirere, quia vae soli ... Et omnia fac cum consilio et postea non poenitebis'. The spiritual aspect of church
government is never very far from Hostiensis' mind and he warns
prelates against negligence in their task: 'Non sit negligens, quia
sanguis subditorum a Deo coram quo tenetur de omnibus rationem reddere de manibus suis in die iudicii requiretur'. [54]

From all this it is evident that Hostiensis thought it the
function of the canon lawyer to provide guidance for the bishop
in his pastoral duties towards the faithful. This comes out
even more clearly in his discussion of the duties of a bishop-
elect where he outlines twelve pastoral duties that the newly
elected bishop should attend to. [55] The list merits consideration
here not only because of its connection with the function of
delineating duties, but also because of the light it throws on

---

[51] *Summa*, I, De officio ordinarii, n. 3.
[52] *Summa*, I, *ibid.*, n. 7.
[53] *Summa*, I, De officio ordinarii, n. 7.
[54] *Summa*, I, *ibid.*, n. 3.
[55] *Summa*, I, De electione et electi potestate, nn. 30-31.

Hostiensis' views of the role of canon law in general. He begins the discussion by stating that the person who is elected to a bishopric is bound by law to receive episcopal consecration within a certain time. He should be an able man, — 'potens in opere et sermone', — a man who practices what he preaches, since his conduct will readily be taken as an example by his subjects. His duty is to preach to the people and provide them with true leadership. Thirdly, he has the duty of teaching, — 'officium magistri; est enim ars artium regimen animarum'. Fourthly, he must shepherd his flock and provide them with the threefold nourishment: the sacramental bread 'de quo dicitur, Ego sum panis qui de caelo descendi'; and also the corporal and spiritual bread, that is to say, good example and the word of God. Fifthly, he has the duty of a prefect of the guard or the watch, and must be on the lookout for negligence in his diocese. The bishop must see that vigilant care is exercised over his priests because of the important work they have to do: 'quia pretiosissima pars fortunarum, scilicet, animarum eis commissa est'. He refers to the whole of Book Three which deals with the clergy in general as well as to the section in the Digest about the duties of the prefect of the guard. It would, he observes, be something if the bishop were as careful as prefects of the guard are held to be in Roman Law; he should, however be even more careful than these since he is charged with greater responsibilities. 'Ergo invigilet quia culpa sua est si lupus ovem rapiat et ipse nesciat'. Sixthly, he has the duty of a nurse who is to provide milk for his subjects. Seventhly, he must play the part of a doctor and take care of those who are in suffering of any kind. Eighthly, he has the duty of an advocate who should plead for those committed to his care. Ninthly, he has the duties of an armed soldier, — 'sed arma nostra lachrymae sunt et orationes'. Tenthly, he must carry out the duty of the swordsman who wields the sword of excommunication. In the eleventh place, he has the duty of the tiller of the soil 'ut evellet et dissipet, aedificet et plantet'. He must, therefore, get rid of evil and provide correction and instruction. And lastly, he has the duties of a moral reformer. All these duties the bishop is bound before God to carry out faithfully and carefully, as well as many others 'de quibus omnibus coram Deo redditurus est rationem'. The list may read more like a moral exhortation than a canonical commentary and provides but another illustration of how blurred the distinction then was between moral theology and canon law. In fact Hostiensis supports almost

every statement with a reference to the *Decretum*, and his delineation of the moral duties of the bishop is in perfect harmony
with medieval canonical tradition.

In the twelfth and thirteenth centuries the office of archdeacon carried considerable powers in the diocese. It was the
highest office after the bishop and involved important juris-
dictional and administrative tasks, corresponding to the modern
vicar general: 'vicarius eius et oculus episcopi appellatur ex
eo quod vices episcopi gerit, inspiciendo et inquirendo quis
qualiter vivat'. [56] Hostiensis begins by counselling the archdeacon
to show reverence and respect to all bishops, even although
they may be poor men, because every bishop is the vicar of
Christ in his diocese. This did not imply, of course, that Hostiensis thought of the bishop as a sort of superior overlord.
He had already made it quite clear in the *Summa* that the
bishop should regard himself as the servant of all, — 'debet
enim praelatus se servum facere ...'[57]. As first assistant to the
bishop it was the archdeacon's duty to carry out correction
and reform, to settle quarrels and disputes that arise between
clerics, to install clerics in their benefices, to carry out visitations, to receive petitions and tokens of allegiance from the
subjects of the bishop. He is also to exercise the care of souls.
In short, he is to be an effective vicar general of his bishop.
His jurisdiction is, of course, much more limited than that of
the bishop. He cannot confer a benefice which carries with it
the care of souls without the knowledge of the bishop. He can
be a judge only in matters of minor importance, and all the
more serious cases are to be referred to the bishop. Local
custom, too, should be taken into account in defining the duties
of particular archdeacons. His power to excommunicate is dis-
puted, and some say that he may be given this, provided he
does not use the solemn form of anathematizing, which is always
reserved to the bishop. A number of duties are prescribed by
the common law for the archdeacon, such as, 'institutio corporalis beneficiorum ecclesiasticorum, sicut ponere abbates et ab-
batissas in sedem, examinatio clericorum ordinandorum et praeficiendorum'. He also has the right and duty of visitation every
three years at least and once a year at the most, 'nisi causa
emergat propter quam necesse habeat saepius visitare'. This
right also belongs to the bishop and to the metropolitan and

---

[56] *Summa*, I, De officio archidiaconi, n. 1.
[57] *Summa*, I, De renuntiatione, n. 6.

sometimes also to others. What is a wretched rector of a parish to do, however, if everybody chooses to exercise his right of visitation? How can he possibly provide for all these men and their retinues? Hostiensis agrees that if all were to carry out visitations each year and demand to be maintained by the rector then this would indeed be an unbearable burden. In actual fact it would be *contra iura* since it would leave the poor man impoverished. What then is to be done? Reduce the number of visitations, say some, and restrict the rights in this matter. This is not the approach that appeals to Hostiensis. He stresses the need for regular visitation, and maintains that it is a duty that ought to be carried out regularly and conscientiously. But this *need* not lead to the impoverishment of the parish. Where the parish is not able to provide then the visitation should be carried out *at the expense of those whose duty it is to make the visitation.* [58]

He insisted on this duty of visitation as very important for the Church:

> Ego puto non debere ius calumniari, nec verba captari, sed qua mente quid constituitur animadvertere convenire ... Puto igitur quod ad hoc ut Ecclesia Dei sanctius regatur, crimina purgentur, et virtutes inserantur, plures visitatores sunt admittendi. [59]

He compares these visitations to the role of the fire brigade in a city. Just as these men have to be prepared and constantly on the watch to protect the city against fire, 'sic multo fortius cavendum est ecclesia ab incendiis spiritualibus'. Hence the need for frequent visitations. He goes on to maintain that this right to visitation cannot be lost through prescription: 'ratio est, quia nisi visitaretur anima periclitaretur'. [60] The duty of visitation is, in fact, so important that even if the parish is too poor to provide for the *visitatores*, Hostiensis holds, as we have seen, that those who have to make the visitation should do so at their own expense.

While noting that it would normally be against the law for a number of churches to be taxed to pay for a visitation, he suggests that the bishops could agree to draw up a special statute in this matter if they so wished. He mentions that

---

[58] *Summa*, I, De officio archidiaconi, n. 4.
[59] *Summa*, I, *ibid.*
[60] *Summa*, I, De officio archidiaconi, n. 5.

he himself had recently done this at a provincial council as
Archbishop of Embrun. [61]   He believed that if the proposals he
put forward were followed both the right and duty of visitation
would be safeguarded and the churches themselves would be
spared impoverishment.

> Occurritur ecclesiarum gravaminibus, iura salvantur, et crimina
> puniuntur. Ergo in his columnis tribus, scilicet episcopo, ar-
> chiepiscopo et legato, qui hoc habent de iure communi, con-
> sistere debet alma mater Ecclesia, ut simul iuncti quo ad
> idem propositum, officium suum recte peragant et perfecte,
> et non sit inter illos invidia neque zelus, id est odium sive
> simulatio.

In his discussion of the clergy's duty to reside in their
benefices Hostiensis goes through the legislation on the subject
and brings out the reasons that lie behind the law. In so doing
he provides another illustration of how the law concerns itself
with the duties of the clergy to the faithful committed to their
care.   Residence is a duty because the church must not be left
'servitoribus destituta'. [62]   This right of the faithful is protected
by canonical sanctions against clerics who neglect their duty
of residence. An incorrigible delinquent is liable to deposition
and privation of his benefice.   The whole point of establishing
benefices, insists Hostiensis, is for the service of the church
not the convenience of the clergy.   'Ad hoc enim constituta
sunt beneficia ut servitium inde fiat: unde ipse non debet recipere qui non servit'. He comments on the legislation on this
and rejects all legal formalism which would try to get round
the law and frustrate its whole purpose. Presence should mean
service.   There may, of course, at times be good reasons for
absence, in which case a 'vicarius' should be appointed, and
he gives a list of the sort of reasons that would justify absence.
Even here, however, care should be taken that the main point
of the law is not neglected. Privileges should be revoked if
they are seen to be endangering the community. Even a papal
indult should be withdrawn, because the pope would not wish
his indult to defeat the whole purpose of the canonical legislation. The rights of the clergy are not forgotten by Hostiensis,
and he maintains that a delinquent should be summoned to
appear and given due warning before he is deprived of his

---

[61] Summa, I, *ibid.*

[62] *Summa*, III, De clericis non residentibus in ecclesia praebendiali,
nn. 1-2.

benefice. The bishop too is advised against acting precipitately in the matter, — 'ideo consulo praelato quod non nimis properet'. The rights of all have to be respected.

On the powers and jurisdiction of the judge-delegate there is a lengthy treatise in the *Summa Aurea* which reflects the juridical development of this office during the previous century. The *Decretales* contained more than forty canons on the subject. On this question of rights and duties it is interesting to note that Hostiensis insists on the need for a clear mandate which will be open to inspection. [63] He also deals in detail with the extent and limits of the powers of legates, emphasising that they may not interfere in *causae maiores* reserved to the Roman Pontiff. [64] The duties and responsibilities of many other subordinate officials in the Church are also fully treated in the *Summa*. The duties that go with the right of patronage, the duties of a *dominus* towards his vassals, the duties of religious who have been given charge of a parish, and so on and so forth. [65] It is a recurrent theme which runs through the whole of Hostiensis' commentary on the law. However, enough has been said to give some indication of how canon law fulfilled this function of delineating duties in the Church and in so doing provided for the protection of the faithful in general.

b) *Limitations on Authority*

It was not enough, however, to specify the rights and duties of those in positions of authority. Safeguards were also necessary against the abuse of authority by Church officials. The *Summa Aurea* provides ample evidence that canon law did attempt to keep such abuses in check, and Hostiensis frequently discusses the subject. Professor Tierney has examined the teaching of Hostiensis on corporation theory and has illustrated how he brought great clarity and precision to this important subject. [66] He was concerned that the rights of the members of a corporation should be respected as well as those of its head. Both prelate and cathedral chapter, for example, had to respect the law as embodied in the *Decretum*, which enjoined coopera-

---

[63] *Summa*, I, De officio iudicis delegati, n. 8.

[64] *Summa*, I, De officio legati, n. 3.

[65] Cf. *Summa*, III, De iure patronatus; III, De feudis; III, De statu monachorum et canonicorum regularium, nn. 3-11.

[66] B. Tierney, *Foundations of the Conciliar Theory*, Cambridge 1955, pp. 108-131.

10

tion between bishop and chapter in important matters that affected the well-being of the whole diocese, such as the conferring of certain benefices, the alienation of church property,
and judging certain cases. Professor Tierney has also shown
how Hostiensis clarified the position of the bishop when he
was acting as proctor for the corporation. 'He realised that
an adequate definition of the prelate's status must concede to
him that freedom of action which was essential for the efficient
transaction of day-to-day business in a litigious age, while ensuring that the authority he exercised was of a purely derivative
nature and could not be used to injure the well-being of the
church'. [67]

In Book Three of the *Summa* Hostiensis discusses this question of when a bishop may not act without the consent of his
chapter and when it is sufficient for him to ask the advice of
the canons. [68]   Although a number of contemporary canonists
apparently tended to confuse counsel and consent, Hostiensis
was insistent that there was an important distinction to be
made.   There are times when the conferring of a benefice will,
by common law, call for the collaboration of the chapter with
the bishop; at other times this may be done by the bishop
acting on his own.   If consent was required and has been omitted,
then the appointment can be rescinded, and the same applies to
other transactions according to local customs or rescripts.   In
such matters the prelate may not act arbitrarily but must respect the rights of each church and of the canons.   Hostiensis
goes on, however, to urge, as he had done earlier, that even
where the law does not demand consent the bishop should nevertheless seek advice.   'Tamen debet hoc facere cum consilio clericorum seu fratrum suorum'. [69]   He has to take advice about
ordinations, though he is not bound to follow the advice given.
When it is a matter, however, of deposing a cleric the bishop
cannot act alone.   He must have the support of other bishops.
For example, if it is a question of a deposing a bishop then
twelve bishops are required.   To depose a priest, seven, and
to depose a deacon, three are necessary.   Nor does he agree
with those who argues that if the bishop is free to ignore the
advice that is given then it is a complete waste of time to

---

[67] Tierney, *op. cit.*, p. 123.
   [68] *Summa*, III, De his quae fiunt ab episcopo sine consensu capituli,
nn. 1-2.
   [69] *Ibid.*, n. 2.

bother giving it. This is by no means the case, he argues, 'licet non teneatur sequi, tamen posset quod consilium capituli traheret praelatum ad se'.[70] Such advice can have great influence, therefore, and should be seriously given. He repeats his advice to prelates that they should make a habit of taking counsel from their fellow-priests before taking action. 'Et breviter, sine consilio fratrum parum aut nihil facere debet praelatus, etiam non obtentu alicuius consuetudinis'. He should moreover respect the dignity of his own clergy and ask their advice about the affairs of the diocese.

> Omnia enim fac cum consilio et non poenitebis ... Ideo regulariter in omnibus clericorum negotiis et ecclesiarum debet canonicorum consilium requirere, ut cum eis peragat et pertractet et quae statuenda fuerint statuat; errata corrigat, deformata reformet, evellenda dissipet et evellat.

Many heads are better than one, — 'firmius est iudicium quod a pluribus requiritur', — and the bishop should beware of acting on his own: 'vae sibi si de se solo nimis confidat'. All this illustrates how concerned Hostiensis was to ensure that purely arbitrary government was prevented. It also shows how he was out to protect individuals from suffering from arbitrary government. When it is remembered that Hostiensis was himself a distinguished archbishop when he published the *Summa* his advice will have carried considerable weight.

A similar function of the law is revealed in Hostiensis' discussion of what is referred to in the Decretals as the *Clericus Percussor*. Hostiensis distinguishes between 'percussio spiritualis' and 'percussio corporalis'. The preacher who indulges in continuous and useless and prolix sermons is guilty of 'percussio spiritualis', and he should avoid inflicting such suffering on the faithful, as he is directed to do in the *Decretum*.[71] Nor should he go in for expounding grammar in the pulpit, but should preach the word of God as the canons instruct him, and as is clear from many passages in the *Decretum* to which Hostiensis here refers. As for corporal punishment, this can be at times quite lawful but all cruelty must be avoided. The canons direct that punishment should be administered reasonably and for a just cause only, 'causa correctionis et non ex odio'. Nor may priests be beaten 'nisi gravissime delinquant'.

---

[70] *Summa*, III, De his quae fiunt ab episcopo sine consenso capituli, n. 2.
[71] D. 43, c. 1. (from Gregory the Great's *Cura Pastoralis*).

And if a superior goes beyond the limits of the canons he stands
in danger of excommunication, especially if he goes so far as
to draw blood. There are heavy penalties laid down against
these who abuse their authority in this matter, and they include
suspension and deposition.[72]

As a last example of this role of law in protecting individuals from the arbitrary abuse of authority, we may consider
Hostiensis's discussion of the penalties that prelates are liable
to incur if they abuse their positions of authority.[73] Prelates
who demand more taxes than are due are liable to a fine 'in
quadruplum' and to restitution, — 'Sed et dignitate privandi
videntur'. They are bound to observe what is laid down in the
law about such exactions. 'Tales igitur debent mandare memo-
riae quod manus suas deberent servare innoxias Deo et Principi
nullumque lucrum contingere'. They may also exceed their authority in excommunicating or suspending a man unjustly, —
either because they do this without the consent of their chapter
or because they fail to observe 'due process' — 'quia non servant ordinem iudiciarium', by, for example, not issuing the warnings that the law requires. Hostiensis cites laws which penalise
such abuses. In a number of cases, too, such unjust actions
can be null and void. 'Unde si sacerdos excommunicetur nisi
furem revelaverit nulla est sententia'. Hostiensis here provides
a whole list of possible excesses of prelates, quoting the relevant
canons from the *Decretum.* All this amounts to a guide towards
just government and it illustrates the care that the law took
to protect the rights of individuals and of subjects. Nor should
a superior be the judge in his own cause, 'Sed coram iudice
contra subditum litigare cogitur'. Superiors should not put unreasonable burdens on their subjects nor treat them dishonor-
ably, 'sed tamquam filios et fratres fraterna charitate tueri et
honorare'. Once again Hostiensis refers to the *Decretum* to
support these directives that he is insisting upon.[74] This whole
section of Book Five shows clearly that Hostiensis thought it
the function of canon law to ensure just government and to
protect the rights of individuals. This is unmistakeable both
from the very clear directives that he gives and his frequent
citation of the *Decretum* in support of his statements.

His concern for justice and for the rights of individuals

---

[72] *Summa*, V, De clerico percussore, n. 2.
[73] *Summa*, V, De excessibus praelatorum et subditorum, nn. 1-2.
[74] *Summa*, V, De excessibus praelatorum et subditorum, nn. 1-2.

is shown also in the directives that he maintains should be carefully followed when there is question of using the penalty of excommunication. The point of such directives is to keep prelates from rushing into excommunications without forethought.

> Primum est quod hodie in civilibus non est aliquis sic excommunicandus nisi mora praecedit. Secundum quod non est excommunicandus aliquis etiam pro commissis vel committendis, nisi exprimatur causa rationabilis in sententia, quare hoc fit. Tertium est quia si aliter fiat, vel causa minus rationabilis praetendatur, sententia relaxabitur et proferens ad arbitrium iudicis punietur, et alias poenas patietur.[75]

Hostiensis warns against the danger of passing unjust sentences of excommunication. Such a penalty should not be inflicted out of envy or hatred or anger. He mentions a number of circumstances that could render a sentence of excommunication unjust, and advises that all of these should be carefully avoided. The sentence itself should always be preceded by due warning. He notes also that for prelates who fail to observe these directives the sanctions can be quite severe, including an action for damages by the excommunicated person.[76]

c) Delineation of Rights

It is clear then, as one would expect, that a major function of canon law was the delineation of duties both for those in authority and for those under authority. But the law was equally clear in the delineation of *rights* and a great part of medieval canon law was taken up with the clarification of rights of all kinds, rights of the Church, rights of communities, rights of individuals. One of the best illustrations of this aspect of canon law to be found in the *Summa Aurea* is the long treatise on elections in Book One. For this reason it is worth considering in detail here. Since the normal procedure for the appointment of a bishop was election by the cathedral chapters clear legislation on this subject was of vital importance for the general welfare of the Church as well as for the protection of the rights of individuals. Gratian devoted three distinctions, containing 58 chapters (DD. 61-63), to the subject and the Gregorian Collection included 60 canons under the *titulus*, *De electione et electi potestate*. Hence the long treatise on the same subject

---

[75] *Summa*, V, De sententia excommunicationis, n. 6.
[76] *Ibid.*, n. 11.

by Hostiensis in the *Summa*, which clarifies the rights of chapter members both to be present at the election and to have full freedom in their voting.

An election is a 'canonice facta vocatio'. The process must be carried out canonically, 'quia si vitiosa fuerit electio, nec transactione nec tractu temporis convalescit, cum tempus electionis inspicitur ...' [77] The canonical form is required 'quae vult quod vitetur dissensionis materia, et ne patiantur ecclesiae detrimenta, quae etiam in minimis sunt vitanda'. It is stressed too that the election must be carried out in common, 'quia singulares consensus non valent'. Only those may vote who have a right to vote; and this right is protected by such rules as those that govern voting by proxy, if there is a good reason for being absent. [78] Hostiensis also spends much time in clarifying the rights of the *eligendus*. Clear grounds must be presented to justify the rejection of someone as ineligible, and if these are not clearly stated then the objection should not be sustained: 'Quid si obiicitur contra personam et electionem et cassatur simpliciter non assignata causa? Non videtur ineligibilis ...' [79] The accused must really be shown to be 'infamis', for example, and if this is not clearly proved then the person's good name stands and he remains eligible for election.

All who are entitled to vote are to be summoned to the election,

> ut praesentibus qui debent et volunt et possunt commode interesse ... Praesentibus, quia omnes vocandi sunt et citandi, alias plus obesset contemptus unius quam contradictio multorum ... Sed tamen contemptus potest ratificare electionem propter bonum pacis ... Omnibus, *quia quod omnes tangit ab omnibus approbari debet* ... Et volunt, quia nec cogitur interesse si non vult, cum quilibet possint renunciare iuri suo. [80]

Of course, the citation must be made 'congruo tempore' and enough time must be allowed for the electors to arrive. Normally this will be about three months. The election should be held 'non praecipiti festinatione nec moratoria cunctatione'. Hostiensis here points out that particular circumstances must also be taken into consideration:

---

[77] *Summa*, I, De electione et electi potestate, n. 2.
[78] *Ibid.*, n. 8.
[79] *Ibid.*, n. 10.
[80] *Ibid.*, n. 11.

Nam quamvis ecclesia ultra tres menses vacare non debeat, non tamen prohibetur praesentibus quo minus intra tres menses eligant: ideo dic quod si usque ad tempus congruum, considerata locorum distantia et aliis circumstantiis assignatum, absentes non venerint, extunc praesentes eligant.

There is a dispute among lawyers about how many should be present for this to happen. Hostiensis is of the opinion that two thirds of the electors should be present and there should be a good reason for going ahead with the election. Otherwise they should wait; and he adds that if any are summoned to the election by mistake their travelling expenses should be paid by those who made the error in citing them. He goes on to be more specific about distances. He wants to avoid all formalism and yet protect the rights of the electors. [81] There are various views on how distances should be estimated. Hostiensis mentions these and gives his own:

Tamen ego potius eligo mentem huius verbi, ut dixi, id solum possumus quod commode possumus ... Plerumque enim nec locus nec tempus patitur plenius deliberandi consilium ... Ergo periculum ecclesiae prae omnibus vitandum dico.

In this whole discussion of election procedure Hostiensis repeatedly mentions the rights of the electors and the elected. He constantly returns to the theme of 'ius suum' for all the parties in any dispute. He stresses the formalities that have to be observed in a valid election because 'tota mens est ut libera sit electio, et discordia fugiatur et malitiis hominum obvietur'. He also emphasises that the good name of any individual should be protected as much as possible. If, for example, the person whose duty it is to confirm an election discovers an impediment in the person actually elected he should not publish this or defame the person but should persuade him to renounce his election of his own free will if this should be necessary.

This concern for the rights of individuals and of groups is a theme that frequently appears in the *Summa*. It was a general principle that any individual was free to renounce his rights if he so desired but qualifications have to be made. Rights can be renounced by the individual 'in quantum tangit privatam utilitatem', but not if they affected the public welfare. [82] Hence

---

[81] *Summa*, I, De electione et electi potestate, n. 11.
[82] *Summa*, I, De renuntiatione, n. 3.

the laws that govern due process must always be observed;
laws protecting the rights of minors cannot be renounced by
tutors, and so on. [83]   There are, moreover, a number of restrictions on the freedom to renounce even private rights and privileges when the good of the church in general is involved. A
bishop, for example, must have very good reasons to resign
from his see. Some of these restrictions have already been
discussed in the last chapter in connection with the need to
protect the 'debitus status ecclesiae'. It should be noted, however, that Hostiensis did not consider these restrictions as a
curtailment of personal rights; they were rather a true expression of what was really in the best interests of all concerned.
What benefited the Church as a whole would also be to the
advantage of each individual: 'Si expediat ecclesiae, pariter et
personis'. [84]   And it was generally accepted by rulers and lawyers,
both secular and ecclesiastical, that the common good or utility
was superior to private rights and interests. Generally speaking,
the ruler, be he pope or king, most effectively preserved the
general welfare of all when he maintained law and justice and
protected private rights in his courts. [85]   But from time to time
the public welfare would demand the sacrifice of private rights
and the law protecting them. This was common doctrine in the
thirteenth century. [86]   Another point that Hostiensis makes in
the matter of renouncing rights is the importance of the person
renouncing being fully aware of what he is doing, — 'nec enim
potest quis renuntiare ei quod ignorat'. [87]

The *Summa Aurea* provides a whole series of specific rights
that had to be respected by all, and it would be tedious to
attempt to list all of these. The following selection will illustrate the point. Much of the legislation specified the rights of
the clergy. They should be provided with sufficient means to
keep them from having to beg for their living. [88]   Among the
rights of the 'vicarius' was included that of not being removed
from his post without reason, and even if there is an adequate
reason, he cannot be removed without the permission of the

---

[83] *Ibid.*, n. 6.
[84] *Ibid.*, n. 3.
[85] Cf. *Summa*, I, De renuntiatione, n. 2: 'Item largo modo publice
interest quod quodlibet ius observatur, ed ideo iudices constituuntur ...'.
[86] Cf. Gaines Post, *Studies in Medieval Legal Thought*, Princeton Univ.
Press, 1964, pp. 12 ff.
[87] *Summa*, I, De renuntiatione, n. 7.
[88] *Summa*, III, De praebendis et dignitatibus, n. 6.

bishop. He also has a right to a fair proportion of the church's revenues. [89] There was also legislation defining the rights of sick and infirm clergy. A prelate should not be deprived of his living because of ill health; he should be given a coadjutor, 'cui portio competens reddituum episcopatus assignatur'. Lesser clerics should be given a 'vicarius'. [90] There was also canonical protection for religious as 'personae ecclesiasticae'. [91]

The feudal principles of mutual obligation and respect for law also finds a place in the *Summa* and Hostiensis notes how the law protects the rights of the vassal against his lord. The rights and duties arising from the oath of fealty are discussed at some length regarding both the lord and the vassal. The vassal, for instance, should lose his *feudum* only for a serious fault and only after a fair trial. [92] On occasion too Hostiensis shows how canon law is concerned to protect the property rights of individuals. [93]

A great number of specific rights are protected by the canonical legislation on marriage. Minors may not be forced into marriage against their will. The freedom of the parties has to be respected and there are a number of safeguards to protect and strengthen their free consent to the marriage. In the matter of the marriage of slaves canon law upheld the right of the individual slave to marry and opposed the civil law: 'Sed licet lex humana ita dicat de servis, non approbat haec lex divina. Servus enim a sacramentis ecclesiae ... non arcetur ... quare et matrimonium contrahere potest'. And the Church defends his right to marry even against the wishes of his master and it is the duty of the ecclesiastical judge to see that these human rights are respected. [94]

Hostiensis specifically mentions that the law of the Church should provide relief for the victims of oppression, — 'ut oppressis compatiatur'. In doing so he was expressing the view

---

[89] *Summa*, I, De officio vicarii, n. 6.

[90] *Summa*, III, De clerico aegrotante vel debilitato, n. 2.

[91] *Summa*, III, De regularibus, n. 3.

[92] *Summa*, III, De feudis, nn. 10-13 (It has been shown that this treatise on feudalism was taken over by Hostiensis from the writing of Pillius de Medina, but the fact that he included it in the *Summa* shows that he thought the Church should support this legislation just as it did the Roman Law in so many cases. Cf. C. Lefebvre, 'Hostiensis', *DDC*, V, 1218).

[93] *Summa*, I, De his quae fiunt vi metusve causa, nn. 4-5.

[94] *Summa*, IV, De matrimoniis, nn. 6-7; De desponsatione impuberum, nn. 5, 6, 7, 11: De coniugio servorum, n. 1.

of medieval canon lawyers in general among whom it was agreed
that the Church had a special duty to protect the rights of
those who were unable to defend themselves. Hence the legislation to protect children and minors from exploitation by their
elders. There were, for example, special laws to protect children
from unreasonable punishment.[95] A minor is not to be forced
to take the oath of fealty until he has attained his majority.[96]
This concern of canon law for the oppressed is particularly
clear in the number of laws whose aim was to protect the
rights of all those who could be considered 'miserabiles personae'. The term appears frequently in the law and was used
of widows and orphans and of all those who could be considered victims of poverty or oppression. Gratian had noted
that the bishop had a particular duty with regard to the poor
and the oppressed: 'Sollicitum quoque ac vigilantem oportet
esse episcopum circa defensionem pauperum, relevationem op-
pressorum, tuicionem monasteriorum. Quod si facere neglexerint,
aspere sunt corripiendi;'[97] Here he was expressing a long-standing tradition of the Church.

> The widow, a *miserabilis persona*, had been a concern of the
> Church from apostolic times. Her freedom to choose her
> state, her property rights and her claim to special legal protec-
> tion were carefully stated by Gratian and were reinforced by
> the decretal literature of the following century.[98]

3. *Due Process of Law*

Clearly then canon law was greatly concerned with the delineation of rights and duties and enacted an abundance of
penalties against infringements of these. But all this legislation
would have been otiose if there had not also been the means

---

[95] *Summa*, V, De delictis puerorum, nn. 1-5.
[96] *Summa*, III, De feudis, n. 10.
[97] D. 84, c. 1, dict. ante.
[98] M. M. Sheehan, 'Canon Law and English Institutions', in *Proceedings
of the Second International Congress of Medieval Canon Law*, Rome, 1965,
p. 395. In this paper Sheehan illustrates the special interest of canon law
to defend the rights of a woman after the death of her husband. Professor
Tierney has provided a full and well-documented discussion of the Church's
defence of the poor and the oppressed in *Medieval Poor Law. A sketch
of Canonical Theory and Its Application in England*, California University
Press, 1959. Cf. also G. Le Bras, 'Le droit classique de l'Eglise au service
de l'homme', in *Congrès de Droit Canonique Médiéval*, Louvain, 1959,
pp. 104-110.

of enforcing rights and duties by means of a recognised court procedure. Hostiensis never tires of repeating the old traditional maxim: 'parum prodest iura habere in civitate nisi sit qui iura reddat'. The saying runs like a refrain throughout the whole of the *Summa Aurea*. Once again Hostiensis is voicing what was the generally accepted view of all medieval jurists, both civil and ecclesiastical.

Due process of law had been developed by the Romans as an orderly means of settling disputes between citizens. Legal procedure was introduced and developed to take the place of the more primitive system of self-help where the only means of enforcing one's rights had been through the exercise of *force majeure* and private vengeance. The developed Roman Law provided a means of obtaining an objective judicial decision which would be in harmony with justice and which would be binding on both parties to a dispute and enforced by the State. [99] Consequently the canon lawyers of the Middle Ages inherited in the *Corpus Iuris Civilis* a highly developed legal procedure for settling disputes of all kinds and they adopted this as the basis of the procedural law of the Church. It was universally recognised that the rights of free men could be effectively defended only if there was an accepted procedure that had to be observed by all. The need for due process of law was taken for granted by medieval jurists. As Professor Plucknett puts it:

> Procedure, considered as a safeguard, played a large part in constitutional struggles. Arbitrary action by the Crown or its officials necessarily involved a breach of procedural rules sooner or later. In 1215 the barons at Runnymede appealed to procedure as the only effective protection for their persons and property, and nearly two centuries earlier the same principle had been formulated in an edict of the Emperor Conrad II (1037) for the Holy Roman Empire. [100]

This was a central factor in the development of canon law in the Middle Ages. Hence the lengthy treatises on the subject by medieval canon lawyers. Nor is this surprising:

---

[99] For a brief history of the gradual development of procedure in Roman law, see J. M. Kelly, *Roman Litigation*, Oxford, 1966.

[100] T. F. T. Plucknett, *A Concise History of the Common Law*, London, 1965[5], pp. 380-381. Canon 39 of Magna Carta reads: 'Nullus liber homo capiatur, vel imprisonetur, aut dissaisiatur... nisi per legale iudicium parium suorum vel per legem terrae'.

For procedure is as much the essence of the law as the ideal and theory; without an adequate, logical procedure the fundamental principles of any body of law are so much ideological wind. The very development of a carefully defined procedure with elaborate rules on informing the defendant, summoning all parties concerned, granting delays that protect challenged rights in certain circumstances, permitting appeals from the decision of lower courts, and, in short, guaranteeing a fair trial and a just sentence, is nothing less than a real and essential expression of the ideal of law and justice — justice according to the famous Roman definition: "iustitia est constans et perpetua voluntas ius suum cuique tribuendi ». All this was especially true in the thirteenth century, when, under the influence of the two laws and the feudal emphasis on individual rights, the ideal of due process, as it is understood in the United States, was virtually stated in the rules of procedure. [101]

Canonical concern for court procedure is shown in a number of the *Causae* in Part Two of the *Decretum* (CC. 2-7) and in Book Two and Book Five of the *Decretales*. Hostiensis' views on the subject will, therefore, be found mainly in his commentary on these two books. Rights could be guaranteed, he thought, only by seeing that a clear procedure is observed, by ensuring integrity in the judges, by requiring clear proof of guilt before conviction, by providing the opportunity for self-defence to all accused persons and by enacting severe penalties for false accusations. Each of these points calls for more detailed consideration.

The importance that Hostiensis attached to the protection of the rights of all in keeping with the law and in the spirit of true canonical equity has already been discussed at the beginning of this chapter. In this matter integrity in the courts was a vital factor. How the law should be administered in ecclesiastical courts is shown particularly clearly by Hostiensis in his lengthy discussion of the duties of the bishop as judge in Book One of the *Summa*. Moreover, as his numerous references to the *Decretum* demonstrate, he was attempting to expound, not his own personal views, but the traditional spirit of canon law. The judge must make it his business to administer justice and protect the rights of all. [102] The passage

---

[101] Gaines Post, *Studies in Medieval Legal Thought*, p. 188.
[102] *Summa*, I, De officio ordinarii, n. 3, (C. 12, q. 2, c. 9).

here referred to in the *Decretum* was taken from a letter by Gregory he Great and expresses an important canonical principle:

> Et quia summum bonum in rebus est iustitiam colere ac sua cuique iura servare, et in subiectos non sinere quod potestatis est fieri, sed quod equum est custodiri.

This was universally accepted, thought Hostiensis. Justice must be granted impartially to all. The pretext that the accused has in fact committed a crime is no reason for denying him justice. Even the excommunicate has the right to a fair trial, 'quia non consideratur in hoc favor excommunicati, sed aequitas iudicantis'. Hostiensis goes on to exhort the ecclesiastical judge to maintain strict impartiality and integrity in his court, steadfastly refusing to be swayed by gifts or by threats:

> Non declinat etiam ad dexteram vel sinistram, non corrumpatur munere, non timore, non odio vel amore; his enim quattuor modis consuevit perverti iudicium; ... unde versus:
>
> Si lis inciderit, te iudice dirige libram
> Iudicii; nec flectat amor, nec munera palpent.
> Munus enim a norma recti distorquet acumen
> Iudicis, et tetra involvit caligine mentem.
> Auri sacra fames, quae non mortalia pectora cogit? [103]

The judge should not, therefore, be out after gain. His duty is to administer the law and provide justice freely. He can, of course, reasonably demand that his expenses be paid provided that he does not turn the administration of justice into a money-making racket. Nor should he allow himself to be influenced by emotional outbursts or floods of tears since this would lead to the breakdown of law and order and encourage crime. [104] Yet this demand for firmness in the judge did by no means imply a rigid juridicism since Hostiensis was equally insistent on the humane interpretation of the law in the spirit of equity, as has already been discussed.

The importance of observance of the procedural law in general is abundantly shown throughout the whole of the *Summa*, and in particular in Book Two and Book Five. The judge is strictly bound to keep within the terms of the law and is not free to act arbitrarily or take the law into his own hands. This

---

[103] *Ibid.*, n. 4.

[104] *Summa*, I, De tempore ordinationum et qualitate ordinandorum, n. 17; cf. also I, De officio ordinarii, n. 7.

was not always observed, Hostiensis remarks, and he refers to
current abuses in the courts. [105]   Nor may judges sell or hire
out their jurisdiction, because this would lead to the exploitation of subjects and the perversion of justice. [106]   He is severely
critical of graft going on in the courts of his time, and castigates
it from time to time in the *Summa*. [107]

The judge too must be above suspicion and Hostiensis comments on the law which allows a man to refuse a particular
judge if there is good reason to suspect that justice and impartiality may be obstructed because of personal relationship be-
twen the judge and the accused or the accuser.   He even added
an extra *titulus* on this subject in his *Summa*, though there is
no corresponding one in the *Decretales*.   *Recusatio iudicis* is
a right that must be respected, and he defines this as 'ob iustam
causam suspicionis contra iudicem propositam audientiae eius-
dem iudicis declinatio'. [108]   He goes on to give a list of the sort
of reasons that would justify such a refusal: if the judge is
the *dominus* of the person seeking justice; if he is on too familiar
terms with either the accused or even with the accuser's lawyer,
and so on.   He also mentions the problem of what might be
termed nationalist prejudice, and refers to his own experience
in England: 'Consuevit etiam livor invidiae regnare inter in-
digenas et alienigenas ... haec causa et quaedam aliae fecerunt
me Angliam elongare'. [109]   Hostiensis thinks that this could be
a good reason for exercising the right of *recusatio*, and indeed
better than many others that are proposed. [110]   The principle
was, of course, recognised in Roman law and recognised too
in the *Decretum*, to which Hostiensis here refers. 'Qui inimici
sunt, iudices esse non possunt' and Gratian comments on the
canon as follows: 'Patet quod, etsi manifesta sunt crimina alicuius, non tamen accusatione inimici condemnandus est'. [111]

---

[105] *Summa*, V, De accusationibus, n. 12.

[106] *Summa*, V, Ne praelati vices suas, vel ecclesias ... pretio concedant,
n. 1 ff.

[107] Cf. *Summa*, I, De officio Ordinarii, n. 4.

[108] *Summa*, I, De recusatione iudicis delegati, n. 1.

[109] *Summa*, I, *ibid.*, n. 3.   The reference to England is clearly to the
violent feeling there against the foreign relations and friends of Queen
Eleanor of Provence who seemed to be receiving preferential treatment
from the king.

[110] *Summa*, I, De recusatione iudicis delegati, n. 3.

[111] C. 3, q. 5, c. 15 and *dict. post.*   Cf. R. Helmholz, 'Canonists and
Standards of Impartiality for Papal Judges Delegate', *Traditio*, 25 (1969),
pp. 386-404.

Hostiensis insisted that legal directives are needed to ensure a fair trial, [112] and clear proof of guilt is required to secure a conviction. 'Imo exigitur quod accusator habeat probationes luce clariores'. The evidence adduced must form a consistent proof that is free from contradictions. If there remains any doubt the accused is to be acquitted, — 'ubi semper tamen obtinet regula ut reus in dubio absolvetur'. [113] — This is to be observed with particular care in criminal trials, — 'et quidem luce clarior si criminaliter proponatur; nam accusanti, et accusato incumbit probatio, et acerrima debet fieri indagatio, non declinando ad dexteram vel sinistram ...'. [114] The same holds good for all legal trials, of course, but in civil actions, Hostiensis admits, there need not be quite the same severity. Another instance where he attacks abuses among judges is to be found in his discussion of the place of confessions in criminal trials. Only in certain specified cases does the law permit the accused to be questioned about the guilt of a third party. These include treason, simony, heresy and crimes connected with these. But Hostiensis insists that these are special cases provided for by the law because of the extreme seriousness of the crimes. They may not be taken as a general rule. [115] And even in those special cases the testimony of the witness does not constitute by itself a legal proof against a third party, and he repeats his principle that in criminal trials 'probationes exigantur luce clariores'. [116] In this same discussion of confessions Hostiensis observes that a son or a slave can bring an action against his father (or master) for cruelty. He rejects the confessions of *furiosi*, as well as those extracted under severe torture, as of no juridical value. The courts should also see that groundless charges are not brought against innocent individuals and should implement the canonical legislation against calumny and detraction. An accuser should be made to realise that if he cannot substantiate his charges then he runs the risk of being charged with calumny. [117] Nor should a man's reputation be blackened by a few malcontents. These should be disregarded. [118]

---

[112] *Summa*, III, De feudis, n. 13.

[113] *Summa*, V, De accusationibus, n. 8.

[114] *Summa*, V, De crimine falsi, n. 6.

[115] *Summa*, II, De confessis, n. 1.

[116] *Ibid.*

[117] *Summa*, V, De accusationibus, n. 8; see also, V, De denuntiationibus, n. 3; V, De Calumniatoribus, nn. 1-11.

[118] *Summa*, V, De inquisitionibus, n. 6.

Above all, every man must be given adequate opportunity to defend himself and his rights against accusers. He must be allowed to answer and defend himself against charges brought against him, even if it seems quite clear that he is guilty, — 'quamvis constat de crimine'. [119] And this right to self-defence is open to *all* without exception, even to heretics and excommunicates. [120] Hostiensis is particularly insistent on this and returns to it again and again throughout the *Summa*. There must *always* be scope for legitimate defence. [121] Even the devil himself should be granted a fair trial!

> Tanta ergo aequitate iura utuntur, quod etiam diabolum non condemnarent iniuste, si in iudicio esse posset; et sic absurdum videtur, quod actore impugnante reo defensio legitima denegetur; quia sic multoties innocens condemnaretur ... [122]

This is the point of the legislation governing the drawing up of a *libellus*. [123] It is also the reason for the importance of the *citatio*. All the parties to a dispute have a right to be summoned and there developed the whole theory of *contumacia* as a protection of legal rights. In this matter the Roman law principle, 'quod omnes similiter tangit, ab omnibus comprobetur' played an important part. Hostiensis referred to this prin-

---

[119] *Summa*, V, De accusationibus, n. 11.
[120] *Summa*, V, De exceptionibus, n. 1.
[121] *Summa*, V, De criminibus sine ordine puniendis, n. 3.
[122] *Summa*, II, De exceptionibus, n. 3. This willingness of Hostiensis to give even the devil the benefit of a fair trial is echoed in a recent play about the great English saint and lawyer, Thomas More. The friends of More are trying to get him to arrest the dangerous informer, Rich, but More refuses because Rich has not yet broken any specific law. The rest of the dialogue runs as follows:
Roper: So you'd give the Devil benefit of law!
More: Yes. What would you do? Cut a great road through the law to get after the Devil?
Roper: I'd cut down every law in England to do that!
More: Oh? And when the last law was down and the Devil turned round on you — where would you hide, Roper, the laws all being flat? This country's planted thick with laws from coast to coast — Man's laws, not God's — and if you cut them down — and you're just the man to do it — d'you really think you could stand upright in the winds that would blow then? Yes, I'd give the Devil benefit of law, for my own safety's sake.
(Cf. Robert Bolt, *A Man for All Seasons*, 1960, Act One: published in *New English Dramatists*, 6, Penguin Books, 1966, p. 60).
[123] *Summa*, II, De libelli oblatione, n. 3.

ciple, as has been already noticed, when he was discussing the
rights of the cathedral chapter.   But it was a maxim that was
very influential in the development of both canonical and civil
institutions of all kinds in the Middle Ages. [124]   Hostiensis' stress
on the right of every man to be given adequate opportunity to
defend himself in the courts illustrates how strongly the maxim
had influenced court procedure in general.   In this, as in so
much else, he was merely expressing what was common canonical teaching.   Medieval canonists emphasised the rights of
all who were in any way affected by a dispute: 'omnes quos
causa tangit vocandi sunt'.   The point of this was

> that all those whose rights were touched by an issue should
> have every opportunity to prepare the defense of their rights,
> to take advantage of all means within the law and to consent
> to the court's decision of the legality of the rights only after
> a full defense and "treatise" or discussion and debate (tractare)
> had taken place. [125]

The principle also affected the procedure of the canonical *in-
quisitio*.

> A decree of the fourth Lateran Council prescribed that when
> an *inquisitio* was to be made against a prelate, the accused
> must be present in court unless he absented himself by con-
> tumacy; and he must be informed not only of what he was
> accused but also of the names of the accusers. [126]

Enough has been said to show how important due process
of law was to Hostiensis and to medieval canonists in general.
They were, of course, all trained in Roman law and nowhere
more clearly is this evident than in their treatises on procedure.
Hostiensis borrowed freely from Azo's *Summa* and from other
Roman lawyers, and the revived Roman law on procedure formed
the foundation of the canonical treatises.   'The twelfth and
thirteenth centuries', writes Professor Post, 'were an age not
only of increasing awareness of rights but of the rise of the
legal science that provided the means of asserting rights in

---

[124] Professor Gaines Post has shown how influential the maxim was
in the Middle Ages in his *Studies in Medieval Legal Thought*, Princeton,
1964, pp. 163-238.   It was universally accepted by canonists and civilians
and also influenced the Common Law.
[125] Gaines Post, *op. cit.*, p. 180.
[126] *Ibid.*

11

courts'. [127]   This brief examination of the *Summa Aurea* has illustrated the truth of this statement as far as the Church was concerned: 'Parum prodest iura habere in civitate nisi sit qui iura reddat'.

---

[127] Gaines Post, *op. cit.*, p. 164.

CHAPTER SIX

CANON LAW AS A GUIDE AND AS A DETERRENT

Throughout this thirteenth-century *Summa*, then, the law of the Church was propounded as a means of promoting unity, stability and concord in Christendom, and as a protection of rights and a defence against oppression. For Hostiensis, however, these roles, though important in themselves, were subordinate to a still higher goal, the attainment of salvation. It was this that he regarded as the supreme criterion of all law and legal interpretation. As he himself stated in his conclusion to the *Summa*, 'doctrinam tradidi non solum ad tuitionem et defensionem rerum et corporum, sed etiam ad salutem medicinalem, ac medicinam salutarem, et antidotum efficax animarum'.[1] The passage is but an echo of the declaration he had made at the very beginning of his commentary:

> Finis autem noster sit, ut hac summa completa, et diligenter ac fideliter compilata, lecta, audita, intellecta, intentione retenta et servata, sic nos ipsos et nobis commissos regamus et instruamus, et canonica negotia quae spiritualia et temporalia sunt taliter pertractemus indefesse continuando ... ut cum in hoc seculo sobrie, iuste, pieque vixerimus, valeamus ad regna caelestia pervenire, et sic veram unitatem et concordiam adipisci, ipso in cuius nomine incepimus praestante.[2]

The primacy of Christian values is a leitmotif that runs through the whole of the *Summa* and is explicitly mentioned in the seventh and last of the functions of law listed by Hostiensis. The law is here proposed as a deterrent from crime and an encouragement for virtue. The fear of punishment is to deter men from evil and compel them to lead a good life, while the hope of reward is to act as a stimulus urging good men on

---

[1] *Summa*, V, De regulis iuris.
[2] *Summa*, I, Prooemium, *ad fin.*

to lead even better lives.[3] Here the canonist is taking over an idea from the Roman lawyers, expressed at the beginning of the Digest,[4] and giving it a specifically Christian slant. 'whether in punishing or in pardoning, what is at issue is this, that the life of men be set on the right course.'

This legal concern with morality has, of course, already cropped up in a variety of ways in the course of this study. In the general survey of medieval canon law, which was given in Chapter Two, attention was drawn to this aspect. It was there pointed out that both in the *Decretum* and in the *Decretales* there are many laws which are really moral rules of conduct for the faithful in general and for the clergy in particular. A large part of Part One of the *Decretum* has been seen to provide a detailed guide for the moral life of the clergy; and the same is true of much of Book Three of the *Decretales*. Also, the legislation on marriage outlines many of the moral duties within the family. Similar directives can be seen in many other parts of the *Corpus Iuris Canonici*. Moral concern, in fact, pervades the whole of canonical legislation which quite explicitly set out to provide a moral guide for the Christian according to his state of life.[5] This same concern for morality has also been adverted to already in the discussion of Hostiensis' approach to canon law in Chapter Three, where a number of illustrations were given of the emphasis he put on the moral character of the law of the Church as a support for and an enforcement of the moral values of Christianity.[6] Three aspects of this role of law as a spur to virtue and a deterrent from crime will now be discussed:

1. In what way did medieval canon law set out to provide a guide for Christian living?
2. How was canon law used as an instrument of reform in the Church?
3. In particular, how did canon law attempt to provide an effective deterrent against the evils of heresy?

---

[3] *Summa*, I, De constitutionibus, n. 10: 'septima, ut metu poenae mali boni, et boni meliores spe proemiorum fiant'.
[4] Digest, I, 1, 1.
[5] Cf. above pp. 55 ff.
[6] Cf. above pp. 71 ff.

1. *A Guide for Christian Living*

It was a common view throughout the Middle Ages that the canonical tradition should embody the norms of conduct for all the members of the Christian community. The laws of the Church were looked upon as an outline of the permanent requirements of the Christian life, — the *sacri canones* of the *Populus Christianus*. During the eleventh-century Gregorian Reform, for example, the writings of the Fathers of the Church, earlier conciliar decrees and canonical legislation were all considered to be sacred texts in a very special way. There was a general belief that their authors had been, in a particularly privileged way, guided by the Holy Spirit. This in effect made the canons and the patristic writings 'inspired' texts for all practical purposes, though, of course, they were not put in the same category as the Bible. Yet the similarity is clear to see in the terms that were used to describe these non-scriptural writings: 'sacra eloquentia', 'sacra pagina', 'sacra scriptura', and so on. The collection of canons was not looked upon as a system of merely human wisdom and prudence produced by ecclesiastical authority, but as an authentic utterance of the Holy Spirit guiding and directing the Church, — a continuation of God's word to his people. The conviction was particularly strong in Pope Gregory VII. When this ardent reformer proclaimed the law of the Church his style was characterised not by juridical logic but by the zeal of a prophet announcing the word of God and applying the 'inspired' law. [7]

The preoccupation about providing a guide for Christian living is clearly expressed by Ivo of Chartres in the prologue to his *Decretum*. Among the functions of law here mentioned, along with the protection of the sacraments and the direction of judicial business, he includes 'ea quae ad instruendos [instituendos] vel corrigendos mores'. [8] The aim of positive ecclesiastical legislation, he tells us, is not primarily to obtain the salvation of souls,

> sed ad cam tutius muniendam ... Habet enim omnis ecclesiastica disciplina principaliter hanc intentionem, vel omnem aedificationem adversus scientiam Christi se erigentem destruere, vel aedificationem Dei, fidei veritate, et morum honestate constantem construere; vel eamdem si contaminata fuerit, poeni-

---

[7] Cf. J. J. Ryan, *Law for Liberty*, (J. Biechler, Editor), pp. 44-45.
[8] Ivo of Chartres, *Prologus in Decretum*, P. L. 161, 47.

tentiae remediis emundare. Huius aedificationis magistra est
charitas, quae saluti proximorum consulens, id praecipit aliis
fieri quod sibi quisque vult ab aliis impendi. Quicumque ergo
ecclesiasticus doctor ecclesiasticas regulas ita interpretatur aut
moderatur, ut ad regnum charitatis cuncta quae docuerit vel
exposuerit, referat, nec peccat nec errat.[9]

A similar approach to canon law has already been noticed in
the *Decretum* of Gratian who reiterates the traditional teaching
that it was the law's task to prescribe what had to be done,
forbid what is evil and permit what is licit.[10]

   This reverence for the law as a guide to perfection, however, was not confined to the canonists. It was shared also
by civil lawyers, who tended to think of Roman law in the
same way. Professor Ullmann has shown how the theory was
propounded by the fourteenth-century post-glossator, Lucas de
Penna. For Lucas, the law in general was to be taken as a
reliable guide for human actions towards man's destined goal.
Law was to be regarded as the translation of the ethical idea
of justice into concrete action. And the role of law was, according to Ullmann:

> that of a directing force, an unfailing and unerring guide of
> human actions in the social field: *Lex est lux et via vitae.*
> Law is the very agency through which the divine power mo-
> tivates human beings and directs their life in society.[11]

If, then, Roman law could be considered as a 'donum Dei' and
the 'divinae voluntatis imago', *a fortiori* canon law would be
regarded by the Christian as an expression of divine guidance.
It is not surprising to find that the principal aim of canon
law, according to Joannes Andreae, was 'ordinare in Deum et
legem evangelicam, ut homo gloriam assequatur'.[12]

   This identification of canon law with Christian morality in
the Middle Ages has been well expressed by Professor Stephan
Kuttner:

> The mutual penetration of two modes of thought of super-
> natural ends and legal means, appears wherever we open the

---

   [9] *Ibid.*, 48-50.
   [10] D. 3,1-2.
   [11] W. Ullmann, *A Medieval Idea of Law*, London, 1949, p. 18. Cf. Cod.
10,5,2, n. 9; 11.18.1, n. 12.
   [12] Joannes Andreae, *Quaestiones mercuriales*, ad reg. 2 (cited by
Kuttner, *Harmony from Dissonance*, p. 60).

books of the medieval canonists. The harmonization of op-
posites here reaches its supreme purpose, that of integrating
human jurisprudence in the divine order of salvation. It is
for this reason that the canonists would not hesitate to employ
scriptural and patristic texts in arguing a technical point of
law, nor to cite texts of Roman civil law in order to prove
a point of moral or sacramental doctrine. At times such
reasonings may appear naive to the modern reader, but they
were not inconsistent with what the classical canonists had
perceived as the ultimate end of all law in the Church: a
common good which includes the natural common good of
human society, and also transcends it because it is essentially
connected with something most individual and personal, "man's
friendship with God, which we call charity". The subject of
all canon law, they would say, is not simply man, but the
spiritual man, a pilgrim on his way between this world and
eternal life. [13]

Such was the tradition that Hostiensis inherited. There
are many indications in the *Summa Aurea* that he wholeheartedly
accepted it and thought that canon law did provide a sort of
Christian 'Torah'. He shared the common conviction that it
was part of the function of canon law to provide a guide for
Christian living, to enumerate the duties that the individual
Christian had to fulfil if he wished to be faithful to his Christian vocation. When he wrote that 'nos tamen considerare non
debemus quid fiat, immo quid fieri possit et debeat', he was
expressing a principle that governed all his canonical writing. [14]
This can be shown in a variety of ways from the *Summa.*

His acceptance of the idea expressed in the phrase, *salus
animarum suprema lex,* can be seen in his consistent concern
for spiritual interests over all other considerations. Mgr Lefebvre has shown how Hostiensis insisted that a preoccupation
with spiritual interests should be a characteristic of the law
of the Church:

> L'un des points qui frappent le plus le lecteur des travaux de
> l'Hostiensis nous paraît être l'effort qu'il tente en vue de
> mettre en relief dans la doctrine canonique le caractère qu'il
> estime devoir lui être propre, celui d'être un droit dominé par
> les préoccupations d'ordre spirituel. [15]

---

[13] S. Kuttner, *Harmony from Dissonance,* Pennsylvania, 1960, pp. 45-46.
[14] *Summa,* IV, De desponsatione impuberum, n. 5.
[15] C. Lefebvre, '*Aequitas canonica* et *periculum animae* dans la doctrine
de l'Hostiensis', in *Ephemerides Iuris Canonici,* 8 (1952), p. 305.

Lefebvre thinks that this tendency is perhaps more pronounced in the *Apparatus* than in the *Summa Aurea,* but it does in fact exist in both. It is shown in his constant emphasis on the need to avoid anything that might endanger the soul's salvation. 'Anima omnibus est praeferenda', and 'Obviandum est periculis animarum' are recurrent themes in both the *Apparatus* and the *Summa Aurea.* Hostiensis thought that the law ought to take positive measures to ward off dangers to the salvation of the faithful. [16] When discussing judicial discretion to adapt or modify legal penalties he points out that the judge must be particularly careful to see that such action does not result in danger to the salvation of the citizen — 'ut tamen caveat ipse iudex quod ubi vertitur periculum animae sine delectu personarum procedat'. [17] The phrase, 'periculum animae' runs throughout the whole of the *Summa,* and is used to indicate any kind of danger to the salvation of the faithful. Many instances could be cited. There is the law which grants the bishop the right to interfere in a parish run by exempt religious if the religious are showing negligence in their duty. The reason for this legislation is the danger that would arise for the faithful from such negligence.[18] The same principle appears in his discussion of the marriage laws. [19] It is because clandestine marriages can be a source of danger to the salvation of the persons involved that they are forbidden by law. [20] Scandal too must always be avoided as far as possible, and legislation to prevent any kind of scandal is another aspect of the law as a guide to Christian perfection. This explains the care that should be taken in the appointment of professors and lecturers in theology. These men may not contradict the teachings of the Fathers of the Church because this would cause harm to the faithful, 'haec etiam requirit salus animarum et publica utilitas'. [21] It is also a principle with Hostiensis that wherever there is any question of endangering one's salvation the safer course must always be adopted. [22]

---

[16] Cf. C. Lefebvre, *op. cit.,* and also 'La doctrine de l'Hostiensis sur la préférence à assurer en droit aux intérêts spirituels', *Eph. Iur. Can.* 8 (1952) 24-41.

[17] *Summa,* V, De accusationibus, n. 12.

[18] *Summa,* I, De officio ordinarii, n. 7.

[19] *Summa,* IV, De desponsatione impuberum, n. 9-10.

[20] *Summa,* IV, De clandestina desponsatione, n. 3.

[21] *Summa,* V, De magistris, et ne aliquid exigatur pro licentia docendi, n. 2-3.

[22] *Summa,* V, De his qui filios occiderunt, n. 3.

Hostiensis, however, was not content to stress in general terms the importance of spiritual and Christian values and leave it at that. He also considered it to be part of his task to provide detailed instructions on the duties of the faithful, both clergy and laity. Attention has already been drawn to the care which he showed in delineating the moral and pastoral duties of the bishop towards his flock.[23] This was a subject which he seemed to take very much to heart and he returns to it quite frequently in the *Summa*. But nowhere does he provide clearer moral guidance for bishops than in his long and detailed list of episcopal misdemeanors in Book Five. The list occurs in the treatise *De poenitentiis et remissionibus* in Book Five of the *Summa* and it constitutes a fairly complete guide to the sort of life that a bishop should be living if he is really taking this office seriously.[24] He enumerates about fifty faults that bishops should guard against and to which they are particularly prone. His reason for doing so is: 'ut sciant episcopi a quibus abstinere debeant et de quibus oporteat confiteri, notent a quibus debeant abstinere et in quibus excedant'. His warnings about the behaviour of bishops may seem somewhat outspoken, and as he himself was an archbishop when he published the *Summa*, he probably knew what he was talking about. Yet he is quite polite about the matter: 'Neminem tamen episcoporum repraehendimus, cum sint patres, sed ut a delictis abstineant admonemus et conscientia conveniat unumquemque'[25]. There is no need to reproduce his list here but a few examples may be considered by way of illustration. The bishop is to ask himself if he is negligent in appointing to benefices. Does he ordain unworthy and untrained candidates? Does he drag monks and other religious out of their monasteries without good reason, and against the will of their abbot? Does he look after the clergy under his charge, administering correction where this is necessary? Is he generous towards the poor? Is he negligent in his duty to defend widows, orphans and the poor and 'alias personas miserabiles' who look to the Church for help? Does he spend too much time on things of the world, when he should be at prayer, study and preaching?

He is warned against pluralism and simony and urged to show proper respect to the priests in his diocese. Does he refuse to allow these men to do their duty and preach,

---

[23] Cf. *Summa*, I, De officio ordinarii, n. 3.
[24] *Summa*, V, De poenitentiis et remissionibus, n. 20.
[25] *Ibid.*

ac si essent gibbosi vel idiotae, vel eis inviderent cum tamen
episcopi ad hoc facti sint ut schismata tollerentur et de con-
suetudine tantum praesunt presbyteris; deberent enim ecclesiam Dei regere in communi; ... cum enim presbyter Christum
consecret, quod maius est, quare praesente episcopo non potest
praedicare? ... Gaudeat ergo episcopus si bonos habeat presby-
teros qui nec habeant ipsum ut principem nisi et ipse habeat
eos ut senatores.

Does he despise those of his own priests who are both able
and willing to provide him with wise counsel, and bring in
advisers from outside? Does he lord it over his clergy instead
of treating them as his colleagues in the government of the
diocese? Is he too credulous in listening to evil reports, against
the advice of St Gregory, 'si quid de quocumque clerico ad
aures tuas pervenerit facile non credas', and he points out that
'non solum ille reus est qui falsum de aliquo profert, sed etiam
ille qui aurem cito criminibus praebet', citing the *Decretum* in
confirmation of this. Does he promote his favourites or those
who will be easily subservient to him instead of those whom
he knows to be more competent? Does he indulge in personal
revenge and try to play the role of both judge and actor in a
lawsuit, whereas he should know that 'cum persona actoris
assumitur, iudiciaria potestas amittitur'? Is he careful in following the directions provided by the ecclesiastical legislation?
'Qui enim nescit obedire canonibus non est dignus altaribus
administrare'. Hostiensis is aware of the hostile criticism of
the law that was current in his time and he mentions only
to reject the idea that the Church should be able to manage
well enough with the Bible and has no need for canonical
legislation: 'igitur praesumptuosum est asserere quod statutis
sacrorum canonum in sua firmitate manentibus, per solam bi-
bliam regi posset ecclesia sancta Dei; sed hoc tantum consue-
verunt asserere ius canonicum ignorantes'.[26]

All this adds up to a rather complete guide to the life a
bishop should be leading. Yet Hostiensis obviously considered
it to be part of his task as a canonist to provide such a guide.
What is more, he supports almost every item in his list with
a reference to the *Decretum* of Gratian, — and mainly to Part
One. Though much of the discussion may today seem to belong
rather to moral theology than to canon law, in fact Hostiensis

---

[26] *Summa*, V, De poenitentiis et remissionibus, n. 20.

was simply expounding canon law as it was then understood.
In this same treatise on penance he goes on to provide similar
guides for abbots, monks, priests, lawyers, kings, emperors, and
so on, [27] and he points out the main faults to be avoided by
the faithful according to their status in the Church. He also
deals with the excesses of prelates in another *titulus* in Book
Five, *De excessibus praelatorum et subditorum*, where he repeats
a number of the faults that he has listed in his treatise on
penance. Again he warns bishops about extortion, living in lux-
ury, unjust excommunications and the like, and he repeats his
advice that the clergy should be treated as colleagues. He adds
that the bishop may not be present at ordeals, nor may he on
any account encourage the infliction of the death-penalty — 'hoc
credo falsissimum, imo si imminet periculum debet instare quod
citra mortem puniatur'. [28]

It has already been noticed how much of medieval canon
law was taken up with delineating the rights and duties of the
clergy in general. Much of Part One of the *Decretum* and of
Book Three of the *Decretales* concerns the moral virtues that
the clergy should possess. This concern is reflected in the *Summa Aurea*. The clearest instance is probably the discussion of
the first *titulus* of Book Three, *De vita et honestate clericorum*.
This is divided into two parts of which the first is entitled,
'clerici qualiter vivere debeant', and the second, 'clericorum honestas in quibus consistit'. Here Hostiensis is quite clearly
providing a guide to the Christian life of the clergy, and for
this reason it is worth looking at in some detail as an illustration of this aspect of the role of law. He begins by addressing
the clergy as follows:

> Sed honestate vitae vacabitis, ut non solum verbo sed exemplo
> nostro, qualiter in domo domini conversari oporteat, laicos
> instruatis. Igitur et si tractatu iudiciorum finito edocti sitis,
> qualiter vos debeatis habere circa iudicia, tamen et nunc
> instruendi estis, qualiter vivere debeatis, vel aliter. Indicabo
> tibi, homo, quid sit bonum, aut quid Deus requirat a te, utique
> facere iudicium et iustitiam, de quibus praemissum est in
> superiori libro, et sollicite ambulare cum domino Deo tuo, per
> vitae sanctitatem, et morum honestatem, quae et si in omni-
> bus hominibus, in clericis tamen potissime requiruntur. [29]

---

[27] *Summa*, V, De poenitentiis et remissionibus, nn. 21 ff.
[28] *Summa*, V, De excessibus praelatorum et subditorum, n. 1.
[29] *Summa*, III, De vita et honestate clericorum, n. 1.

Hostiensis then goes on to give an outline of how precisely
they ought to live. He observes that the common life, though
not absolutely necessary, does have many advantages for the
clergy. They are to remain unmarried and live chaste and continent lives, observing temperance too in eating and drinking.
'Fabulationes et comessationes' should be avoided and they
should spend their time in the study of the sacred scriptures.
Nor should they attend gathering 'ubi amatoria cantantur, et
inhonesta exercentur spectacula, ne per hoc contaminentur'. Once
again Hostiensis backs up his statements with frequent references to the *Decretum*.

He then goes on to consider in what this *honestas* consists.
In an infinite number of things, he says, but he will mention
a few. The clergy should not mix with the laity, 'quia sunt
diversae professionis'. They should wear the tonsure, and secu-
lars and regulars should be clearly distinguished by their dress.
They should be sober in their appearance. They should be
humble and modest and avoid any kind of ostentation in their
clothes which should be neither red nor green, nor too long
nor too short. They should also keep away from inns, unless
they happen to be on a journey, 'et aleas et taxillos non debent
ludere, nec ludis interesse'. In short, the whole of the priest's
life is here under discussion and Hostiensis is providing moral
exhortation in his canonical commentary. Yet again he supports his advice with citations from Part One of the *Decretum*.
A frequent topic in these exhortations to priests is the care
that they have to take in their dealings with women, and in
Book Three of the *Summa* the second *titulus* deals with this
question, *De cohabitatione clericorum et mulierum*. The point
of the legislation in this subject is to protect clerics from dangers which threaten their commitment to celibacy. [30] The priest
must exercise great care about the women he allows to stay in
the same house as himself. He should do all he can to see no
grounds for scandal or suspicion are provided. Women may be
permitted to live in the same house as clerics, — 'dummodo
personas suspectas secum non teneant'. It is probably all
right to have one's mother or sister or aunt staying with one,
but as for others one must be careful about the dangers involved.
While it is permissible to have close relatives in the house, one
should bear in mind, remarks Hostiensis wrily, that 'non omnes
quae cum sorore mea sunt, meae sorores sunt'. Nuns should

---

[30] *Summa*, III, De cohabitatione clericorum et mulierum, n. 1.

not live in the same house as clerics, nor should clerics be
frequent visitors to the monasteries of nuns; nor should monks
and nuns share the same monastery.[31] Hostiensis goes on to
discuss the penalties that may be inflicted on clerics and others
who disobey this legislation on cohabitation; suspension, interdict and excommunication may all be used. Those that are
inflicted, however, should be intended to bring the delinquent
to repentance. And in all cases he advises that idle gossip
should be disregarded, — 'vanae voces populi non sunt audien-
dae'.[32]

These are only a few samples of the sort of canonical legislation that governed both the public and the private life of
the priest. But the subject was a central concern of canon law
which set out to provide a complete guide for clerics. Special
penalties were enacted against criminous clerics, 'quia non debet
praebere laicis pravum exemplum'.[33] Dicing and gambling and
hunting are all forbidden to clerics. Fishing is all right, thinks
Hostiensis, but hunting with hounds or hawks is certainly
wrong.[34]

Hostiensis composed his *Summa* for the instruction of
priests and one of the main pastoral duties of priests was the
hearing of confessions. Hence he spends a great deal of time
in giving careful and detailed instructions on how this important
task should be carried out. As has already been mentioned,
the long treatise in Book Five, *De poenitentiis et remissionibus*,
is really a manual for confessors in which every aspect of the
sacrament of penance is discussed. The treatise is full of quotations from Scripture, and from the Fathers and it includes brief
exhortations on the mercy of God and the Passion of Christ.
He begins by discussing the nature of the sacrament of penance
and its twofold aspect, — 'quoad Deum and quoad ecclesiam'.
He distinguishes mortal from venial sin and outlines the difference between mortal sins and crimes: 'omne criminale peccatum mortale est, sed non convertitur'.[35] He enumerates the
eleven major crimes: those against the Trinity, *contra naturam*,
homicide, treason, sacrilege, incest, conspiracy, adultery, false
testimony, simony, and usury. He then discusses the qualities

---

[31] *Ibid.*, n. 2.
[32] *Ibid.*, n. 6.
[33] *Summa*, V, De maledicis, n. 1.
[34] *Summa*, V, De clerico venatore.
[35] *Summa*, V, De poenitentiis et remissionibus, n. 7-9.

that the penitent's confession should have, — voluntary, integral, and so on; and this is followed by a discussion of the faculties for hearing confessions and a list of reserved sins. He goes on to provide the detailed guides for the examination of conscience of Christians which have already been discussed. He stresses the need for regular confessors and discusses the proper age for the confessions of children, and so on. He does, however, insist that he does not expect a rigid adherence to all the detailed suggestions that he proposes as guide-lines in this matter. The discerning priest will use what he finds helpful. [36]

What follows is largely an instruction on how to bring men to the sacrament of penance and how to administer it fruitfully. Students of the *Summa* would find here useful outlines for their preaching, complete with scriptural references, — especially to the Psalms and the New Testament, with Seneca and Cicero thrown in for good measure. They would also find guidance about what sort of questions they should put to their penitents, bearing in mind that in the sacramental forum the priest must perform the role both of the judge and of the 'medicus spiritualis'. [37] He ought therefore to proceed discreetly and with great caution. Warnings too are given about the seal of confession, and Hostiensis proposes that the simple rule to be followed in this matter is the rule of silence, — 'Do not talk about confessions at all'. He castigates the behaviour of many priests who act carelessly in this matter — even although they do not actually name their penitent. In his advice about the sort of penances that should be given he states that the confessor should be familiar with the 'canones poenitentiales' which specify particular penances for particular sins; but he should always bear in mind that the circumstances in each case must be taken into consideration. Rigidity is to be avoided and equity preserved at all times. The conclusion to the whole treatise is in fact an exhortation on the need for prudence and discretion. Confessors and judges must at all times be careful to see that their judgments are tempered with equity and that their motivation is the salvation of the souls entrusted to their charge. Such considerateness for their penitents should determine the advice that confessors give in confession. [38]

A very large proportion of canon law was, therefore, taken

---

[36] *Ibid.*, n. 46.
[37] *Ibid.*, n. 49.
[38] *Summa*, V, De poenitentiis et remissionibus, n. 62.

up with providing precepts and directives for the clergy, but canonical legislation also provided quite a substantial amount of moral guidance for the faithful in general. There were, for example, the precepts of the Fourth Lateran Council on annual confession and communion. There were also the general laws on fasting and abstinence, which were rather severe and applied to all Christians. There were also numerous enactments contained in Part Two of the *Decretum*[39] and in the *Decretales*[40] whose aim was to provide protection for the Christian ideal of marriage and provide guidance on the morality that should obtain between husband and wife and within Christian families. All this is reflected in the *Summa Aurea*, particularly in Book Four. There were, too, the laws whose aim was to foster reverence and respect for sacred places and persons, for the sacraments, and so on that have already been mentioned. There are also numerous occasions in the *Summa Aurea* where Hostiensis plays the role of the spiritual director and provides guidance concerning moral problems of the faithful. Instances of this are his lengthy treatment of vows in Book Three, where he discusses the nature of the obligation, various reasons that would excuse, and the courses of action that he thought would be morally sound. The same may be said of his treatment of the duty of paying tithes, and the morality of oath-taking. Hostiensis was insistent that once an oath had been taken then it had to be carefully respected, and if a Christian undertook to perform a task under oath he was bound to fulfil what he had undertaken, in spite of legal subtleties that might seem to free him from the obligation. Spiritual interests must prevail over purely temporal advantages.[41]

He also thought, in common with his contemporaries, that it was part of the function of law to protect the faithful from dangerous occasions of sin. Tournaments, for instance, were forbidden 'propter mortis hominum et animarum pericula quae inde saepe proveniunt'.[42] Ecclesiastical burial was refused to anyone who was killed in such a tournament. Another clear example of this approach is provided by the legislation against fortune-telling and lotteries. Drawing lots cannot be considered

---

[39] Cf. *Causae* 27-36.
[40] Cf. Gregorian Decretals, IV.
[41] Cf. C. Lefebvre, 'La doctrine de l'Hostiensis sur la préférence à assurer en droit aux intérêts spirituels', *Eph. Iur. Can.*, 8 (1952), pp. 24-44.
[42] *Summa*, V, De torneamentis, n. 2.

an evil thing in itself, he admits, since there are examples of
it in the Old Testament, and it was through the drawing of
lots that Matthias was elected to the college of the Apostles.
But, he argues, such examples do not prove that it is now lawful
for Christians to take part in these practices. 'Dic enim sors
non est, id est non erat aliquid mali dum permittebatur. Sed
hodie mala est ex quo prohibetur'. Convincing arguments cannot be drawn from the Old Testament practice in the matter;
because the coming of the Gospel has enjoined a more perfect
way of life than that which was permitted earlier, and he mentions a number of other examples. If, then, *sortilegium* is not
an evil thing in itself why is it forbidden by the law of the
Church? Because, replies Hostiensis, it is a source of danger
to the Christian. [43] The faithful must be protected by the law
from such dangerous occasions of sin. It was for similar reasons that clerics were forbidden to play games of dice.

All this raises the question about how the law should be
used to enforce morality. The medieval canonists certainly considered that the suppression of vice was as much the law's
business as the suppression of any kind of subversive activity;
and they would have justified this as necessary for the preservation of society in general. This leads into the next question
that has to be discussed: how far was canon law used as an
instrument of reform within the Church?

2. *The Law an Instrument of Moral Reform*

In this seventh function of law, according to Hostiensis'
list, which is here under discussion, the law is proposed as
a deterrent from crime and an encouragement for virtue. Fear
of the penalties which may be inflicted upon them should deter
evil men from crime and impel them to lead better lives. 'Septima, ut metu poenae mali boni, et boni meliores spe praemiorum fiant'. This reforming function of law was stressed in the
Middle Ages. Professor Hart, in a discussion of law in general,
has remarked that 'legal enactments may set standards of hon-
esty and humanity which ultimately raise the current morality'. [44]
And history demonstrates that it has always been a function
of law to uproot social evils and abuses. This is particularly
true of the Church in which canonical legislation has often in

---

[43] *Summa*, V, De sortilegiis, n. 1.
[44] H. L. Hart, *The Concept of Law*, Oxford, 1961, p. 172.

the past been a not completely ineffective instrument of renewal
and reform, although, of course, no one would claim that it
ever achieved complete success. Consider, for instance, the part
played by positive legislation in the Carolingian and in the
Gregorian reforms. Here the aim was to remove by legal enactments obstacles which seemed to be preventing or stifling the
sound development of the Christian community. It was an
attempt to foster, through the law, conditions in which the
following of Christ would be for most men less difficult. The
penal law was to protect men against themselves as much as
to prevent them from coming to harm at the hands of others.
Penal legislation was perhaps primarily meant to protect innocent men from criminals, but the penal law of the Church
was also out to deter men from evil and lead them to repentance.

A study of the activity of St Peter Damian illustrates this
approach to law in the eleventh century. 'Norms of conduct
for all members of society', writes J. J. Ryan, 'were embodied
in the canonical tradition of the Church, which regulated institutional and individual life within the Church and the activities
of the Church itself within the Christian world. It was to this
canonical tradition that the men filled with the new spirit appealed *to eradicate flagrant abuses*, which grew increasingly intolerable to awakened consciences, and to render a permanent
and closer conformity to the requirements of the Christian life'. [45]
Professor Kuttner agrees with this judgment:

> It has become clear in particular that the burning desire
> for a restoration of the "ancient" canonical traditions was one
> of the chief motivating forces in the reformers' thought and
> action. As they saw it, spiritual renewal and repression of
> abuses was not a matter of single disciplinary measures but
> was contingent upon establishing the right order of Christian
> society as it shone forth in the *sacri canones* and *decreta
> sanctorum patrum;* the great issues of the Reform [the eleventh-
> century Gregorian Reform] were fundamentally issues of canon
> law. [46]

---

[45] J. J. Ryan, *St Peter Damiani and His Canonical Sources*, Toronto,
1956, p. 9.

[46] S. Kuttner, in the preface to J. J. Ryan's *St Peter Damiani & His
Canonical Sources*, p. x-xi. Cf. also, P. Palazzini, 'Il diritto strumento di
riforma ecclesiastica in S. Pier Damiani', in *Ephemerides Iuris Canonici*,
11 (1955), pp. 361-408; 12 (1956), pp. 9-58; J. T. Gilchrist, 'Canon Law Aspects
of the Eleventh Century Gregorian Reform Programme', in *Journal of
Ecclesiastical History*, 12 (1962), pp. 21-38.

There were, of course, a number of currents of reform in the eleventh, twelfth and thirteenth centuries, of which the juridical current was only one. The religious revival which can be seen in the Cluniac Movement, the Cistercian Expansion, and the rise of the Franciscan and Dominicans are eloquent witnesses to this deeper search for religious renewal and reform in the Church. The law was used to promote such interior renewal and reform. If men were not impelled by noble desires to live according to the Gospel then the law was there with its severe legal penalties if they strayed too far from the path of Christian perfection.

The movement for reform under Pope Gregory VII was continued and consolidated by the Lateran Councils of the Twelfth century (1123, 1139 and 1179) and a large body of penal legislation was enacted against simony, clerical concubinage, usury, pluralism, heresy and many other crimes. Severe sanctions too were threatened against any who ignored the prohibitions. Legislation is, of course, no substitute for interior religious renewal and the very bulk of the penal legislation and its frequent repetition are an indication that it was not really very effective against the abuses that were undermining Christendom. Lateran IV in 1215 added to this body of reform legislation and initiated a century of reform. All these laws and penal sanctions were incorporated into the *Decretum* and the *Decretales* and were commented upon by Hostiensis. What did he make of it all? The frequency with which he quotes Augustine on the need to correct Christian behaviour indicates that he, with most of his contemporaries, would have agreed with Augustine's approach to the reforming function of law. Augustine's justification of the suppression of the Donatists was to have a lasting influence in the Church. What was the argument that he proposed in defence of what amounted to a full-scale persecution of the Donatists by the State? It was the need for what he called 'disciplina'. Augustine would have agreed that for each individual the final act of choice between good and evil, — for God or against God, — has to be spontaneous and free if it is to have any real spiritual value. But, he argued, this final act has to be prepared by a long process which the individuals need not necessarily choose for themselves, but which can be imposed upon them against their will by God. This was what he meant by 'disciplina'; it was a corrective process of teaching, even through fear and pain, a sort of softening-up process, a 'per molestias eruditio'. Consider, for instance, the whole series

of divinely ordained disasters in the Old Testament. Carnal
men, he maintained, can only respond to fear and so there are
sound uses for the strait-jacket! 'Take away the barriers created
by the laws! Men's brazen capacity to do harm, their urge
to self-indulgence would rage to the full'. The 'sheer sweet taste
of sinning', thought the Bishop of Hippo, would be too much
for them![47] More will be said about this augustinian approach
to penal law later when the laws against heresy are being examined, but it does seem to indicate an approach that was
quite common in the Middle Ages and shared by Hostiensis.

The aim of canonical penal legislation was twofold: to reform actual criminals and to deter those who might otherwise
become criminals. Moreover, medieval canon law did not restrict
itself to what might be considered ecclesiastical crimes such
as simony, pluralism, nicolaitism and the like. It also added
ecclesiastical sanctions to the penalties enacted in the civil law
against criminal offences, such as homicide. This is evident
from a number of the *tituli* of Book Five of the *Decretales*:
*De his qui filios occiderunt, De infantibus et languidis expositis,
De homicidio voluntario et casuali, De furtis*, and so on. Hostiensis expounds the Roman law on all these issues and adds
the canonical penalties that had been enacted by the Church.
These took the form of excommunication or a period of canonical penance. He states that crimes should not be allowed to
go unpunished and that the legal sanctions should not be lightly
put aside in case such leniency be taken as an encouragement
to criminals.[48] The judge must always bear in mind the effect
of his actions on the general state of the Church as well as on
the individual whose case is being tried in court.

In Book Five he outlines all the penalties that the Church
has the right to inflict, and he divides them into personal, real
and mixed. The Church has the power to inflict all of these
and in the opinion of Hostiensis it is the penalty that is most
feared that should be inflicted. 'Poena quae magis timetur in-
fligenda est'.[49] This is so because then the penalty will be most
likely to produce the desired effect, which is the correction of
misbehaviour and the reform of the Church.[50]

He argues that some kind of penal legislation, including

---

[47] Cf. Peter Brown, *Augustine of Hippo*, London, 1967, p. 238.
[48] *Summa*, I, De treuga et pace, n. 5.
[49] *Summa*, V, De poenis, n. 3.
[50] *Summa*, V, De poenis, n. 4.

sanctions, is needed within the Church since otherwise the jurisdiction of the authorities would be quite powerless, 'nam iuris-
dictio sine modica coertione nulla esset'. Moreover, the infliction of excommunication, although in itself an extreme penalty,
can, he thinks, be regarded in fact as 'modica coertio' for the
simple reason that worldly people tend to think very little of it:
'quia modice appretiatur hodie, et modica est inter mundanos
qui tantum sectantur temporalia, de spiritualibus non curantes;
verum quo ad periculum sive ligamen animae nulla maior re-
peritur'.[51] A little later when discussing the restrictions placed
by papal authority on the power to absolve from ecclesiastical
censures, he cites and rejects a number of views proposed by
others and then gives his own opinion, which throws some light
on what he thought was the function of such penalties:

> Dic quod haec est ratio: remissio, quamvis favorabilis, ideo
> restringitur ne vilescat ecclesiastica iurisdictio, et ne poeniten-
> tiae satisfactio enervetur. ... Excommunicatio vero ideo dila-
> tatur ut is qui in factum damnatum scienter et pertinaciter
> incidit, maxime in eo quo delinquit puniatur; nec enim debent
> remanere maleficia impunita.[52]

This is an idea to which Hostiensis returns on a number of
occasions, and it shows that he thought there should be a vin-
dicative aspect to the penal law as well as a corrective one.
Penalties, however, must be administered only according to the
law and due process is to be observed.

It will be remembered from the discussion of the duties
of those holding posts of authority in the Church that Hostiensis
stressed their duty to eradicate abuses from the diocese and
punish delinquents. The bishop has to perform the role of
watchman and see that negligence in the clergy does not go
unpunished and unreformed. He has to provide correction and
instruction and encourage moral reform.[53] Papal legates are
also instructed to see that reform is carried out in their province.[54] It is also one of the duties listed for the archdeacon
that he assist the bishop in carrying out correction and reform,
— 'est quidem corrigere et reformare'.[55] Regular canonical visi-

---

[51] *Summa*, V, De sententia excommunicationis, n. 5.
[52] *Summa*, V, De sententia excommunicationis, n. 5.
[53] Cf. *Summa*, I, De electione et electi potestate, nn. 30-31.
[54] *Summa*, I, De officio legati, n. 3.
[55] *Summa*, I, De officio archidiaconi, n. 4.

tation was another means of carrying out programmes of reform in the Church and this is why Hostiensis insisted so strongly on its being carried out carefully and conscientiously. It was important for the general welfare of the Church.[56] Such visitations should also be carried out in religious orders to see that the rule is observed, to get rid of abuses and suggest reform.[57]

Part of the reform programme of the Fourth Lateran Council consisted in the re-establishment of annual provincial councils and two of the conciliar canons are concerned with this. One of these reminds metropolitans of the obligation to hold such a council every year with their suffragan bishops for the purpose of reform. The other warns provincial councils to pay particular attention to the abuse by which bishops and chapters often appoint unworthy clerics to ecclesiastical benefices.[58] Hostiensis urges the observance of this legislation.[59]

Another canonical institution whose purpose was moral reform primarily was the 'denunciatio evangelica'. Mgr Lefebvre has published a study of this procedure in which he traces its history from the time of Gratian until the time of Hostiensis, who, he notes, brought a greater degree of clarity and order into the institution.[60] It has also been mentioned by Professor Kuttner as yet another instance of the spiritual concern which is characteristic of canon law:

> Another corollary of the spiritual aspect of ecclesiastical jurisdiction originated in the interpretation of the words of Christ, "If thy brother sin against thee, go and show him

---

[56] *Ibid.*

[57] The right to visitation was a very ancient canonical right. Cf. *Decretum*, C. 18, q. 2, cc. 16-17.

The Fourth Lateran Council imposed this duty on bishops. Const. 12, in singulis. It is interesting to compare the modern Code of Canon Law with what Hostiensis wrote on the subject. CIC 343:1 reads as follows: 'Ad sanam et orthodoxam doctrinam conservandam, bonos mores tuendos, pravos corrigendos, pacem, innocentiam, pietatem et disciplinam in populo et clero promovendam ceteraque pro ratione adiunctorum ad bonum religionis constituenda, tenentur Episcopi obligatione visitandae quotannis dioecesis vel ex toto vel ex parte, ita ut saltem singulis quinquenniis universam vel ipsi per se vel, si fuerint legitime impediti, per Vicarium Generalem aliumve lustrent'.

[58] Cf. X. V, 1, 25 (sicut olim); and X. III, 5, 29 (grave nimis). E. W. Kemp, *Counsel and Consent*, London, 1961, discusses these decrees.

[59] *Summa*, V, De Iudeis et Sarracenis, n. 5.

[60] C. Lefebvre, 'Contribution à l'étude des origines et du developpement de la *Denunciatio Evangelica* en droit canonique', in *Ephemerides Iuris Canonici*, 6 (1950), pp. 60-93. Cf. also P. Bellini, '*Denunciatio evangelica*

his fault ...; but if he do not listen to thee, take with thee
one or two more so that on the word of two or three witnesses
every word may be confirmed. And if he refuse to hear them,
appeal to the Church" (Mt 18:15-17). On the strength of this
text, medieval canon law gradually developed the equitable
procedure of *denunciatio evangelica*, as a remedy for the correction of faults, *ratione peccati*, without the solemnities normally required in canonical trials. [61]

Hostiensis expounds this institution in Book Five of the
Summa. It was an institution peculiar to the Church and it
served both for the emendation of the sinner and for the repression of evil within the Church. He defines it as follows:
'criminis alicuius apud iudicem sine inscriptione legitime facta
delatio, ad poenitentiam peragendam, vel aliam poenam legitime
imponendam'. [62] It differed from the normal procedure of
accusation in an important respect: 'Haec est differentia inter
denunciationem (sc. charitativam) et accusationem, quia in denunciatione attenditur emendatio fratris, in accusatione autem
punitio criminis'. Moreover, the person making such a denunciation had to be motivated by 'bonus zelus' and charity, and
possess the 'animus corrigendi et emendandi'. Hostiensis distinguishes between sins that are occult and those that are publicly known. 'Quando occultum est, non potest denuntiari crimen, nisi ad poenitentiam peragendam, et in hoc casu quilibet
Christianus admittitur'. [63] But there are a variety of *denuncia-
tiones* and these must be carefully distinguished from each other.
The strictly evangelical denunciation has as its aim the emendation of the delinquent and his soul's salvation. The procedure
is quite simple. The sinner is summoned before the judge and
both he and the person denouncing him are obliged to take an
oath to tell the truth. If the delinquent then confesses, 'cogetur
poenitentiam agere et satisfacere per censuram ecclesiae'. Similarly if he denies the accusation but it is proved by witnesses.
If, however, he cannot be convicted, 'et nullae probabiles coniec-
turae apparent, absolvi debet, et iniungi poenitentiam denun-
tianti, ex eo quod iniuste praesumitur denuntiasse'. [64] The other

---

e *denunciatio iudicialis privata*', in *Ephemerides Iuris Canonici*, 18 (1962),
pp. 152-210.
   [61] S. Kuttner, *Harmony from Dissonance*, Pennsylvania, 1960, p. 45.
   [62] *Summa*, V, De denunciatione, n. 1.
   [63] *Summa*, V, De denunciatione, n. 2.
   [64] *Summa*, V, De denunciatione, n. 3.

type of denunciation is called by Hostiensis *canonica et iudicialis*, and this involves temporal penalties, such as removal from one's benefice and the like. For this sort of denunciation strict legal procedure must be fulfilled, and the same rules which apply to those who may bring an accusation before the court apply here. The procedure too has to follow the same rules as other judicial processes; there must be the citation, the *contestatio litis*, and so on. Hostiensis also observes that there are severe penalties for detractors, including an action for damages, as well as degradation and excommunication. [65]

Enough has now been said to demonstrate how the law of the Church was regarded and used as an instrument of reform and a deterrent from crime. But there is one last point to be made before passing on to the examination of the laws against heresy. This concerns the specifically deterrent nature of a number of penalties. When explaining what he meant by equity Hostiensis, as will be recalled, also discusses the meaning of *rigor iuris*. [66] The phrase, he tells us, could be used to describe an excessive severity in a law whose purpose is primarily to act as a deterrent from crime; and he instances the law which prohibited the granting of communion to anyone who brought false accusations against the clergy. Communion was not even to be granted to such a criminal on his death-bed. Such severity, however, was included in the law to frighten people from committing such a crime; it was meant *ad terrorem*, and Hostiensis states that he did not think it should normally be observed in practice, — 'sed iste rigor non est servandus nisi ubi timetur exemplum mali'. This idea of extremely harsh penalties being used as a threat to frighten prospective criminals, while it was generally accepted that they would not really be used in earnest, is an important factor that must be borne in mind when medieval penal law is being considered. What was written down in the law cannot always be taken as a completely reliable guide to what in fact happened in the courts. A number of laws were dead letters which had arisen out of some panic measures against particular dangers but which had never really been put into execution. Hostiensis' statement that the *rigor iuris* should not normally be observed in practice is perhaps a better source of information about court practice than the written law by itself. And this goes some way towards mitigating the charge of bar-

---

65 *Summa, ibid.*
66 Cf. *Summa*, V, De dispensationibus, n. 1.

barity against medieval penal law in the Church. However, the
deterrent element in penal law was common and Hostiensis
frequently refers to it. A public sinner, for instance, may be
avoided by the faithful, 'ad hoc ut rubore confusus retrahatur
a peccato et caeteri terreantur'. [67] The ecclesiastical judge 'crimine crescente debet maiorem [poenam] imponere ad terrorem'. [68] There may even be occasions when it would be right
to deny Christian burial to a criminal, even although he had
repented at the last minute and had received Viaticum. This
would be done, states Hostiensis, 'ad terrorem et propter in-
obedientiam et contumaciam suam in qua longo tempore fuit'. [69]
Similarly, the harsh penalties of public flogging and deportation
were fulminated against calumniators and false denouncers 'ad
terrorem' and 'causa exempli ... ut caeteri terreantur'. [70] This
desire to warn the faithful against the danger of being led into
sin and also to win back the criminal himself is an important
element in the use of penal law as a deterrent and as a means
of reforming Christian life. The main purpose, too, of the penalty of excommunication was to bring the sinner to his senses
and make him repent of his sins and do penance. It was, as
Hostiensis stresses, a medicinal penalty — 'nam et excommunicatio medicinalis est, non mortalis'. [71] This was also the purpose behind the handing over of excommunicates to the secular
arm. The idea was that if the fear of damnation was not sufficient to bring the criminal to repentance, then the fear of
imprisonment and temporal penalties would be more successful.
Nowhere is the more clearly to be seen than in the legislation
against heresy; and this must now be examined.

3. *The Deterrent against Heresy*

The medieval conviction that the salvation of souls should
be the primary criterion in all ecclesiastical legislation has already been discussed at the beginning of this chapter, and it
has been shown that the phrase, *salus animarum suprema lex*,
expressed a principle whose influence is evident throughout the
whole of the *Summa Aurea* of Hostiensis. It is just such a conviction that leads him to argue forcefully that a crusade can

---

[67] *Summa*, III, De cohabitatione clericorum et mulierum, n. 6.
[68] *Summa*, V, De poenis raptorum corporum, n. 2.
[69] *Summa*, V, De poenis raptorum corporum, n. 3.
[70] *Summa*, V, De calumniatoribus, n. 11.
[71] *Summa*, V, De sagittariis et balistariis, n. 2.

be proclaimed against schismatics and disobedient Catholics as well as against Saracens and heretics. He puts this view forward even although there is no express sanction for it in the law. The argument that he puts forward in defence of this view is a deeply religious one: 'Nec enim filius Dei in mundum venit, nec crucem subiit ut acquireret terram, sed ut captivos redimeret et peccatores ad poenitentiam revocaret'.[72] Hostiensis views the whole problem as a case of removing obstacles to the redemption and salvation of mankind. A man's soul is more precious than any other possession — 'pretiosior est anima quam res' — more precious even than life itself; and it is with a man's soul that canon law is primarily concerned.[73] Moreover, since Hostiensis, along with most of his contemporaries, makes little or no allowance for the possibility of good faith in heretics or schismatics, he firmly believes that it is in the best interests of these men themselves that they should be compelled by the severest penalties available to return to the one true Church, the haven of salvation, and abandon their self-willed and sinful life. It is the desire for the eternal salvation of these erring Christians that motivates the taking up of arms in a crusade against them. These poor misguided souls must be constrained by the law to return to the Church.

The large body of canonical legislation enacted in the twelfth and thirteenth centuries against heresy is the most striking example of canon law being used as a deterrent and an instrument of reform. *Causa* 24 of the *Decretum* is devoted to heresy, and it contains three *quaestiones* and almost ninety canons; there are also sixteen canons of anti-heretical legislation in the *Decretales*, including the important decretals, *Ad abolendam* and *Vergentis in senium*, as well as the decree of the Fourth Lateran Council. The background to this severe legislation was the deep conviction, which has just been mentioned, that heresy constituted one of the greatest dangers to salvation against which the Church had a strict duty to protect the faithful in every possible way. It was also partly due to the particular nature of the predominant heresies of the period, which were regarded

---

[72] *Summa*, III, De voto et voti redemptione, n. 19. Cf. M. Villey, *La Croisade*, Paris, 1942, pp. 256-262, where it is shown how Hostiensis constructed his crusade theory on the basis of customary law. Villey describes Hostiensis as 'the father of the juridical theory of the Crusade' (p. 256). Cf. J. Brundage, 'The Votive Obligations of Crusaders', in *Traditio*, 24 (1968), pp. 117-118.

[73] Cf. *Summa*, III, De sepulturis, n. 8-9.

as an attack not only on the Catholic faith but also on the very foundations of society as it was then constituted; Catharism, for instance, was seen as a threat to the structure of civilised society, which if allowed to develop would lead to general anarchy. Added to this, of course, was the general refusal to allow for good faith in heretics. Not much respect was then accorded to what are now revered as the rights of the individual conscience. Such intolerance had a long history in the Church prior to the Middle Ages, and this is worth glancing at.

'Credere non potest homo nisi volens'.[74] In this formula, which has often since been used in defence of religious toleration, St Augustine summed up the Christian teaching that it is only through personal conviction, and not under compulsion, that anyone can come to true faith in Christ. Conscious of his own past errors and of the difficulties he had experienced in extricating himself from these, Augustine was at first naturally inclined to adopt a policy of patient understanding in dealing with heretics. 'No, I cannot be harsh with you', he wrote to the Manichaeans in 397, 'I must now bear with you as others bore with me then; I have to treat you with as much patience as I received from my friends when I myself wandered astray in a blind and senseless manner concerning that teaching of yours'.[75] A similar refusal to force people into the Church appears also in a letter to the Donatist bishop, Maximinus, in which he advocates calm and peaceful discussion, with the Scriptures as their common authority. Yet it is notorious that Augustine came to abandon this tolerant and magnanimous approach. Later ages have seen him as the doctor of 'compelle intrare' and regarded him as the spiritual father of the Inquisition. What brought about this remarkable change?

Augustine did in fact for years believe in the efficacy of gentle means to bring back heretics to the Church, even when urged to more violent measures by his colleagues in North Africa. Gradually, however, as the controversy with the Donatists dragged on and civil violence and disorder increased, he came to change his mind. Peace had to be restored somehow; the faithful had to be protected from the hooliganism of roving bands of Circumcelliones. Forceful intervention by the civil

---

[74] *In Joannem*, XXVI, 2; (P. L. 35, 1607); cf. also, P. L. 44, 235; 33, 985. For what follows I am indebted to Joseph Lecler, *Histoire de la Tolérance au Siècle de la Réforme*, Paris, 1955, vol. I, pp. 65-126.

[75] P. L. 42, 174-175; (cited by Lecler, *op. cit.*, p. 82).

authorities seemed to be the only effective way of excising what was seen as a cancerous growth in the African Church. So, against all his natural instincts, Augustine came to the conclusion that he ought to give positive support to the imperial legislation which ranged heresy among the civil crimes of *laesae maiestatis*. In several of his letters he has explained this change of mind. A certain amount of constraint, he argued, is a good thing because it makes the heretic reflect and, in the face of severe physical penalties, reconsider his position. He quotes the experience of a number of people who had in fact been reconverted in this way and were grateful for it afterwards.

> We did not realise, they said, that this was the truth and we had no desire to learn it; but fear made us reconsider the matter and we recognised it. We give thanks to God for having pierced our negligence with the sting of fear. [76]

Augustine also turned to the Bible for support and he quoted a number of passages from the Old and the New Testaments to back up the imperial legislation. What is particularly interesting for the understanding of the later medieval mentality is the use that he made of the phrase, 'compelle intrare', from the parable of the supper in St Luke's Gospel (Lk 14:23). Augustine proposed quite a novel interpretation of this parable, and in so doing he turned it into a proof-text for all future defenders of the Inquisition. [77] He explains the parable as follows:

> Those who came of their own accord represent perfect obedience; those that were compelled represent suppressed disobedience ... That is why if the Church, by the power God has bestowed on it, at the appropriate time and with the assistance of pious and faithful kings, forces those that are found in the highways and hedges, (that is to say, in schism and heresy), to come in, let them not complain of being forced, but let them rather consider where they are being compelled to go. The Lord's banquet is the unity of the body of Christ, not only in the sacrament of the altar, but also in the abode of peace. Of the Donatists, however, we can say that no one is

---

[76] *Retractationes*, II, 5; (P. L. 32, 632); J. Lecler, *op. cit.*, p. 86.

[77] Cf. J. Schmidt's comment on this passage: 'Augustinus hat als erster in folgenschwerer Missdeutung dieses Sinnes ("compelle intrare") hier die biblische Grundlage für die Erlaubtheit von Gewaltmassnahmen gegenüber Ketzern gefunden, wodurch er der geistige Vater der Inquisition geworden ist'. *Das Evangelium nach Lukas*, Regensburg, 1951, p. 200.

forced by them to what is good, but that all who are compelled
by them are driven to what is evil. [78]

This was the first time that the supper parable had been
put to such use, and although the Gospel text itself and the
majority of the patristic commentaries on it do not permit such
an interpretation, yet Augustine's invocation of 'compelle intrare'
in favour of the use of physical compulsion against heretics was
to have a long and influential history. Future zealots for the
faith were to take it as their guide. A few even extended it to
cover pagans as well, but these were exceptional and isolated
cases. [79] In the twelfth and thirteenth centuries political and
religious conditions had led to the development of the idea of
the *Respublica Christiana*, the City of God, in which all the
citizens were bound together in the unity of the one faith. *Ecclesia* and *imperium* were but different aspects of the one reality. It is this that explains the relatively tolerant attitude towards Jews and infidels and the utter intolerance of any kind
of heresy. The militant expansion of Islam had created within
Christendom an atmosphere of siege, and it was not unnatural
that the crusading spirit should look upon heretics as a sort
of fifth column within the city walls. A point of view which
becomes even more intelligible when one considers the nature
of the dominant medieval heresy of Catharism and its violently
anti-social implications. It was a view too which was shared
by both civil and ecclesiastical authorities. This is the background that must be kept in mind in examining the canonical
legislation against heresy. It also throws some light on St
Thomas's attitude to the problem. For him 'compelle intrare'
had become 'compelle remanere'. In his treatment of tolerance
he makes a sharp distinction between pagans and Jews on the
one hand, who had never accepted the Catholic faith, and heretics
on the other, who have abandoned the true faith. Pagans and
Jews, states St Thomas,

> nullo modo sunt ad fidem compellendi ut ipsi credant; quia
> credere voluntatis est ... Alii vero sunt infideles, qui quandoque
> fidem susceperunt, et eam profitentur, sicut haeretici, et qui-

---

[78] Epist. 185, 24; (P. L., 33, 804).
[79] Cf., for example, Bruno of Querfurt, who in 1018 urged the German
king to bring about the conversion of the pagans by force of arms,
(Lecler, *op. cit.*, pp. 100-101).

cumque apostatae; et tales sunt etiam *corporaliter compellendi,*
ut impleant quod promiserunt. [80]

And one of his proof-texts here is the 'compelle intrare' of the
supper parable in St Luke's Gospel. To accept the faith in
the first instance, he admits, is a matter of the free will, but
to remain true to the faith once it has in fact been accepted is
a matter of necessity.   Hence the authorities are entitled to
make use of physical compulsion. He agrees with St Augustine
in holding that the parable of the tares does not forbid the
weeding out of obvious evils from the Church, provided there
is no real danger of being mistaken. But he goes far beyond
the position of Augustine when he supports the infliction of
capital punishment for heresy, as he does in the *Summa Theologica*:

> Ex parte quidem ipsorum est peccatum, per quod meruerunt
> non solum ab Ecclesia per excommunicationem separari, sed
> etiam per mortem a mundo excludi; multo enim gravius est
> corrumpere fidem, per quam est animae vita, quam falsare
> pecuniam, per quam temporali vitae subvenitur. [81]

During the patristic period the death-penalty for heresy was
almost universally condemned, and it was due to the influence
of Church leaders that the more severe imperial laws against
heresy were not carried into effect, but remained primarily as
threats. [82]   This was also true as late as the twelfth century.
The view of St Thomas, just quoted, shows how the atmosphere
had changed by the middle of the thirteenth century. 'Compelle
intrare' had by then become one of the standard weapons in
the Inquisitorial armoury and it was to be used for many centuries still by Catholic and Protestant alike in support of policies
of intolerance and suppression.
     The views of such influential theologians as Augustine and
Aquinas have been mentioned here in order to give some illustration of the theological thinking that lay behind the canonical
legislation against heretics in the Middle Ages. The policy of
suppression was not an invention of the canonists. It was sup-

---

[80] 2a 2ae, q. 10, 8.
[81] 2a 2ae, q. 11, 3; cited in Lecler, *op. cit.*, pp. 110-112.
[82] Cf. M. Bévenot, SJ, 'The Inquisition and its Antecedents, II', in
Heythrop Journal, 1966, pp. 381-393; especially pp. 382-384.

ported by the vast majority of Christians, both clergy and laity, and regarded as essential for the welfare of both Church and State. While a great many opposed the use of the death-penalty, there were few who were averse to the use of coercive measures, such as fines and imprisonment, to deter men from heresy and protect the Church. As has been seen, it was common practice to attach canonical penalties to all kinds of crimes in order to protect the purity of the faith and deter men from evil. Heresy, as an aberration from the true faith, was looked upon as an attack on God's revelation and as such it came to be looked upon as a more serious crime than treason. Strenuous measures were considered necessary to preserve the faithful from such contamination. Hence the stern measures that were enacted against heresy in the twelfth century. Both the Second and the Third Lateran Councils passed anti-heretical legislation, ordering the prosecution of heretics and stressing the duty of secular rulers to assist in the extermination of heresy from their territories. The policy of systematic investigation and repression was further developed by Pope Lucius III at the Council of Verona in 1184, when, in agreement with the Emperor Frederick Barbarossa, he promulgated the constitution, *Ad abolendam* (X, V, 7,9). This laid down severe penalties for heresy and enjoined on bishops the duty of visiting their diocese regularly and searching out all who were suspected of heresy. Suspects and accused had to clear themselves on oath and if they refused to do so they would be convicted of heresy, excommunicated and handed over to the secular authority to be punished 'debita animadversione'. Civil authorities were obliged to take an oath to assist the bishop in carrying out these duties, and if they refused to do so they were to be deprived of their office and excommunicated. Nor did papal exemption obtain in charges concerning heresy.

Fifteen years later Innocent III felt that since, in spite of previous firm legislation, the cancer of heresy was continuing to spread, even more severe measures were called for. So, in 1199, he issued *Vergentis in senium*. This confirmed the previous measures, but it went a bit further in that it drew a clear parallel between heresy and treason and stated that the same penalty should be inflicted for both these crimes; and it extended these penalties to the children of heretics whether they were orthodox Catholics or not. The severity of the penalties enjoined by this papal constitution was clearly derived from a harsh imperial measure of the late fourth century, — the constitution 'Quisquis' — which had been an emergency measure to meet a particular crisis, and which in fact does not seem to have been put into effect, though, of course, it was included in the *Codex*. [83] That the sanctions were adopted from the Roman law is indicated by the wording of the papal decree:

> Quum enim secundum legitimas sanctiones, reis laesae maiestatis punitis capite, bona confiscentur eorum, filiis suis vita solummodo ex misericordia conservata: quanto magis, qui aberrantes in fide Domini Dei filium Iesum Christum offendunt, a capite nostro, quod est Christus, ecclesiastica debent districtione praecidi, et bonis temporalibus spoliari, quum longe sit gravius aeternam quam temporalem laedere maiestatem? [84]

Innocent III does not stipulate the death-penalty for heresy; 'ecclesiastica districtione' obviously refers to the penalty of excommunication. But on the matter of the disinheritance of the children the papal decree goes further than the imperial legislation, since it enjoins that not even orthodox Catholic children are to be allowed to inherit, — 'cuiusdam miserationis praetextu'. [85] Roman law, on the other hand, did permit the or-

---

[83] X, 5,7,10 (Vergentis in senium). Cf. *Codex* 9,8,5 *Quisquis*. This was promulgated in 397 as an emergency measure because of certain conspiracies that had been discovered against the imperial entourage. It is a particularly savage piece of legislation, issued in a moment of panic. Those condemned under it were considered guilty of treason, sentenced to death, and had their property confiscated; even their children were to be deprived of their inheritance and excluded from any office in the State. For a discussion of this law and its relation to *Vergentis in senium*, cf. M. Bévenot, SJ, 'The Inquisition and Its Antecedents, III', *Heythrop Journal*, 8 (1967), pp. 61-62. Also, W. Ullmann, 'The Significance of Innocent III's Decretal "Vergentis" ', in *Etudes d'histoire du droit canonique dédiées à Gabriel Le Bras*, vol. I, pp. 729-741.

[84] X. 5. 7. 10 (Vergentis in senium).

[85] Professor Ullmann is severely critical of this harsh legislation. ' However much Innocent himself may have stressed that the descendants were to suffer merely in a temporal manner, the fact remains that even only a temporal punishment was a severe enough penalty. This is a standpoint which strikes some harsh and discordant notes in those who considered the Roman Church as the *sedes iustitiae*. Whether one views the assistance which Roman law rendered to canon law and to the papacy favourably or unfavourably, the stark and incontrovertible fact remains that by using the juristic category of the Roman *crimen laesae maiestatis* Innocent adopted — and from his own contemporary point of view he was indubitably correct in so doing — the inhuman and very late Roman law sanctions concerning the descendants and thereby began a development in criminal law in the thirteenth century

thodox children of condemned heretics to succeed to their inheritance. [86] This contradiction between the Roman law and
canon law led, as will be seen shortly, to a controversy among
later canonists. *Vergentis in senium* also forbade lawyers to
assist heretics in any way under pain of *infamia* and deprivation of office.

All this very severe legislation was confirmed by the Fourth
Lateran Council, but neither Innocent III nor the Council had
advocated the death-penalty for heresy. Fines, confiscation of
property, disinheritance of heirs, imprisonment and exile had
all been permitted by the Church, but that was as far as it
went. The last step was taken by the Emperor Frederick II
when in 1224 he decreed that those convicted of heresy in certain
of his territories were to be burnt alive. [87] This was later accepted by Pope Gregory IX, and in 1231 he decreed that life
imprisonment should be the penalty for repentant heretics, —
'damnati vero per ecclesiam saeculari iudicio relinquantur, animadversione debita puniendi, clericis prius a suis ordinibus de-

---

which extended this deterrent of punishing descendants to a number
of other offences. It is one of the great legal-historical paradoxes that
the thirteenth century on the one hand witnessed the height of medieval
jurisprudential thought, and yet on the other hand also witnessed
the adoption of such deterrents which cannot be justified by any juristic
principle'. W. Ullmann, 'The Significance of Innocent III's Decretal
Vergentis', *op. cit.*, p. 741. Ullmann also points out that these measures
run counter to a canonical principle which Innocent himself claimed to
respect. In a letter written in the same year in which *Vergentis* was
promulgated, the pope expressed concern for the protection of innocent
persons: '... sollicite debet attendere ne vel damnet innoxios vel noxios
absolvet. Non est nostrae intentionis innoxios cum nocentibus condemna-
re'. Ullmann, *op. cit.*, p. 741. It would appear, however, that Innocent
himself did not observe this part of his own decree and did in fact
allow sons of convicted heretics to inherit. Cf. M. Bévenot, *op. cit.*,
pp. 65-66. Perhaps this is but another example of strict penalties being
used *ad terrorem*, — a threat which was not really meant to be put
into effect!

[86] Cf. Cod. I. 5, 19: 'Cognovimus multos esse orthodoxos liberos, quibus nec pater nec mater orthodoxae sunt religionis, et ideo sancimus,
non tantum in casu, ubi alter orthodoxae religionis est, sed etiam in
his casibus, in quibus uterque parens alienae sectae sit, id est pater
et mater, ii tantum liberi ad eorum successionem sive ex testamentis
sive ex ab intestato vocentur et donationes seu alias liberalitates ab his
accipere possint, qui orthodoxorum venerabili nomine sunt decorati'.
Cf. also Cod. I, 5, 15.

[87] Cf. M. Bévenot, SJ, 'The Inquisition and Its Antecedents, III', in
Heythrop Journal, 8 (1967), pp. 66-67.

gradatis'.[88] In 1231, however, it was quite clear that the *debita animadversio* meant burning at the stake. By appointing special envoys to ensure that his anti-heretical legislation was carried out in various parts of the Church, Gregory IX also established the Inquisition, empowering judges delegated by himself to search out and condemn heretics. The process was completed by Pope Innocent IV who, in 1252, made the imperial constitutions applicable throughout the Church, and by the bull, *Ad extirpanda*, he allowed civil authorities to force heretics under torture to confess their error and denounce their accomplices, — although he did stipulate that there should be no loss of limb or danger of death in the torture used.

How effective all this legislation was and how it can really be justified on Christian principles is beyond the scope of this study. How much of it was meant to be carried out to the letter remains perhaps a matter of dispute. What there can be no doubt about is that we have here a clear example of canon law being used as a deterrent from evil. Most of the legislation that has just been discussed was certainly intended to frighten the faithful against the danger of being led into heresy and also to compel the heretics themselves to come to their senses and repent. It is a classic example of the law being used as a deterrent and as an instrument of reform. And all of it was in force by the time that Hostiensis published his *Summa Aurea* in 1253.

It is quite clear from the *Summa* that Hostiensis shared the common conviction about the evils of heresy and that he accepted the severe legislation that had been enacted against it. Drastic measures were justified against such an evil, — 'ut metu poenae mali boni ... fiant'. His treatment of heretics in Book Five is simply a résumée of the anti-heretical legislation that has just been outlined and it reveals how important he thought it was that the law should do all it could to stamp out heresy. 'Et quia inter solicitudines nostras illa debet esse praecipua, ut vulpeculas, id est haereticos qui latent ad modum vulpeculae, capiamus'.[89] He draws attention to the wide range of meaning that the word, heretic, could have in the language of his time.

---

[88] Decree, *Excommunicamus*, X, 5, 7, 14.

[89] *Summa*, V, De haereticis, n. 1; the phrase about vulpeculae is an echo of an expression used in the papal decretals and is, of course, an allusion to the Canticle of Canticles, 2:5 — 'Capite nobis vulpes parvulos quae demoliuntur vineas'.

A Christian who entertains any doubts about the faith could be called a heretic; so could an infidel. A person guilty of simony could also come under the term, as well as an excommunicated Christian, — 'nam qui non est membrum ecclesiae haereticus iudicatur'. Similarly, anyone who distorted the meaning of sacred Scripture could be called a heretic, even although he did not leave the Church. According to the strict meaning of the word, however, a heretic was one who differed from the Roman Church in his interpretation of the articles of faith:

> sed stricto modo dicitur haereticus qui aliter sentit de articulis fidei quam Romana ecclesia, et qui non recipiunt quattuor concilia ... Item de eucharistia, poenitentia, matrimonio, et aliis sacramentis ecclesiae, non est aliter sentiendum quam Romana ecclesia sentiat, nec docendum. [90]

He points out that even a slight deviation from accepted teaching is enough to justify the charge of heresy: 'Notandum est quod haereticus deprehenditur etiam is qui levi saltem argumento a iudicio catholicae religionis et tramite, sive a fide catholica detegitur deviare'. Anyone who dares to oppose the Church's teaching in such a manner is to be excommunicated, — 'perpetuo vinculo anathematis innodati', and he refers to the legislation of Pope Innocent III, 'pater iuris divini canonici et humani'. For Hostiensis the unity of the Church was of primary importance, and there could never be any justification for leaving or separating oneself from this unity of the one true faith that was to be found within the Catholic Church.

Heresy is to be combatted by the procedures of accusation, inquisition and denunciation, and Hostiensis refers his reader to earlier *tituli* in the *Summa* for a detailed exposition of each of these procedures. He draws attention to the inquisitorial duty that had been enjoined upon all bishops and archbishops by the Lateran Council to search out all those suspect of heresy within their territories:

> Ut quilibet per se vel archidiaconum suum, vel alias honestas idoneasque personas, bis aut saltem semel in anno propriam parochiam circumeat in qua fama est haereticos habitare; et ibi tres vel duos boni testimonii viros, vel etiam totam viciniam, si expedire viderit, iurare compellat quod si quis haere-

---

[90] *Summa*, V, De haereticis, n. 1.

ticos ibidem scierit vel aliquos occulta conventicula celebran-
tes, quare habentur suspecti ... [91]

They are to be asked to reveal to the bishop the names of
any who have given any grounds for suspicion by their way
of life — 'a communi conversatione fidelium, ita et moribus
dissidentes, id est discrepantes'. If anyone refuses to clear himself on oath when ordered to do so by the bishop, he is to be
canonically punished. But if a man confesses his error and
repents he should be treated mercifully by the bishop who
should impose upon him a salutary penance. If, however, he
denies the charge and is then convicted he is to be condemned
by the ecclesiastical judge and left to be punished in a fitting
manner by the secular power.

Hostiensis clearly thought that this legislation should be
put into effect and that all forms of heresy should be hounded
down and destroyed. To start an inquiry even slight deviations
from normal behaviour can be sufficient. All that is needed is
a probable indication, one that can easily be noticed. A man,
for instance, who refuses to take oaths, regarding this as a
sinful practice, could be convicted of being a Waldensian. Again,
if a person has frequent dealings or is on familiar terms with
a known heretic then it should be taken as not unlikely that
he himself is also guilty of heresy; if he is a cleric he should
be suspended from his post. He may be allowed to go free
if he agrees publicly in his preaching to reject the heretics he
had befriended. Similar treatment is to be meted out to all
who encourage or defend heretics. No one, however, should
be condemned if he is willing to renounce or deny the heresy
and promise obedience to the Church, and the judge should
use his discretion in the matter and consider carefully all the
circumstances of the case. [92]

Hostiensis emphasises that it is the ecclesiastical authority
that is principally competent to judge the crime of heresy, while
it is the duty of secular authorities to put into effect the penalties laid down by the state after the Church has delivered
her judgment. Secular authorities are obliged to swear publicly that they will do their best to exterminate heretics from
their territory and that they will cooperate with ecclesiastical

---

[91] *Summa*, V, De haereticis, n. 3, expounding X. 5.7,13 Excommunicamus itaque.
[92] *Summa*, V, De haereticis, n. 3.

judges in this matter when asked to do so. It is, after all,
an important part of the duty of Christian rulers to suppress
heresy and see that Christian virtues are fostered in the territories under their charge — 'totum studium imperatoris est ut
subditi Deum recognoscant et honeste vivant'. [93] They should
not meddle in ecclesiastical affairs nor attack the Church's jurisdiction. In fact the secular judge has to take an oath not to
oppose the Catholic faith nor to permit others to do so. If a
secular ruler refuses to take the oath to assist the Church
against heresy he should be deprived of his office. If he treats
with contempts the Church's warnings in this matter, he is to
be excommunicated by the metropolitan and the other bishops
of the province. If, even then, he refuses to yield, and persists
in his excommunication for a year, the case is to be referred
to the pope who at the end of a year will declare the vassals
of the guilty man freed from their oath of allegiance and will
allow his territory to be taken over by Catholics. If the Church
does hand the heretic over to the secular arm the military are
to confiscate all the property of the heretic, — 'quia secundum
Isidorum et Augustinum et alios sanctos, et ipsa bona nullo
iure possunt haeretici possidere'. They cannot claim to have a
natural right, because according to the natural law all property
is held in common. Nor can they be said to have a right, *iure
divino*, as is clear from the saying of Christ: 'auferetur a vobis
regnum et debitur genti facienti fructum eius'. [94] It will be
noticed, of course, that all this is simply a summary of the
papal anti-heretical decretals of the late twelfth and early thirteenth centuries. Would it be lawful for Catholics to proceed
to despoil heretics on their own authority without waiting for
official action from the Church? Hostiensis thinks that this
would not be unlawful, but he advises against it because it
could lead to private greed, spitefulness and revenge. If a
bishop is negligent in the business of exterminating heresy he
should be deposed and replaced by another who will prove
more effective in carrying out the commands of the Church.

Hostiensis goes on to discuss the penalties that are to be
inflicted for the crime of heresy. [95] These ought to be severe,
he argues, because heresy is a public crime which causes injury
to the whole state since it attacks divine religion, — 'quia longe

[93] *Ibid.*, n. 5.
[94] *Summa*, V, De haereticis, n. 5.
[95] *Summa*, V, De haereticis, nn. 8-11.

gravius est divinam quam temporalem offendere maiestatem' —
a direct reference to *Vergentis in senium* of Innocent III.   There
will, of course, be different penalties for different types of heresy.
'Quod autem ad poenas pertinet, notandum est quod leges distin-
guunt inter haereticos, nam quidam sunt qui turpia praedicant
et in maximo sunt errore, ut Manichaei'.   Such men may not
enter into legal contracts with others nor may they bequeath
their property to others after their death.   What about orthodox
descendants?   Are they too to be disinherited?   As has already
been noticed, Innocent III's decretal, *Vergentis in senium*, deprived even Catholic children of the right to inherit from a
heretical parent whereas the imperial legislation was milder and
did allow orthodox children to retain the right to their inheritance.   There was a variety of views among canonists on the
matter.

> Vel dicatur quod bona haereticorum devolventur ad agnatos
> vel cognatos orthodoxos; nec debet dici secundum Goffredum
> quod corrigantur leges per decretum [*Vergentis*], nisi in terris
> quae temporaliter subsunt iurisdictioni Romanae ecclesiae, ut
> in principio decreti innuitur manifeste. Nam *leges maiori aequi-*
> *tate nituntur quam decretum,* nec puniendus filius pro patre, ...
> et poena suos debet tenere authores.

Those who put forward this point of view argue that the Church
should demonstrate its love for all men and should close its
heart to no one.   'Ergo aequitas legum praeferenda est in re-
stricto et rigore canonico'.   Nor should the objection be raised
that in the case of the crime of *laesae maiestatis*, it is not only
the criminal himself who is included in the penalties but also
his heirs; — 'quia ibi timuerunt leges ne filii essent paterni
criminis imitatores'.   This argument can be discounted if it
is a known fact that the children of the convicted heretic are
orthodox Catholics.   This was one point of view but it was
not universally accepted.   Other canonists argued that the *leges*
are to be interpreted and corrected in accordance with the papal
decretal, *Vergentis*.   This clearly stipulates that the sons of
heretics are to be disinherited in the same way as the sons of
those who have been convicted of treason.   Nor, the argument
continues, should a judge allow pity to distract him from his
duty in this matter:

> nec moveat te filiorum exhaeredationis misericordia, quia (as
> Innocent III declares in his decretal) in multis casibus filii

etiam secundum divinum iudicium corporaliter puniuntur ...;
et secundum canonicas sanctiones aliquando fertur ultio non
solum in authores scoeleris, sed etiam in progenies damna-
torum. ... Et est ratio, quia forte pater magis verebitur ex-
haeredationem filii quam propriam.

Which of these two views does Hostiensis himself support?
He tries to save something from each opinion by proposing that
the *leges* should be allowed to prevail over the decretal, *Vergentis*, in cases where the heretic dies before the accusation or
the denunciation was made against him, because then the crime
would have been occult. The second, and harsher, view should,
however, according to the strict letter of the law, be followed
in those instances where the heretic is publicly accused and
condemned in his lifetime. Yet even in such cases, thinks
Hostiensis, the more lenient view may be followed in practice,
provided that it is made perfectly clear that this leniency is
due to the mercy of the authorities and cannot be claimed as
a right in law. In this way, then, without having to reject the
harsh legislation of Innocent III, Hostiensis manages to mitigate
its severity and reach a more equitable solution in practice.

He does, however, seem quite content to accept the heretic's
deprivation of a number of legal rights and remedies. Heretics
may not be allowed to give evidence against orthodox Catholics,
teachers of heresy are to be deported, those who assemble to
spread heresy are liable to lose their property, or be fined or
beaten. Hostiensis accepts all these harsh measures because
in his view all heretics are heading straight for damnation.
Hence they deserve to be anathematised and to undergo temporal penalties as soon as they have been found guilty. If they
are clerics they are to be degraded and receive due punishment
from the state.

But what exactly is meant by this handing over to the
secular arm? Some say that this means that the Church should
physically hand over the convicted person to the secular authorities. Hostiensis does not accept this understanding of
canon law, — 'iste pravus intellectus corrigendus est'. [96] The
Church may not hand over the heretic to the secular authority
because she has the serious duty of interceding for clemency
for him. The secular authority should therefore be present
at the ecclesiastical process and after this has been completed

---

[96] *Summa*, V, De haereticis, n. 9.

it is up to the state to take over. 'Debet tamen ecclesia *efficaciter* intercedere', so that the death-penalty, for example, is not carried out, even although the law does impose capital punishment for heresy. It will be recalled that in his guide for the prelate's examination of conscience, Hostiensis mentions that the bishop may not on any account encourage the infliction of the death-penalty. Some other canonists clearly thought that he should, but Hostiensis rejects this view very firmly: 'Hoc credo falsissimum, imo si imminet periculum debet *instare* quod citra mortem puniatur'.[97] He suggests the alternative of life imprisonment as a 'conveniens satisfactio' et 'ratio est quia si haberet liberum aditum et exitum, timendum esset ne alios corrumperet'.[98] He draws attention to the fact that vassals may be released from their oath of allegiance not only on account of the heresy of the lord himself but also if he neglects to clear his territory 'ab haeretica foeditate'. This is permissible, he argues, because an oath of fealty is taken on the implicit condition that the lord remains faithful to his Christian duties.

The next question to be discussed is how heretics should be reconciled with the Church. Such reconciliation should take place preferably before any condemnation or immediately after it; but if a period of time is allowed to elapse between a condemnation and an attempt at reconciliation then the case is to be referred to the pope. Hostiensis does insist that the Church should never close her heart to anyone, but he thinks that a reconciled heretic who later reverts to his old crime should be treated with great severity.[99] He goes on to discuss the penalties that may be incurred by those who aid and abet heretics in any way. Those who encourage heretics or help them or do business with them are excommunicated *ipso iure*. Advocates too are warned to be particularly careful in this matter since the penalties can be very severe. There are, of course, a number of exceptional cases where communication with excommunicates is permitted for various reasons.[100]

Canonical legislation against schismatics is the next topic for discussion. Schismatics too are liable to severe ecclesiastical penalties, 'ut sciant homines quam grave et quam detestabile

---

[97] *Summa*, V, De excessibus praelatorum et subditorum, n. 1.
[98] *Summa*, V, De haereticis, n. 9.
[99] *Summa*, V, De haereticis, n. 12.
[100] *Summa*, V, De haereticis, n. 13.

sit hoc crimen'. Grave penalties too are incurred by apostates and these can include confiscation of property. Where the apostates are clerics they are to be expelled from the city in the same way as heretics. They should not be allowed to remain in case they infect the healthy members of the flock of Christ. They may also be imprisoned 'quousque a tanta nequitia resipiscant'. Here again the aim of the penal law to act as a deterrent is clearly apparent. 'Et sic oderunt peccare boni virtutis amore, oderunt peccare mali formidine poenae'. [101] Hostiensis continues to maintain in all this that the main point of the penalty of excommunication is to bring the guilty persons back to the Church and to repentance for their crimes, — to startle them back to their senses. 'Nam et excommunicatio medicinalis est, non mortalis', as the *Decretum* teaches. [102]

The legislation against heresy, then, provides a particularly clear example of canon law being used 'ad terrorem' to reduce crime. It was meant to terrify Christians to mend their sinful ways and do penance. Heresy was numbered among the most serious crimes possible. It merited very special treatment 'propter periculum fidei' and 'propter immanitatem criminis'. So much so that even those who normally enjoyed certain privileges lost these, including that of papal exemption, if they were convicted of heresy. [103] Hostiensis shared the general intolerance of his age towards all forms of heresy. It was a plague that had to be suppressed by all the means that were available. The dogmatic and moral traditions of the Church had to be safeguarded at all costs. In a matter of such public interest the freedom of the individual could only take second place. In any case, Hostiensis, along with most of his contemporaries, could not really accept the possibility that a heretic might be acting in good faith. He was considered a criminal and treated as such and it was for the law to do what it could to bring him back to his senses.

The Church's anti-heretical legislation has here been discussed in some detail, not only because it forms a large and important part of medieval canon law, but also because it is the clearest example of the law of the Church being used as a deterrent. The extremely severe penalties enacted in the Middle Ages against heresy have been condemned by later ages as both

---

[101] *Summa*, V, De haereticis, n. 15.
[102] *Summa, ibid.;* cf. *Decretum*, C. 2, q. 1, c. 18 (from St Augustine).
[103] Cf. *Summa*, V, De privilegiis et excessibus privilegiatorum, n. 10.

unchristian and unreasonable. This is not the place to attempt an evaluation of the judgment of history on such legislation, but the study of the *Summa Aurea* does make clear the motivation which lay behind the medieval laws. Medieval Christendom was not the modern pluralist society and there was as yet little understanding of the liberty of the individual or of the possibility of good faith in anyone who might decide that he could no longer accept the teaching of the Catholic Church once he had accepted the faith. Such a person was considered either evil or deluded and in both cases it was thought to be in his own best interests that he be compelled to return to his senses and to the truth; he had also to be prevented from leading others astray. The penalties were harsh but, as Hostiensis emphasises, they were meant to warn the faithful against the danger of being led into heresy and to win back the heretic himself. The law was to be that 'medicina salutaris' and 'antidotum efficax animarum' that Hostiensis mentions in his conclusion. What was considered of primary importance was that the Christian life be fully lived, — 'hoc solum bene agitur, ut vita hominum corrigatur'. The medieval anti-heretical legislation does, however, exemplify in a most striking manner Hostiensis' seventh function of law, — 'ut metu poenae mali boni, et boni meliores spe praemiorum fiant'.

CHAPTER SEVEN

SUMMARY AND EVALUATION

1. *Summary of the Results of the Investigation*

At this point, before going on to try to evaluate Hostiensis' teaching in the light of modern thought, it may be helpful to provide a brief summary of the results of the investigation. It has been shown that Hostiensis did not think that there was one single function which could be applied to the whole *corpus* of canonical legislation. Canon law was expected to fulfil a variety of functions.

The first function to be examined was that of making provision for security against violence and fraud and of promoting stability and concord within the Christian community. Examination of the *Summa Aurea* has shown how in practice Hostiensis thought that the law fulfilled this function. It was a constant preoccupation of canon law to guarantee the security of innocent people by offering them legal protection against violence, trickery and deceit of all kinds.

It has also been seen how the law tried to promote stability and concord through the clear delineation of areas of responsibility within the Church. It was for the law to clarify the juridical structure of the Church and afford protection against anything that would undermine or disrupt the ecclesiastical order. Hence the medieval respect for the hierarchical principle which was considered essential for the existence of true peace and concord. It is this that explains the care shown by Hostiensis in clarifying and defending the plenitude of papal power. The Church is the one body of Christ; therefore it can only have one head on earth, and this one head is obviously the pope, the Vicar of Christ. Hostiensis believed this conclusion was firmly rooted in Scripture and theology and that to question it was to undermine the whole structure of Christendom. There had to be one source of unity and one final court of appeal if peace was to be preserved and justice promoted

throughout Christendom. Hostiensis' enthusiasm over papal
prerogatives did at times lead him to strange exaggerations in
his language about the pope which give the impression that he
regarded secular rulers as mere servants of the papacy. Such
a view however of Hostiensis' teaching on papal supremacy is
inaccurate. He did think that the secular and the ecclesiastical
were two distinct jurisdictions which should cooperate with
each other for the good of Christendom as a whole and refrain
from meddling in each other's business. Only in exceptional
circumstances, when there seemed to be no other way of ensuring peace and harmony or of maintaining the rule of justice,
did he think that the papal plenitude of power should come
into play and make provision for justice and peace.

Within the Church, however, the absolute supremacy of
the pope is clearly depicted in the *Summa Aurea*. There is no
convincing evidence here of conciliarist tendencies. He fully
accepted and handed on the current canonistic teaching that
the bishops derived their authority from the pope, who called
them, — 'in partem sollicitudinis' — to share in the government
of the Church. He appears to be a solid supporter of the papal
centralization which had been developing with an ever increasing rapidity throughout his lifetime. By his plenitude of power
the pope can supply for any deficiencies in the law, convalidate
invalid transactions, and grant dispensations from all purely ecclesiastical legislation. Yet, in spite of occasional rhetorical
flourishes, Hostiensis did not regard the papal *plenitudo potestatis* as entirely unrestricted and unconditional. He thought
that it should not be used excessively but only when the good of
the Church demanded it. Moreover, it had to be used in harmony
with the faith and within the limits of the divine law.

It would, therefore, be a mistake to conclude from Hostiensis' defence of papal plenitude of power that he approved of
arbitrary or despotic government of any kind. On the contrary,
he insisted on the due observance of the whole juridical structure. Only through the proper observance of this hierarchical
structure would true peace and harmony be maintained throughout the Church. So he is careful to note how the law defines
and protects the competence of the local ordinary and of other
officials. He was not in favour of a one-man-rule either over
the universal Church or over particular Churches. He stoutly
defended the dignity of the college of cardinals and maintained
that they should share with the pope in the government of the
Church. A similar concern for collegial government is apparent

in his discussion of the duties of the local bishop. One of the faults that he draws attention to in the guide for the examination of the conscience of the bishop is precisely this failure to treat his clergy as colleagues. Both bishop and priests 'deberent enim ecclesiam Dei regere in communi'. A similar preoccupation lies behind his stress on the importance of cooperation between the bishop and his chapter. 'Vae sibi si de se solo nimis confidat'; so he should make a habit of taking counsel.

Examples have also been discussed of another function of law which is closely related to that of promoting order and security in the Church. This is the legal protection of both the spiritual and the material interests of the Church which had to be safeguarded against the harmful passions of men. Hence the numerous laws whose role it was to protect the Church against undue interference from the temporal authorities and from irresponsibility and negligence on the part of churchmen themselves. The good of the Church had always to be preferred to private advantage. Allied to this is the vast *corpus* of canon law which aimed at protecting the dignity, rights and privileges of the clergy. This also was out to promote a right order in the Church and preserve it from the harm that would result from negligent or incompetent ministers.

One area in which these spiritual interests of the Church are particularly involved is the administration of the sacraments. In a matter so closely related to the practical life of all Christians it was important that orthodoxy and unity were preserved. This was the aim of the canon law on the subject. Hostiensis' commentary on this legislation, as has been seen, forms a large part of the *Summa Aurea*. This is also one of the areas where the close connection between theology and canon law, which Hostiensis advocated, is most apparent. In his clear and authoritative presentation of the traditional teaching on the sacraments the canonist is in fact doing much to preserve and protect the Church's dogmatic traditions as well as providing the pastor with a reliable and practical guide.

The second function of law that Hostiensis mentions is the need to keep in check the recklessness of mankind and to protect innocent people from criminals. His third function was the provision of special protection for those who were the victims of cruelty, injustice or oppression of any kind. Examination of the *Summa* has shown that he thought these functions would be fulfilled if a real respect was fostered for

justice and equity and legal protection provided for the rights
of all men.

One of the most effective ways of protecting the rights
of the innocent and the oppressed is clearly to delineate such
rights by law and enact legal penalties against their infringement. Hostiensis indicates that medieval canon law attempted
to fulfil this function by specifying the duties of Church authorities towards the faithful entrusted to their charge. He insisted on the pastoral responsibility of these men and regularly
warned them that they would have to answer before God for
negligence in this important task. Nor was he content with
a purely juridical approach; he frequently includes moral exhortation in his advice to prelates and provides them with an
admirable guide towards good Christian government.

To guarantee protection, however, it was not enough for
the law to delineate rights and enact penalties against any
infringement of these. It had also to make provision for the
enforcement of rights through a recognised court procedure.
This is the point of Hostiensis' fourth and fifth functions of
law. It had to provide clear directives to ensure the fair completion of legal proceedings and afford legal remedies for victims
of injustice in the courts. Hostiensis has much to say about
the importance of due process of law. He thought that rights
could only be guaranteed if a clear and recognised court procedure was observed by judges who were concerned to see that
justice was done and whose integrity was above suspicion. He
insisted on the need to have clear proof of guilt before conviction and to provide every accused person with a fair opportunity for self-defence. There were, of course, abuses —
which Hostiensis mentions and condemns, — and there were
elements in the procedure which would not today be considered
in harmony with justice, — such as, the obligation put upon
the accused to answer every question of the judge, even if this
meant self-incrimination; but Hostiensis does reveal that there
was real concern for a fair trial and for due process as this
was then understood.

Finally, Hostiensis thought it part of the function of canon
law to provide both a deterrent from evil and an incentive
towards virtue. The fear of punishment was to deter men from
sin and the hope of reward was to spur them on to virtue. The
reward promised was eternal salvation, but the penalties could
include not only spiritual censures such as excommunication,
but also severe temporal penalties like imprisonment, fines

confiscation and exile. There was also the general effort at a legal enforcement of Christian morality which can be clearly seen in the canonical penalties enacted not only for specifically ecclesiastical crimes but also for what were civil crimes. Canonical penal law was used to protect the faithful from dangerous occasions of sin or from anything that might endanger their eternal salvation.

The suppression of vice and the reformation of Christian morality was also considered to be part of the role of law. And this has been illustrated by the examination of a number of medieval canonical institutions. Canonical penalties were also used to frighten men from sin and their severity was specifically meant to act 'ad terrorem'. Nowhere is this more clearly apparent than in the anti-heretical legislation. Heresy was numbered among the most serious crimes against both Church and State and in consequence a series of quite savage penalties were enacted against it. All this was accepted by Cardinal Hostiensis who felt that the most drastic measures were justified to eradicate such an evil from Christendom and preserve the unity of the one true Church.

2. *Hostiensis and the Medieval Legal Tradition*

Such in outline were the views of one medieval canonist on the function of canon law in the Church. But, it may be asked, how far can Cardinal Hostiensis be taken as a reliable spokesman for his period? Can his views be considered as representative of those of the medieval Church in general? The reading of the *Summa Aurea* alone would suggest that he can and ought to be taken as such a representative. Throughout this commentary on the *tituli* of the Decretals of Gregory IX he consistently claims to be expounding the law of the Church as this was to be found in the *Decretum* and in the teaching of popes and canonists. Every page contains numerous references to the *Decretum* and to papal decretal legislation. The very passage in which he outlines the main functions of law and which has provided the pattern for this investigation, is not an original composition. It is woven together from quotations from Gratian, Gregory IX, Innocent III, and St Augustine. So that even here he was claiming to present, not simply his own opinion, but the traditional and generally accepted views on the role of law.

The general survey of medieval canon law that was presented

in Chapter Two supports this impression. There the views of
Gratian, Rolandus Bandinelli, Paucapalea, Rufinus, Honorius III,
Gregory IX, Boniface VIII and John XXII were briefly sketched.
These medieval popes and canonists put forward a variety of
functions for the law to perform within the Christian community.
Canon law was proposed as the means for securing order peace
and harmony in the Church. It was to be an instrument of
moral reform and provide instruction for the faithful, protecting
them from harm and guiding them towards Christian perfection.
It was for the law, these men thought, to clarify the hierarchical structure of the Church and outline the rights and
duties of Church officials; and it had to regulate the procedure
for ecclesiastical trials. The study of the *Summa Aurea* has
shown that Hostiensis was completely faithful to this tradition
he had inherited.

But one can go further. In Chapter Two an attempt was
made to give a bird's-eye view of the contents of the major
medieval canonical collections, the *Decretum* and the *Decretales*.
If one approaches these collections from a practical point of
view and asks what the law was actually doing, the following
appear as the principal preoccupations of medieval canon law.
There was, first of all, the attempt to clarify and consolidate
the position of the pope as the supreme authority throughout
the Church. This can be seen in the large volume of decretal
legislation and the use of rescripts. There was also the common practice of appointing judges delegate to hear cases in
first instance. The same centralizing tendency shows itself in
papal reservation of benefices and the growing practice of papal
provision. This control over ecclesiastical benefices of all kinds
was of primary importance in the growth of papal sovereignty.
There were too the increasing papal demands for money. By
the mid-thirteenth century the theoretical monarchical claims
of Gregory VII had become a practical reality and canon law
reflected and consolidated this development. After all, 'it was
only after the papacy had created the institutions through which
to make its authority effective that it was in a position to exercise the judicial, legislative, financial and administrative powers
it had gradually accumulated'. [1]

---

[1] G. Barraclough, *The Medieval Papacy*, p. 120. Church organisation
was in fact a main theme in canonical writing. 'In the *Decretum*, the
problems of governing the Church were, of course, a paramount concern.
Many chapters discuss in general the governing authority inherent in

Then there was a large body of legislation whose aim was to promote the spiritual reform of the Church by providing for a carefully-chosen and well-disciplined clergy. It is this that lies behind the large volume of legislation on the rights and duties of the clergy, and, as has been seen, almost the whole of Part One of the *Decretum* and much of Book Three of the Gregorian Decretals are taken up with the moral virtues that the clergy should possess. The qualities required in candidates for orders are discussed in detail. Clerical celibacy is emphasised and severe penalties are laid down against simony. Pluralism too is forbidden. Thirdly, much of the law was concerned with organising and protecting the beneficiary system. Benefices were regarded as a necessary condition for the mission of the clergy and there is much legislation on the rights and duties of the beneficed cleric, the rights of patronage, presentation, election and so on. The growth of ecclesiastical property led to conflicts of interests at many levels in the Church and this called for detailed canonical legislation. It was also a major concern of the law to defend the Church's immunity from taxation. Only the pope was to have the right to tax Church property. [2]

Fourthly, a large part of the law directly with due process in ecclesiastical trials. Most of the rules were in fact taken over from Roman law but canon law did have its own contribution to make here. Le Bras has noted that canon law allowed great freedom for the exercise of judicial discretion and did much to reduce formalism in judical trials. [3] In the fifth place there were the regulations for the administration of the sacraments and these form another large block of the legislation to be found in the *Decretum* and the *Decretales*, particularly concerning matrimony, holy orders and penance. Then there was the great variety of laws whose purpose was to protect the oppressed and the poor, and in general to provide for security and stability in society.

There was also the zealous desire to preserve the unity of the Church and maintain orthodoxy in the faith. The unity of

---

the Church and its higher officers, and more specifically, many chapters treat the legislative, judicial and coercive powers'. R. L. Benson, *The Bishop Elect*, Princeton, 1968, p. 45. See also M. van de Kerckhove, 'La notion de juridiction chez les Décretistes et les premiers Décretalistes (1140-1250)', *Etudes Franciscaines*, 49 (1937), pp. 420 ff.

[2] Cf. E. W. Kemp, *Counsel and Consent*, London, 1961, p. 57.

[3] Cf. G. Le Bras, 'Canon Law', *The Legacy of the Middle Ages*, p. 358.

faith had to be preserved at all costs and so a large volume of medieval canonical legislation is taken up with heretics and schismatics and the inquisitional courts of the thirteenth century. Related to this was the attempt to enforce Christian morality through the imposition of canonical penalties of all kinds, both spiritual and temporal. A glance at Book Five of the Gregorian Decretals, for example, will indicate the great variety of delicts which were subject to ecclesiastical penalties: usury, homicide, theft, rape, and so on. It should be borne in mind that seems to have been a lack of a clear distinction between *crimen* and *peccatum* in the writings of many canonists. Another apparent defect of this penal system seems to be its acceptance of the idea of group responsability for crimes. This has been remarked on by Professor Le Bras:

> It must be added, however, that while in general the canon law maintained the principle of personal responsibility for faults, it did not altogether escape the tendency common to all medieval legal systems, which is, in determining the penalty, to take account of the group as much as of the individual, and to obtain reparation, which should be complete, exemplary and deterrent, by demanding it from the innocent if it could not be paid by the guilty. Canon law thus adopted the idea of group responsibility, the penal responsibility of the heir, of corporations and associations, of the family of the offenders who had injured the rights of the Church. It borrowed from the secular law the majority of its vindictive penalties, sometimes with modifications. [4]

An important factor in the thirteenth-century political and religious scene were the military expeditions organized by the Church for the liberation of the Holy Land. The First Crusade had been proclaimed at the close of the eleventh century but by the thirteenth the idea had been extended to include wars against heretics within Christendom and against enemies of the Church anywhere. Crusades were preached against the Albigensians in 1208 and against schismatic Greeks in 1237 and Gregory IX and Innocent IV made use of the crusading ideal in their struggle with Frederick II. All this was reflected in the canonical legislation. In the Gregorian collection there are eleven decretals under the title, *De voto*, which show the increasing tendency of the papacy to commute crusaders' vows when the

---

[4] G. Le Bras, 'Canon Law', *The Legacy of the Middle Ages*, p. 361.

military usefulness of the individuals concerned was not clear.
What was needed in such wars, it was soon realized, was not
a horde of pious and enthusiastic incompetents but a well-
equipped army of soldiers. The widespread crusading enthusiasm had, therefore, to be converted into some form of material
support which would be a real contribution to the war effort.
This became papal policy under Innocent III. It led to the
development of the law on commutation and redemption of
vows and was the source of a variety of canonical problems. [5]
The crusades also led to an important development of the financial resources of the papacy through the introduction of an
income tax on the clergy.

> This was introduced in aid of the crusades, but was later put
> to any and every use. Furthermore, it could be levied at
> various rates; and though the assessment was standardized
> by Nicholas IV in 1291, in principle at least it related to real
> income and grew with it. The first income tax, a fortieth,
> was levied for the crusade by Innocent III in 1199. The rate
> was stepped up in 1215, and already in 1228 a tenth was raised
> to finance the war against Frederick II. There-after the impost
> soon became a general tax, which provided a regular and
> substantial income, levied on the pope's own authority. Already
> by the time of Innocent IV the papacy, ahead of most secular
> rulers, was exercising a well-established power of taxation. [6]

There were, of course, many other problems dealt with by
medieval canon law, but these topics illustrate the main preoccupations of the law contained in the *Decretum* and in the
Decretales.

---

[5] J. A. Brundage has shown how the whole development of the
canonistic theory of vows and commutation is parallel to the rise and
decline of the crusading idea. Cf. J. A. Brundage, 'The Votive Obligations
of Crusaders: The Development of a Canonistic Doctrine', *Traditio*, 24
(1968), pp. 77-118; J. A. Brundage, 'The Crusader's Wife: A Canonistic
Quandary', *Studia Gratiana*, XII (1967), pp. 425-441; J. A. Brundage, 'The
Crusader's Wife Revisited', *Studia Gratiana*, XIV (1967), pp. 241-251;
J. A. Brundage, *Medieval Canon Law and the Crusader*, Wisconsin, 1969.
M. Villey, *La Croisade: Essai sur la formation d'une théorie juridique*,
Paris, 1942; M. Villey, 'L'Idée de la croisade chez les juristes du moyen
age', *Relazione del X congresso internazionale di scienze storiche*. 6 vols.
Florence, 1955, vol. 3, pp. 565-594; S. Runciman, *A History of the Crusades*,
3 vols. Cambridge, 1951-1954.
[6] G. Barraclough, *The Medieval Papacy*, London, 1968, p. 121.

Not surprisingly, these same preoccupations have been found to characterise the *Summa Aurea* which, after all, was intended to be an explanatory commentary on the medieval *corpus* of canon law. Here again there is confirmation of the conclusion that Hostiensis may safely be taken as typical or representative of his time in the views he propounds about the role of law in the church. There appears to be no reason to think of him as a radical innovator in the matter. This opinion gains further support, as we have seen in Chapter One, in the writings of modern scholars who have seriously studied the work of Hostiensis. 'The reading of Hostiensis, writes J. A. Watt, 'in the light of the antecedent canonist tradition — as it always should be to be properly appraised — has brought the conviction that the bases of his thought were rooted deeply in a century or more of the discipline of canonical science, that he was its full embodiment and logical product'. [7] 'It was as if he typified the canonist writing of the thirteenth century'. [8] For Mgr Lefebvre, the *Summa Aurea* is 'l'une des plus représentatives du droit médiéval'. [9] Professor Le Bras, to mention one other authority, has divided the canonical activity that followed the publication of the *Decretum* into three periods. First of all, there was all the ingenious ardour of the early decretists, then came the calm solemnity of the authors of the *summae*, and finally there was the ponderous erudition of the commentators. And he remarks: 'S'il nous fallait citer des noms représentatifs de ces trois époques, nous choisirions Rufin, Hostiensis et Jean André'. [10]

This does not imply, of course, that Cardinal Hostiensis can be dismissed as a mere compiler of other men's opinions. By any standard he must be ranked among the most distinguished canonists of the Middle Ages. Little attempt has been made in this study to single out and comment upon his original contribution to canonical thought. The omission has not been accidental. A discussion of the originality of Hostiensis would have involved a different approach. It would have involved the detailed investigation not only of the writings of Hostiensis but also of the writings of a large number of the principal canonists of the twelfth and thirteenth centuries. Only the

---

[7] J. A. Watt, 'The Theory of Papal Monarchy', *Traditio*, 20 (1964), p. 185.
[8] *Ibid.*, p. 282.
[9] G. Le Bras, C. Lefebvre, J. Rambaud, *L'Age Classique 1140-1378*, Paris, 1965, p. 312.
[10] *Ibid.*, p. 25, n. 4.

careful and comparative study of a great number of such canonistic compositions would permit one to speak with any measure of authority on the originality or lack of originality of any single individual. As Professor Stickler has warned us,

> Definite attributions can never be made without a thorough study of the whole line of tradition. Anyone familiar with the methods of the glossators and with the often arbitrary transmission of their sigla, will always be on guard against identifying a master as the originator of a doctrine on the mere strength of the fact that he is explicitly named in a gloss as holding this doctrine. [11]

Moreover, it can seriously be questioned whether such an exercise is possible — in so far as the subject of this investigation is concerned — without the prior existence of a number of monographs on individual writings, such as has been attempted in these pages. It would certainly be a lengthy undertaking. What has to be borne in mind in this matter — and it is a point that has already been made a number of times in the course of this investigation — is the fact that the role of canon law was not a subject that had a neat compartment already allotted to it in the canonical collections. The aim of this study has not been to demonstrate or discuss the originality of Hostiensis, but simply to give an account of his views on the role of canon law in the church as these are presented in the *Summa Aurea*. It is, however, also being suggested that there is sound evidence for thinking that these views may safely be taken as representative of the thought of medieval canonists in general.

Hostiensis did, in fact, have an original contribution to make to canonical thought and his originality in a variety of fields has been studied by a number of modern scholars. Professor Le Bras and Mgr Lefebvre, — among others, — have drawn attention to Hostiensis' profound knowledge of Roman law and to his attempt in the *Summa Aurea* to present a systematic combination of Roman and canon law concerning ecclesiastical matters, — a decisive step towards the *ius commune* that was to be developed in the following century. [12] This view has been supported by Professor Caron, who thinks that Hostien-

---

[11] A. M. Stickler, 'Concerning the Political Theories of Medieval Canonists', *Traditio*, 7 (1949-1951), p. 456.

[12] G. Le Bras, 'Théologie et Droit Romain dans l'oeuvre d'Henri de Suse', in *Etudes Historiques à la mémoire de Noël Didier*. Grenoble, 1960, pp. 195-204. C. Lefebvre, 'Hostiensis, in *DDC*, vol. V, col. 1219.

sis, particularly in his teaching on canonical equity, achieved
a brilliant synthesis between Roman law and canon law, — 'affermandosi in tal modo come il sommo artefice del *ius commune*,
e raggiungendo in tale opera una delle più alte vette del pensiero giuridico'. [13] Mgr Lefebvre has also devoted a number
of important studies to Hostiensis' teaching on equity and he
has tried to show the originality that he demonstrated in his
insistence that spiritual and Christian values must always prevail over purely temporal advantages, — an insistence that at
times led him into conflict with the views of other canonists,
and even popes. [14] He also had an important contribution to
make to the development of the doctrine of votive obligations; [15]
and Dr Watt has maintained that Cardinal Hostiensis ,— 'perhaps the most interesting of thirteenth-century canonists', —
was the author of the most complete analysis of papal power
of any produced up to his time, and that on a number of
aspects of the supremacy of the pope he had something new
and significant to say. [16] And finally, to bring this incomplete
list to a close, Professor Tierney has shown how Hostiensis
did much to clarify canonical teaching on corporation theory,
which was to exercise considerable influence later on the development of conciliarism. [17] Such studies, — and these are
but a selection, — give some indication of the originality and

[13] P. G. Caron, '*Aequitas* romana, *Misericordia* patristica ed *Epicheia*
aristotelica nella dottrina decretalistica del duecento e trecento', *Studia
Gratiana*, XIV (1967), 307-47, cf. pp. 316-17.

[14] C. Lefebvre, 'La doctrine de l'Hostiensis sur la préférence à assurer
en droit aux intérêts spirituels', in *Ephemerides Iuris Canonici*, 8 (1952),
24-44. — ' "Aequitas canonica" et "periculum animae" dans la doctrine
de l'Hostiensis', in *Ephemerides Iuris Canonici*, 8 (1952), pp. 305-321.

[15] J. A. Brundage, 'The Votive Obligations of Crusaders', *Traditio*, 24
(1968), pp. 111-118.

[16] J. A. Watt, 'The Theory of Papal Monarchy in the Thirteenth
Century', *Traditio*, 20 (1964), pp. 179-317; esp. 281-308.

[17] B. Tierney, *The Foundations of the Conciliar Theory*, Cambridge,
1955, pp. 108-31. Professor R. L. Benson has drawn attention to the
original contribution that Hostiensis had to make in the development of
the theory of papal elections by his insistence that the pope derives
his jurisdiction not from the electors or the election, but from the
moment that he *consents* to his election. Cf. R. L. Benson, *The Bishop-
Elect*, p. 164. And Fr J. Russell, SJ, has pointed out the important
contribution that Hostiensis made to the development of the theory
of *Sanatio in Radice*, by his clarification of the pope's powers of
legitimation. Cf. J. Russell, *The Sanatio in Radice before the Council
of Trent*, Rome, 1964, pp. 48-49.

brilliance of the canonist whose work has been the subject of this study. They give grounds for ranking him among the most distinguished and influential of medieval canonists. His views, then, on the role of law in the Church may be considered not only as representative of the thirteenth century, but perhaps also as an influential factor during the following centuries as well.

3. *An Evaluation*

In this final section an attempt will be made briefly to assess in the light of modern thought the current value of those functions of canon law which were enumerated by Cardinal Hostiensis. The same order that was followed in the investigation into the *Summa Aurea* will be observed in this assessment.

Many modern writers agree that one of the main functions of law in the Church — as in any human society — is to provide good order. Law should set out to reduce to a minimum the clash of conflicting interests which can lead so easily to insecurity, exploitation and even chaos. Life in any community demands a certain amount of order. Moreover, it is argued that law in itself need not imply a lack of liberty, since by ensuring order and security sound law will encourage the development of true human freedom. A group of theologians and canonists in the United States recently agreed that 'a regulatory or legal system of some sort is essential for the Church ... because without the order and the unity which such a system safeguards, the free development of the human personality and the achievement of the collective goal become impossible'. [18] Others maintain that the role of law in the Church should be 'to help the community by human means to establish good order so that order should produce peace and tranquillity: the best

---

[18] J. Biechler (Editor), *Law for Liberty*. (A symposium on the role of law in the Church), 1967, p. 197. In this context the following remark by one of the members of this symposium is worth quoting. He thought that 'Trinitarian principles are violated by what Richard Niebuhr called the "unitarianism of the Third Person", in which the freedom of the Spirit to blow where it wills, becomes *the* theological norm. This is, in a sense, to forget that God is a God who *orders* life as well as breathing into it a new spirit. At this point it is a matter *not only* of finding prudential grounds for insisting on the necessity for organization, *but also* of keeping a balance in the fundamental theological conviction of the Christian community that the God in whom we believe is a God of order and not just a God of freedom. Order itself liberates'. *op. cit.*, p. 87.

dispositions for receiving the prompting of the Holy Spirit'. [19]
This same point has been made by Cardinal Felici, the President
of the Commission for the Revision of Canon Law:

> La legge nella comunità ecclesiale, he writes, è espressione
> di giustizia, ma anche di carità, la virtù che tutte le altre
> rende perfette. Proprio per questo essa « la legge » contribuirà:
> non solo a salvaguardare gli inderogabili diritti della persona
> umana dei figli di Dio, ed il retto ordine della società ecclesiale,
> ma a creare altresì tra i fedeli e, per riflesso, tra tutti gli
> uomini il vincolo che di tutti farà una sola cosa in Cristo,
> nella *tranquillitas ordinis* che è propria della pace. [20]

These writers would agree with Hostiensis in his insistence on
the task of canon law to promote peace and concord within
the Christian community, although, of course, they differ considerably from him about how in particular this task should
be accomplished.

How does canon law fulfil this function of providing order
and promoting concord? Modern writers would agree with
Hostiensis that this is done principally by defining and establishing the structures that are necessary for the Church's mission. To quote one recent writer, 'The structures of the Church
can illumine or obscure the idea of the community of Christ;
they can make it a beacon of light or they can so disfigure it
as to make it virtually unrecognizable'. [21] But what in fact are
these structures that are considered necessary for the Church's
task? There would seem to be few essential structures in the
ecclesiastical order that go back to the foundation of the Church
and can claim the authority of Christ and the Apostles. Clarification about what precisely these essential structures are is
the task of theology and in particular of ecclesiology. The current revival of ecclesiology in the Catholic Church is revealing
a desire to ensure that the structures of the Church do in fact
faithfully express the teaching of dogmatic theology. Much of
Hostiensis' emphasis on the papal plenitude of power, with its
authority to intervene in temporal affairs, depose rulers and
release subjects from their oaths of allegiance, while meaningful

---

[19] L. Orsy, 'Quantity and Quality of Laws after Vatican II', *Jurist*,
1967, pp. 385-412.

[20] *Osservatore Romano*, May 29-30th, 1967.

[21] F. Klostermann, 'Structures of the Church of Tomorrow III', *Information Documentation on the Conciliar Church* (IDO-C), Doss. 67/29,
p. 13.

perhaps in the context of a united Christendom of the Middle Ages, would be rejected today. Yet, as the two Vatican Councils have stressed, papal authority in the Church remains of vital importance for the maintenance of order and concord in the Church. But this is no longer a matter that can be settled by the canonists. The conciliar constitutions contain authoritative theological teaching on the hierarchy of the Church. It is for the law to reflect this teaching. The laws that regulate papal authority, collegiality, ecumenical councils, and the like should be the practical implementation of sound ecclesiology. These laws should be seen as dogmatic theology in the concrete, theology in action. Such a desire is in harmony with Hostiensis' view that canon law should always be closely related to theology.

Similarly, canonical legislation on the sacraments and on worship is expected to be a faithful reflection of sacramental theology. Canon law, by its directives on the valid administration of the sacraments, can and does provide a pastoral help of great value towards the safeguarding of unity and orthodoxy in this matter which is of practical importance in the life of every Christian. Here again there seems to be substantial agreement between modern thinkers and Hostiensis's approach to the sacraments. What is being stressed today, however, is that in such matters, which concern the essential structures and institutions within the Church, the role of canon law should be to formulate in clear and practical terms the Church's dogmatic tradition. Incidentally, this may be one of the most effective ways of safeguarding and transmitting this tradition. In doing so, however, the law is to be guided and controlled by theology, and more firmly perhaps than in the past. Some think that for too long canon law has tended to be studied in a rather positivist fashion, purely as a legal system parallel to the civil law or the common law, and that this has led to a sort of divorce of law from theology. [22]

---

[22] P. Lombardia has indicated the need for reform in the teaching of canon law: 'First and foremost legal studies must be soundly based on theology. We will have to get over the so-called tension between the Ecclesia Iuris and the Ecclesia Caritatis and approach the question in a much more positive way: the ecclesiological bases of juridico-canonical relationship must be studied in such a way that the jurist can discover the norms of divine law which indicate the scope of that personal autonomy, which is completely necessary if one is to speak in legal terms of mutual dignity and responsibility — just in the same way as the norms of divine law are being studied which support the hierarchical principle. In this area the Constitution *Lumen Gentium*

In all this it is pointed out that the canonist must play his part as a member of a team. Fr. Huizing writes:

> 'The proper function of the canonist is a technique rather than a science. The scientific study of the Church's reality in all its aspects is the function of the exegete, the patrologist, the historian, the theologian, the moralist, the liturgist, the sociologist, the missiologist, etc. The canonist [qua canonist, that is], is only concerned with the various ways in which this reality can be given a certain order by means of authoritative regulations. For instance, the theologian studies what the college of bishops *is*, and what must be the necessary relationship between the pope and the bishops as well as among themselves. The canonist examines the way in which these relationships can be expressed coherently and conveniently in a set of ecclesiastical regulations. Pastoral theology establishes the best way for the exercise of authority, for the administration of the sacraments and for the various forms of the apostolate. The canonist decides how far and which authoritative regulations are most useful in bringing about the conclusions of pastoral theology in the community of the Church. The canonist, therefore, constantly depends on others to find out what his set of regulations is supposed to achieve. By itself, the system is worthless'. [23]

Fr. Huizing is here giving expression to what is felt by many Catholics in the Church today. Those who agree with this point

---

is an invaluable guide.' In this training he stresses also the need for the serious study of the history of law and the philosophy of law. Cf. P. Lombardia, 'Canon Law Today', *The Furrow*, September, 1969, pp. 444-453. Similar points have been made by G. Lesage who asks for a closer cooperation between theology and canon law in order to clarify the role of law in the church. He insists that canon law cannot be regarded as self-sufficient since it is for theology to explain what precisely the law of the church is and what it should be doing (and he refers for confirmation of this to Suarez, *Tractatus de Legibus*, Proemium, in Opera Omnia, t. 5, Parisiis, 1856, p. ix). Cf. G. Lesage, *La Nature du Droit Canonique*, Ottawa, 1960, chapter one. Other writers too have advocated that much more attention should be paid by students of canon law to ecclesiological studies, and in particular to those which deal with the juridical structure of the church. Examples cited include the following: O. Semmelroth, *Church and Sacrament*, Dublin, 1965; K. Rahner, *The Dynamic Element in the Church*, and *The Church and the Sacraments*, Herder, London, 1963; T. Sartori, 'The Church and the Churches' in *Theology Today*, Herder, 1965, pp. 148-193; P. Smulders, 'Ecclesia, Ius et Sacramenta', *Periodica*, XLVIII (1959), pp. 3-53. See also R. Latourelle, *Theology, Science of Salvation*, New York, 1969, pp. 175-186.

[23] P. Huizing, SJ, 'The Reform of Canon Law', *Concilium*, 8 (1965), p. 60.

of view are by no means intent on encouraging narrow-minded legalists. Breadth of knowledge and experience will always be necessary. The canon lawyer must be familiar with modern thought and modern needs if he is to appreciate the nature of the problems that call for solutions. He must be aware of the pastoral aims of the law if he is to be able to interpret the law correctly according to the mind of the Church. In short, he must be a fully committed Christian who is alive in the community of today. But, 'non omnia possumus omnes', and he has to realise that, as a canonist, he has a limited and specific task to perform, not in isolation, but as a member of a team. He should bear in mind, too, that technical mastery of the law can easily lead to narrowness. Yet, as a canonist, his specific contribution to the good of the Church is precisely this technical mastery of the law, a practical knowledge of the legal tradition, a solid grasp of the underlying principles, the lawyer's precision in thought and language. This is what people come to a lawyer for, — at least for this, though, of course, perhaps not only for this.

It would appear, then, that the canonist's role in the Church is to provide the precision of thought, the accuracy and lucidity in language which are needed if theological truths are to be effectively reduced to action within the community. It is for this reason that a number of writers look to the revision of canon law to provide a valuable instrument in consolidating and perpetuating the ideals put forward by the Second Vatican Council. Hostiensis' acceptance of the growing centralization of the medieval papacy is rejected today; but there is one aspect of his teaching which has a very modern ring. This is his persistent advocacy of the need for collaboration in government. He maintained that the cardinals should be given a share in the government of the universal Church and he insisted on the bishop's duty to rule his diocese in consultation with the rest of his clergy. His exclusion of the laity from all such matters would, of course, be unacceptable today, but his stress on collegiality as a general principle of government would be welcomed. It is here that canon law could play an important part today. The Vatican Council gave many new directives and pointed the way towards a more harmonious and constructive collaboration within the Church — between pope and bishops, between bishops and priests, between priests and laity. Specific directives have been issued concerning episcopal conferences, senates of priests, diocesan pastoral commissions, and so forth.

These new structures can strengthen the bonds of unity within the Church and within each individual diocese. Unity is made more manifest in a concrete form and regular and constructive dialogue is rendered easier. Because of the great importance of these new means of collaboration it is thought by many that their existence and structure should not be left to the whim of individual bishops. And it is argued that if the Council directives are not crystallised into clear laws they will evaporate into thin air. Moreover, in such matters a certain amount of clear legislation is considered necessary in order to avoid misunderstanding about roles and competence and responsibility. In short, the law of the Church is expected to strengthen these structures by providing clarity and precision about their function. [24] Canon law is expected to be a support for collegiality in action. It is expected to embody in a practical way the principles of collegiality, equality and subsidiarity. If this is the case, then canon law should cease to be regarded as a mere list of legal prescriptions arbitrarily laid down by authority. On the contrary, it should increasingly be seen as a pastoral instrument of great value, a positive help for Christian to 'live' their theology. From all this it would appear that there is substantial agreement between Cardinal Hostiensis and modern Catholics on the role of law in providing for order and peace and harmony in the Church through the definition and clarification about ecclesiastical structures and institutions.

But the area of agreement is much wider than this. Another aspect of the *Summa Aurea* that would be welcomed by modern Catholics is the emphasis which Hostiensis consistently placed on the importance of justice and equity. It was for the law to protect innocent and upright men, and this could be done, thought Hostiensis, only by an assiduous cultivation of justice in the spirit of canonical equity. Innocence would be effectively protected if there was general respect for the rights of all men. He was equally insistent that true justice must always be tempered by compassion and administered in a humane manner

---

[24] Discussing the way collegiality should be practised, Karl Kahner wrote: 'Nevertheless, one thing should be — but is not — clear and undisputed: the specific methods of collaboration between the pope and the bishops should be broadly established in definite norms of human canon law which the pope and the bishops should keep to (as the pope and the secular governments have to keep to a concordat); they should not simply be left to the unpredictable "wise judgment" of the pope on each individual case'. *The Tablet*, June, 27th, 1970, p. 630.

and in accordance with the spirit of the Gospel. It is this that explains his preoccupation with canonical equity. The law of the Church, he maintained, can only be correctly interpreted in the light of Christian principles and priorities, and it is the duty of the ecclesiastical judge to see that these take precedence over all other considerations. Such principles would be approved by most modern writers who are strongly advocating that the function of canon law should be to ensure the protection of the rights of all Christians.

It is also thought that these rights will be more effectively protected if they are clearly delineated in the law of the Church. This, then, is another area where agreement in principle between medieval and modern thought is quite marked, although once again there is a great deal of difference when it comes to deciding which particular rights ought to be so protected. The Vatican Council stressed the dignity of all the members of the People of God, their dignity and freedom as children of God. [25] Canon law is expected to remain faithful to this theological principle. It follows that the law of the Church should openly recognise and protect a whole series of rights and duties of her members, — rights and duties which they possess 'ratione iuris naturalis et ratione Baptismi'. [26] Moreover, there are specific rights and duties possessed by different groups within the Church. Canon law should protect these rights also and provide a reliable guide for these duties. And one effective protection for such rights and duties would be their clear and precise formulation by the law of the Church. Hence a number of modern Catholics have been asking for a 'Bill of Rights' for the various sections of the Church — laity, clergy, and religious. They maintain that since the values of democracy have now become so widespread it is becoming increasingly important that canon law should display a deep respect for the dignity and freedom of each Christian and for his inalienable rights. They want to see the basic rights and duties of the Christian written into the new canon law, 'including the right to protection from arbitrary denunciation, the right to be heard, to defend oneself, to appeal'. [27] It is suggested too that protective measures and controls should be added where necessary. [28]

---

[25] *Lumen Gentium*, n. 9. Cf. also, *Dignitatis Humanae*, n. 1.

[26] *Lumen Gentium*, n. 36. Cf. also, *Gaudium et Spes*, n. 75.

[27] F. Klostermann, 'Principles of a Structural Reform', IDO-C, Doss. 67/23, p. 5.

[28] F. Klostermann, *ibid.*

It is also pointed out that canon law should emphasise 'the
duties and obligations of those in authority at least as much
as it stresses the duties and responsibilities of obedience'.[29]
Presumably Hostiensis' plain speaking on the duties of prelates
and on the reasons that would justify their removal from the
administration of a diocese would be acceptable to such men.
Another point that these men would like to see in the renewed
law of the Church is a 'reformulation of the presumptions of
law to favour persons rather than institutions, in acknowledgement of the fact that rights are primarily inherent in persons'.[30]
It is argued, for example that if there is real doubt about the
validity of a marriage the benefit of the doubt should be given
to the individual so that he or she be allowed to re-marry.
Limits to authority should also be provided by the law. Some
admit that a service of authoritative guidance should be provided in the Church, but they do not think that this need assume
the forms of an absolute monarchy. 'Should not a renewed
canon law clearly indicate the limits of power, and should it
not take precautions and introduce safeguards against despotic
caprice, and effectively ensure that no *de facto* power systems
develop which would be contrary to the spirit of Christ?'[31] The
principle is already exemplified in the Code of Canon Law,
which does provide a number of traditional safeguards against
the abuse of episcopal authority.[32] It will be recalled too that
Hostiensis discusses a number of checks and limitations on ecclesiastical authority and was opposed to capricious and arbitrary government.

What is often mentioned in this context is the parallel relationship that should exist between canon law and civil or common law, — between ecclesiastical and political authority. The
explicit safeguards of individual rights that are provided by
common law are put forward as a pattern which canon law
would do well to follow. The Church's teaching is quite explicit about this duty of political authority.

It is agreed that in our time the common good is chiefly
guaranteed when personal rights and duties are maintained.

---

[29] J. Biechler (Ed.), *Law for Liberty*, p. 195.
[30] J. Biechler, (Ed), *Law for Liberty*, p. 200.
[31] F. Klostermann, 'Structures of the Church of Tomorrow II', IDO-C,
Doss. 67-28, p. 7.
[32] See the procedure outlined in the *Codex Iuris Canonici* for the
removal of pastors, for determining competence, for the alienation of
Church property, and the like.

> The chief concern of civil authorities must therefore be to ensure that these rights are acknowledged, respected, coordinated with other rights, defended and promoted, so that in this way each one may more easily carry out his duties. [33]

This teaching was repeated by the Second Vatican Council, which drew attention to contemporary man's concern for freedom and his demand 'that constitutional limits be set to the powers of government, in order that there be no encroachment on the rightful freedom of the person and of associations'. [34] And it put forward the need for a positive system of law in which there should be established 'a division of governmental roles and institutions, and, at the same time, an effective and independent system for the protection of rights. Let the rights of all persons, families, and associations, along with the exercise of those rights, be recognized, honoured and fostered'. [35] While these statements refer directly to civil government, it is thought by many that they should also be applied to the law of the Church which should also make it its business to provide effective protection for the rights of the faithful. Cardinal Felici has, in fact, maintained that the revised canon law should observe these principles, stressed by the Council, about the dignity and inviolable rights of the human person. 'Nel futuro codice,' he writes, 'si stabilisca uno statuto comune giuridico che deve valere per tutti a motivo della fondamentale uguaglianza che esiste tra i fedeli di Cristo'. [36] And he added that the Church's law should aim at safeguarding the freedom of physical and moral persons in the Church. This was supported by the first Synod of Bishops in 1967. There is, therefore, a large measure of agreement among modern thinkers that the Church should provide some sort of constitutional guarantees of liberty. These will include the delineation of rights and duties, and also opportunity for redress where these rights are violated.

The question about the legal protection of human rights is regarded as a vitally important one in the current discussion

---

[33] *Pacem in Terris*, n. 60.

[34] Concilium Vaticanum II, *Dignitatis Humanae*, n. 1. See also *Gaudium et Spes*, n. 41: 'In virtue of the Gospel entrusted to it the Church proclaims the rights of man: she acknowledges and holds in high esteem the dynamic approach of today which is fostering these rights all over the world.'

[35] *Gaudium et Spes*, n. 75.

[36] *Osservatore Romano*, October 1st, 1967. See also the official prin-

on the role of law in the Church. In a recent report of a
committee of the Canon Law Society of America, the following
rights were listed as belonging to every member of the Church:
the right to hear the Word of God and participate in the sacraments; the right to share in the apostolate and mission of the
Church; the right to have some say in and be given information about the pastoral needs of the Church; 'the right to educa-
tion, to freedom of inquiry and to freedom of expression in
the sacred sciences'; the right to free assembly and association
in the Church; and such inviolable and universal rights of the
human person as the right to the protection of one's reputation,
to respect of one's person, to activity in accord with the upright
norm of one's conscience, to protection of privacy'. [37] Each of
these was supported by a reference to the teaching of the Second
Vatican Council. But how is the Church to protect the rights
and freedom of the individual? Much can be done in a negative way by insisting only on what is really necessary and reducing laws to the bare minimum, and by inculcating a truly
Christian interpretation of ecclesiastical law rather than a wood-
en rigidity. In this matter attention is drawn to the teaching
of St Thomas, who advocated moderation in the making of
laws in the Church. These should not be unduly multiplied so
as to become an unbearable burden on the faithful. St Thomas
also taught that in the interpretation of law the moral virtue
of *epikeia* should be cultivated. [38]

It is also maintained, however, that the common rights of
all the faithful should be positively and directly protected by
canon law. 'Rights without legal safeguards, both preventive
and by way of effective recourse, are often meaningless. It is
the noblest service of law to afford effective safeguards for
the protection of rights, and, where rights have been violated,
to afford effective means for their prompt restoration'. [39] That
there should be legal guarantees of freedom is proposed as a
particularly crucial aspect of the revision of Church law, 'for

---

ciples that are to govern the revision of the Code of Canon Law where
it is clearly stated that one of these principles must be that 'unicuique
christifidelium iura agnoscenda ac tuenda sunt', noting that this is to
be observed by all who hold authority in the church, since 'usus huius
potestatis in Ecclesia arbitrarius esse non potest'. *Principia Quae Codicis
Iuris Canonici Recognitionem Dirigent*, Vatican City, 1967, n. 6.

[37] *Report of the Ad Hoc Committee on Due Process*, (Ohio, 1969), p. 1.
[38] S. T., 2a 2ae, 95, 5; 120, 1.
[39] *Report of the Ad Hoc Committe on Due Process*, p. 2.

the experience of the recent and contemporary Church would seem to advise that this "just freedom" can hardly come to life in the Church unless it is somehow guaranteed by law. The issue of legally protected freedom is essential, as freedom is a *sine qua non* condition as well as a goal of Church reform'.[40]   It is worth remarking that this was an aspect of canon law that was mentioned by Pope Paul VI in his speech at the celebration of the fiftieth anniversary of the promulgation of the Code of Canon Law.   The pope was making the point that canon law formed an important part of the Church's activity:

> Essa non è l'unica, ne forse la prima, ma è necessaria — come è stato detto — giacchè la Chiesa, essendo una comunità non solo spirituale, ma visibile, organica, gerarchica, sociale e ordinaria, ha bisogno anche di una legge scritta e postula organi adatti che la promulgano e la fanno osservare, non tanto per mero esercizio di autorità, ma proprio per la tutela della essenza e della libertà sia degli enti morali, sia delle persone fisiche che compongono la Chiesa stessa.[41]

This same point of view was spelled out in greater detail at the American symposium on the role of law.   These theologians and canonists agreed that,

> Among the cardinal goals of the Church law there should be included the protection of the dignity, freedom and responsibility of the individual member of the People of God, not merely because he experiences such protection from his civil law but also and especially because the values of the Church dictate such protection.   Far from merely reflecting the respect for human freedom of civil law, the Church ought to show the way to even greater respect for this right.   Thus we deem that Church law should incorporate the full range of regulations and procedures which can be subsumed under the heading "due process", — and in particular, the existence of an independent and impartial judiciary, the right to a speedy and public hearing, the right of counsel and cross-examination, the right to judgment by one's peers, the right of appeal and the more recently established right of recourse from inequitable bureaucratic decisions.[42]

---

[40] Ben F. Meyer, SJ, in *Law for Liberty* (Ed. J. Biechler), p. 125.
[41] *Osservatore Romano*, May 29th, 1967.
[42] From the consensus statement in *Law for Liberty*, (Ed. J. Biechler), p. 195.

This desire for the extension and more efficient structuring of
due process in the Church is a frequent theme in writings on
the revision of canon law. Due process does in fact exist in
the Church but it is thought to be too exclusively used for
marriage cases, and even here it stands in need of revision.
There is an increasing demand for really competent regional
tribunals throughout the Church and a reduction of the formalities surrounding nullity proceedings. In this matter of due
process reference is often made to the sound common-law tradition and it is advocated that canon law stands to learn much
from the common law whereas at present it seems to be dom-
inated by Roman law traditions. [43] This is a fair point. Canon
law should draw advantage from all the current legal traditions
and not just from one. However, in forwarding the advantages
of the common law tradition, one must be careful to avoid
romantic idealism. Due process in common law has its own
difficulties and has been severely criticised in recent years. [44]

It is urged, then, by many modern critics of canon law
that there should be more clear formulation of rights and duties
in the Church, — and even, perhaps, a sort of 'Bill of Rights', —
and also that due process should be more extensively used in
the protection of these rights. [45] Such critics would, therefore,
presumably agree with many of the points made by Cardinal
Hostiensis on the importance of granting a fair trial to anyone
under accusation. They would endorse his frequent insistence
that 'parum prodest iura habere in civitate nisi sit qui iura
reddat'. In the investigation into the Summa Aurea an attempt
was made to bring out the respect with which due process of
law was regarded by medieval canonists. Hostiensis makes it
clear that rights could only be guaranteed by making sure that
a fair procedure was observed, by doing everything possible
to ensure integrity in the courts, by requiring clear proof of
guilt before conviction, and providing an opportunity for self-
defence to all accused persons. So, once again, there seems
to be basic agreement in principle between Hostiensis and
modern thinkers. But only in principle, because there are a

---

[43] Cf. S. Kuttner, 'The Code of Canon Law in Historical Perspective',
The Jurist, 1968, pp. 146-148.

[44] See, for example, M. Zander, Lawyers and the Public Interest,
London, 1968.

[45] The letter published by thirty-eight Catholic theologians in 1968
stipulated a number of rights that should be protected. Herder Correspondence, 6 (1969), 46-49.

number of details in medieval procedure that would not be accepted in the Church of today. The inquisitorial procedure that was used against heretics would be rejected out of hand. Also, modern writers would grant the accused more rights than were granted him in the Middle Ages. The right to confront one's accusers and those who give evidence in support of the accusation would be among these. And they would reject completely the place that was given to juridical confessions in medieval trials. No man should be obliged to incriminate himself, and confession should not be treated as a legal proof of guilt. However, it is only fair to point out that the accused's right to silence took a very long time to receive recognition in both civil and ecclesiastical courts. In this matter Hostiensis was simply reflecting the common views of medieval society in general. [46]

It does appear, therefore, that there is a considerable measure of agreement between the thirteenth-century cardinal and modern Catholic writers about a number of functions that canon law may be expected to perform in the Christian community. Agreement, however, ceases over the proposed role of canon law as a deterrent from evil and a guide to Christian living. It is here that the difference between the medieval and the modern mentality is most clearly marked.

Some would deny that there is *any* place for a system of penal law within the Church. All would reject the widespread use of canonical penalties that was common in the Middle Ages. Even the penal legislation that is contained in the current Code of Canon Law would be rejected by most modern Catholics as excessive. Though the general principles about culpability and imputability and so on are recognised as excellent, it is still thought that there are too many censures and too many automatic penalties. Some modern writers, while admitting that canonical penal legislation has led to serious abuses in the past, do not think this necessarily implies that it should now be abandoned all together. They do not propose it as a deterrent from evil because as such it is usually quite ineffective, but they think it can serve a useful function. A minimum of penal legislation can have an educative value in underlining the seriousness of certain contraventions of Christian teaching, and it can help to preserve the Church's visible identity. That is

---

[46] Cf. P. Granfield, OSB, 'The Right to Silence', *Theological Studies*, 27 (1966), pp. 401-20.

to say, the Church should have the right to declare publicly that certain members have rejected essential points in the Church's mission or have refused to acknowledge the Christian Tradition as proclaimed and believed by the community. Moreover, it is also maintained that the Church should in certain cases state quite clearly what penalties may be inflicted if certain specific duties are not carried out by Church officials, such as bishops and parish-priests. This would be regarded as a protection of the right of the faithful to efficient service from the ministers of the Church. But all this would require only a very little penal legislation.

The medieval use of canon law, however, as a deterrent from heresy would be rejected by all modern Catholics both in principle and in practice. In principle, because it made no allowance for the rights of the individual conscience and paid no respect to the principle of religious liberty. And in practice, because of the injustice and cruelty of the procedure and the penalties.

The Catholic Church is not by its Christian principles committed to a policy of forcible repression of rival sects. And the fact that the Church has in the past used physical force — not excluding the death-penalty — to protect the faithful from the evils of heresy is regarded by many as an aberration from the teaching of Christ. It is rejected by the modern conscience as going beyond the limits of justice and contradicting Christian principles. To quote from the Vatican Council's *Declaration on Religious Freedom*, 'while the people of God pursued its pilgrim-way through the vicissitudes of human history, there has at times appeared in its life a way of acting that conforms little with the spirit of the Gospel, and indeed contradicts it'.[47] This is not the place to attempt to explain how the anti-heretical legislation of the Middle Ages was the product of a complex set of circumstances in which political, religious, philosophical and legal influences all intermingled with each other to produce a mentality which is quite different from that of the mid-twentieth century.[48] Many of those who defended that legislation, such as Hostiensis, did so from the highest religious motives and were themselves conscientious Christians. But it can no longer be defended as being in har-

---

[47] Concilium Vaticanum II, *Dignitatis Humanae Personae*, n. 12.
[48] Cf. M. Bévenot, SJ, 'The Inquisition and Its Antecedents I-IV' in *Heythrop Journal*, 1966, pp. 257-268; 381-393; 1967, pp. 52-69; 152-168.

mony with the teaching of Christ. The Vatican Council has affirmed that the dignity of man consists in his responsible use of freedom. It teaches that a man has a right to the free exercise of religion in society, and that he should not be driven by coercion but motivated by a sense of duty.[49] For these reasons the anti-heretical legislation, so vehemently defended by Hostiensis, would be rejected today on principle.

It would also be rejected because of the manner in which it was implemented. The procedure that was used in the trials of heretics would be repudiated as contrary to justice and the whole idea of due process. The accused was not permitted to know who were the witnesses for the prosecution and therefore was not given a fair opportunity to answer their charges; testimony was accepted against the suspect heretic from criminals and others who were normally debarred from giving evidence; the heretic was obliged to become an informer on others; even the use of torture was permitted by the Church in order to extract confessions and information from heretics. Then there were the savage penalties that were enacted against the crime of heresy, which went so far as the death-penalty for the convicted heretic and disinheritance even of his innocent children. Added to this was the whole inquisitorial method of inquiry where men were encouraged to inform on one another, and compelled on oath to incriminate themselves and others. All this cannot be harmonised with modern ideas about due process of law and fair trials. In any case, it is no longer accepted that the Church should make use of temporal penalties at all, and certainly not to compel a person to accept the Catholic faith. Moreover, the whole idea of using the law as a deterrent from evil, — *ad terrorem*, — is repugnant to the modern Christian. 'Credere non potest homo nisi volens', expresses a principle that is fully accepted by modern man. The attempt, therefore, to force a man to believe, or to compel him to be good through the fear of punishment is utterly rejected, as having no place in the law of the Church.

Finally, what is one to think of the function of canon law to provide a guide for Christian living? This is more controversial. Many Catholics today would reject the idea completely, maintaining that it is opposed to the teaching of Christ who set his followers free from all external law. Attention has been drawn throughout this study to the apparent confusion

---

[49] Cf. Concilium Vaticanum II, *Dignitatis Humanae Personae*, n. 2.

that seems to have existed in the Middle Ages between canon law and moral theology. The *Decretum* and the *Decretales* contain a great number of moral rules of Christian conduct. Professor Le Bras has praised medieval canon law for embodying what he calls 'the highest moral tradition of the West'.[50] This, as has been seen, is embodied in the *Summa Aurea*, which shows quite plainly that its author thought it part of the function of canon law to provide a guide for Christian living. The idea is shared by some modern writers who would maintain that the Church's legal code cannot be a mere collection of laws; 'it must be a *Torah* in which all law is illuminated by doctrine. Only in this way will the law of the Church serve its true purpose of bringing men to see that the conduct prescribed reflects the will of God and leads to God'.[51] Others think that the old charismatic approach to the law of the Church which is reflected in the terms, *sacri canones*, and the like should be preserved in the revised canon law to keep before the minds of all that the spiritual rights and obligations of the faithful are in quite a different category from civil rights and obligations.[52] There are, however, many modern Catholics who find this approach quite unacceptable. 'Love', writes Fr. John McKenzie, 'is not the fulfilment of an obligation but a spontaneous movement. The Christian would be incapable of this spontaneous movement were the spontaneity not given him by the indwelling Spirit. But it is given him, and words like law and obligation become meaningless',[53] Such a view is not uncommon in the Church today.

Not all critics of the law, however, would go as far as this, though they all want to reduce law to a minimum within the Church. Some reluctantly agree to keep a modicum of law, but only because they see this as a necessary evil, — an external restraint, needed only because of man's sinful state. 'Law is for the ungodly', such people maintain, 'and it becomes functional to the extent that the option to live a life of Christian liberty is not seized upon'.[54] The implication here seems to be that there is and that there must be real opposition between

---

[50] G. Le Bras, 'Canon Law' in *The Legacy of the Middle Ages*. Oxford, 1926, p. 361.

[51] B. Ahern, in *Law for Liberty* (Ed. J. Biechler), p. 104.

[52] See, for example, S. Kuttner, 'The Code of Canon Law in Historical Perspective', *The Jurist*, 28 (1968), p. 146.

[53] J. McKenzie, SJ, *The Power and the Wisdom*, London, 1965, p. 207.

[54] See J. Biechler, (Ed.), *Law for Liberty*, p. 135.

the Spirit of God and any kind of external law. It is presumed, apparently, that the transforming power of the Spirit cannot be fully operative in anyone whose actions are 'constrained' by law in any way. To observe a law is to be shackled in some way; it is to be unfree. Hence it is argued that there should be no question of constructing anything like a Christian *Torah*. On the contrary, canon law should sedulously avoid laying down legal prescriptions about how to live the Christian life. Canonical legislation will be fulfilling a useful function if it keeps to what is necessary for the social structure and for order within the Church, but it would do well to exclude from its concern pastoral norms and moral directives. In such matters each Christian should be left to follow the teaching of Christ according to his own conscience. There is, of course, the need for guidance in such matters, but this should be the function, not of canon law, but of preachers, catechists and moral theologians. This would do much to avoid legalism and pharisaism in the Christian life. If morality is outlined in clear prescriptive legislation, then, these critics argue, it becomes difficult if not impossible to avoid constructing a 'morality of law', and this in turn becomes self-righteous and unchristian.

So it is urged that there be eliminated from the law as such all specific injunctions regarding, say, penance and worship, behaviour, and so on, leaving all such matters to be decided by the conscience of each individual in the light of the Gospel principles. It would seem that canon law should not aim at establishing or positively fostering what is right, but should protect the rights of the individual to do what he thinks is right, — provided that he does not interfere with the like freedom of others. [55] It is probably this aspect of the law as a moral guide that those writers have in mind when they ask that canon law should provide directives and exhortations rather than juridical norms. The idea was proposed at the first Synod of Bishops in 1967: 'La Chiesa, infatti, ha il fine di salvare le anime; ma vi è da domandarci se tale compito essa lo deve raggiungere attraverso leggi giuridiche. Sarebbe forse più opportuno che il Codice indulgesse nelle esortazioni, nei consigli, nelle persuasioni, piuttosto che nell'elencazione di vere e proprie leggi'. [56] It is not easy to see how this could apply to the structure of councils, election procedure, the protection and

---

[55] Cf. John Stuart Mill's teaching on liberty.
[56] *Osservatore Romano*, October 4th, 1967.

defence of rights and so on; but it could be applied to guidance on Christian behaviour concerning such things as fasting and abstinence, the obligation of going to Mass on Sunday, and the like.

Most Catholics today would agree that the main purpose of the Code of Canon Law should not be to provide a complete guide to Christian living. They would reject the paternalism that appears to characterise much of medieval canon law. They would reject the rigidity and formalism that have not always been avoided in the Church. A morality of law is objectionable because one cannot pretend to approach God and love God through the mere observance of external laws. This is true. It has always been true, as the teaching of Deuteronomy makes plain even in the Old Testament. Cardinal Hostiensis would also agree with this, as has been shown by his comments on St Paul's teaching on the need to be led by the Spirit. [57] How, then, is this danger to be avoided? By abolishing the law, suggest some writers, or at least by reducing it to the absolute minimum and keeping off all moral matters. [58] But this is not the only possible approach. Others suggest that another way of avoiding a morality of law is to clarify the proper use of law in the Christian moral life. It may after all be feasible for a sound moral tradition to be at least partially embodied in the law of the Christian community. Such a law could then be taken as a reliable guide towards living the Christian life, although, of course, the fully Christian life would always mean much *more* than simply observing a law. This implies, too, a truly Christian way of interpreting law and a rejection of all rigidity and formalism. It is of course, extremely difficult to express moral direction by means of *absolute* rules, but this need not entail that there should be no rules at all about Christian behaviour. It may, after all, be possible to have some *general* laws which would indicate the direction that the Christian life should take if it was being true to the Gospel teaching. It is, of course, beyond question that the important thing is obedience to the Father's will rather than the observance of laws. Yet, as a number of contemporary thinkers point out, laws give general and helpful guidance. They can guide the faithful in the process of maturing in Christ. They can embody

---

[57] *Summa Aurea*, I, De his quae vi metusve causa fiunt, n. 6.
[58] Cf., for example, R. Haughton, 'The Changing Church: the Ending of the Law', *Doctrine and Life*, 18 (1968), pp. 86-90.

the Christian moral tradition, just as the dogmatic tradition may be partially embodied in the structure of the Church and in the sacraments.

It is thought by some that many Catholics are afraid of what is termed 'the freedom to decide for ourselves'. But what precisely is meant by the phrase is not completely clear. Freedom here would seem to imply a certain amount of independence, and it may be asked in what sense or to what extent the Christian may be considered independent in the matter of Christian morals. He presumably wishes to be guided by the teaching of Christ in his moral life. Moreover, any really responsible moral decision must be based on sound knowledge concerning the teaching of Christ; the Christian normally obtains this knowledge from the New Testament and from the traditional teaching of the Christian community; and all this is bound to affect in an important way the individual Christian's freedom to decide for himself. Perhaps what is being implied is that each individual must commune with the Spirit in his own heart, and that if only he would listen to the Spirit of God he would have no need for laws of any kind. The need for laws would arise then solely from the fact that men are sinners and so deaf to the voice of the Spirit. 'If all Christians were just', writes Fr. Lyonnet, 'there would be no need to restrain them by laws. Law generally does not enter upon the scene except to repress an existing disorder'.[59] Here Fr. Lyonnet is expressing a view that is widely held among Christians today and one that is put forward as the authentic teaching of St Paul. Yet it is a view that seems to rest upon a number of questionable assumptions.

First of all, it seems to presume that the Spirit of God will speak always directly to the individual's own heart and conscience without the use of any intermediaries. It seems to take for granted that the just man is at every moment under the immediate and palpable direction of the Spirit. But that this is verified in normal Christian experience is seriously open to question. Does not the Spirit of God usually act through the ordinary events of everyday life, content that his inspirations should seem, to us, bright ideas of our own?

Secondly, the view seems to consider the Christian purely as an individual rather than as a member of the Christian community who is, to a large extent, dependent upon the support of the community. The Spirit works, after all, not just on the

---

[59] Stanislas Lyonnet, SJ, *St Paul: Liberty and Law*, Rome, 1962, p. 17.

individual but also on the collectivity, and it is not often that
an individual is directly and unmistakably guided by the Spirit
in such a way that he becomes independent of his fellow Christians. All are members of One Body, dependent upon each
other. Therefore, as one recent writer has observed, it does
appear to be the case that

> here on earth, where the children of God must walk by faith,
> live in dependence upon one another, and be protected from
> thoughtlessness, our Father has to remind us through the
> Church's laws and precepts of all that life in his family really
> means. [60]

Thirdly, does not the view that is here being questioned
tend to presume that the guidance given by the Holy Spirit will
always be self-authenticating? And yet St Paul and St John
warn all Christians to be alert to the need to discern the spirits,
since Satan himself can appear as an angel of light. It is not
every movement of the spirit that is to be trusted. Even granting the authentic guidance of the Spirit, however, can any Christian ever consider himself as self-sufficient? Can it be presumed
that each just man receives *all* the gifts of the Spirit? St Thomas
Aquinas, while stressing that the law of the Spirit is superior
to any law made by man, goes on to say:

> It follows that spiritual men who are led by the Holy Spirit
> are not subject to the law when it is contrary to the leading
> of the Holy Spirit. But nonetheless it is an element in the
> leading of the Holy Spirit that spiritual men are subject to
> human laws. [61]

And Melchior Cano included canon law among the *loci theologici*:
'Deus itaque, quoniam non deficit in necessariis, non in theo-
logos solum sed et in iuris pontificii peritos spiritum veritatis
infudit'! [62]

Lastly, it appears to some a peculiarly narrow view of law
which considers it merely in terms of restraint and repression.
Cannot the law of the Church be so formulated as to be a
positive guide to an authentic Christian life? The Spirit of
God draws men to the Father in all kinds of ways. But he
does not reject man's reason and his intuitions of the natural

---

[60] B. Ahern, in *Law for Liberty* (Edited by J. Biechler), p. 106.
[61] S. T., 1a 2ae, q. 96, art. 5 ad 2.
[62] Melchior Cano, *De Locis Theologicis*, VIII, 7.

law. The Spirit does not normally by-pass the moral instruction that Christ gave to his followers and which has been handed on by the Apostles and developed within the Christian community. [63] Hence, it is argued, a Christian should remain alert to all these various manifestations of the Spirit. Moreover, unless one is willing to settle for some sort of 'inner light' theory, one has to acknowledge than man — even the just man — needs some sort of guide, some kind of external aid in the discernment of spirits. Of course, there does remain the danger of constructing a morality of law. There have been serious aberrations within the Christian community, — narrowness, rigidity and pharisaism. But such aberrations are not regarded by all as inevitable.

There are many, therefore, who remain unconvinced that the narrow view of law which regards it solely in terms of restraint and repression is the only possible one. Professor Dodd writes:

> The Church is bound, to take seriously the work of establishing a specific discipline for its own members, which shall bring the fundamental principles of the Gospel and the law of Christ to bear upon actual situations in the world as it is. [64]

In doing so, the Church is simply carrying on the work that was done by the early Christian teachers when they constructed the primitive catechesis. The written law has been in the past and can still be in the future a positive guide to the individual to help him live up to his Christian vocation. It can be a lamp to guide man in his search for the good pleasure of the Father. It can provide an outline of the sort of life that is proper to the Christian. Law can, therefore, be a help, — only *secondary* in the Christian life, but still a help. For this reason there are many who would be sorry to see this aspect of the law abandoned.

So the complete rejection of law is not advocated by all modern writers. Many still insist on the positive role which regulations ought to play in the formation of the consciences of individuals. They maintain that one of the functions of law in general is and always had been to educate the citizen in the

---

[63] Professor C. H. Dodd has made out a strong case for the existence of a Christian moral tradition in the New Testament epistles. Cf. *Gospel and Law*, New York, 1951.

[64] C. H. Dodd, *Gospel and Law*, p. 80.

knowledge of what is right and what is wrong. Should not this also be true of the law of the Christian community? Should not the Church's law embody the community's sense of what is right? Sincere Christians do desire to fulfil Christ's commandment of love; but how to do this in practice is not always immediately apparent, and so they look for authentic direction and positive guidance. These writers would like to see canon law including a sort of 'Highway Code' for the Christian pilgrim, a clear expression of the Christian moral tradition. In this way the laws of the Church might play an important part in the Christian life if only they could be seen to be, not an arid list of prescriptions rigidly interpreted and woodenly applied, but a reliable guide to the following of Christ, an external expression of the internal law of love. [65] Disciplinary laws could then help Christians to practice Christian charity. Some think too that canon law could be a positive instrument of the Spirit in 'pointing out the demands of the Spirit for the community and for the individual Christian'. [66] Others would like to see the Church's legislation as a 'sign of salvation' in the world through its clear display of truly Christian wisdom and understanding.

Moreover, canon law in its function of giving clear expression to certain aspects of the Christian moral tradition could provide valuable guidance about the relative seriousness of various Christian duties. But the common use by Hostiensis of sin as a sanction for ecclesiastical laws would not be acceptable to many modern Catholics. In actual fact the Code of Canon Law does not use the expression 'under pain of sin'; but it is true that a number of canonical commentators and moralists in our own time have been rather free in brandishing the penalty of grave sin, and that by so doing they have helped to bring canon law in general into disrepute. This abuse should be avoided and yet the law, if it were to distinguish more clearly between what is of great importance and what is of less importance for the Christian life, could do much towards the formation of the Christian conscience. [67]

---

[65] Cf. D. O'Mahoney, 'Canon Law in the Seminary Today,' in *Irish Theological Quarterly*, 1967, pp. 231 ff.

[66] Charles Curran, in *Law for Liberty*, 1967, p. 158.

[67] The old expressions, 'sub gravi' and 'sub levi' have often been caricatured and laughed out of court. But in fact they do not, or they *should not*, imply the attitude which can say: 'It doesn't really matter; it is

In all this, however, canon law should not be confused with moral theology. Nor should it be substituted for moral theology. The two subjects should be regarded as distinct disciplines, although of course they are not unrelated to each other. Hence the general mixture of moral theology and canon law that has been displayed in the *Summa Aurea* of Hostiensis — and in the canonical collections, — would be unacceptable to most modern Catholic thinkers. Until quite recently in many institutes of ecclesiastical training the role of the canonist was quite clear: he was expected to teach moral theology; and it was quite normal for the prospective moral professor to prepare for his task by taking a doctorate in canon law. This encouraged the confusion between two distinct disciplines and between the respective roles of the moralist and the canonist. This confusion in turn tended to encourage a certain legalism and even perhaps minimalism in the following of Christ. A clearer distinction between the roles of the canonist and the moralist should help to remove the dangers of constructing a morality of law and permit moral theology to develop according to the guide-lincs laid down by the Second Vatican Council. The primary object of moral theology should be the exposition of the good news of the Christian's vocation in Christ and his response to this vocation.[68] Moral theology should, therefore, present Christian morality as the personal response of the Christian to this vocation in Christ, rather than as a doctrine of mere obedience to laws. Moral theology will, of course, have to deal with the Christian attitude to law in general and to canon law in particular, but this is only a small part of its task. Canon law will be but one of the standards with which Christian behaviour ought normally to conform. The technical interpretation of the law of the Church, however, should be the task of the canonist.

At the Synod of Bishops in 1967 it was urged that the new Code of Canon Law should be an instrument of salvation, a positive help for the pastoral ministry. In this sense perhaps canon law should try to express more clearly that Christian tradition which down the centuries has been inspired by the

---

only a venial sin!'. These terms are simply short-hand expressions for drawing attention to the greater or less importance that can attach to particular duties. All laws are not of equal importance in the Christian life, and this was one way of trying to make the distinction. But perhaps it was not an entirely happy use of language!

[68] Concilium Vaticanum II, *De Institutione Sacerdotali*, n. 16.

Holy Spirit in response to the Gospel. However, as has already been shown, there are many today who reject the duty or the right of the Church to try to further the salvation of men by means of juridical prescriptions. They do so mainly for two reasons. Their first reason is that such a procedure would contradict the teaching of St Paul on the Christian's freedom from all law. The second reason is that such juridical prescriptions have frequently in the past led to formalism, rigidity and other abuses which run counter to the Gospel and which tend to dehumanise the human person. Such argumentation does not, however, convince everyone. As to the first reason, it has been well argued that St Paul's teaching, far from ruling out all legislation within the Christian community, in fact laid firm foundations for the Christian moral tradition that can partially be embodied in the Church's law. As to the second, it can be pointed out that the evils of legalism and rigidity can and should be averted by sound instruction on the proper interpretation of law and by encouraging the practice of the Christian moral virtue of *epikeia*.

Cardinal Hostiensis, along with other medieval churchmen, regarded canon law as an important instrument for helping to reform the Church. Many today would reject some of the ways it tried to do so, and in particular its use of penal legislation as a deterrent. They would also maintain that Hostiensis tended to exaggerate the importance of law in the Church. And yet, in spite of this, many would still agree in principle that canon law can still be a useful instrument in the renewal of the Church, provided that it is used in the right way. But it is only an *aid* to renewal and too much should not be demanded of it. The rules and constitutions, for example, of a religious order are not intended to be a complete and accurate translation into legal terms of the original charismatic experience of the founder. This simply cannot be done. Mere observance can never take the place of sincere performance. The function of such rules and constitutions is to indicate clearly, and to protect or foster, a certain type of life within the Christian community. Similarly with the canon law of the Church. It does not, — or rather, it should not, — attempt the impossible task of trying to translate the Gospel into legal terms and clear-cut prescriptions. What it can do, however, is to indicate the direction in which the Christian should travel. Canon law has been accused of causing many evils in the Church, and where this has been the case, then the law must be reformed. But one must be wary of indulging in romantic dreams. The reform of canon law can provide substantial help in eradicating a number of evils from the Church. This was true in the Middle Ages and it remains true today. But there is a limit to what one can reasonably hope for from legal reform. This can only be a help towards — never a substitute for — the true interior Christian renewal.

> The new vigour that St Francis gave to the life of the Western Church had a very different character from the stimulus given by the reforming legislators of the age. These latter sought to impose an order and a discipline upon the discordant and flaccid elements in the body of the Church by means of a legal code and measures of administration; learning, law, organization were to be the instruments of their policy; they followed a rationally calculated method of action based on a careful study of the discipline of the past, the conditions of the age and the external ends to be attained. Though the goal they aimed at was spiritual rebirth, and though many of them were, like Grosseteste, men of evangelical zeal, they thought and acted as rulers and legislators in a world of men and things. St Francis moved upon another and far deeper plane. [69]

Conclusion

Several conclusions may be drawn from the preceding investigation. The first of these is that in fact a variety of meanings can be attached to the word, law, and a variety of functions that the law may be expected to perform. Much confusion has arisen in current discussion about the function of law in the Church because of a lack of clarity and precision about what is meant by the words used. Apart all together from the numerous theories about what law is — and this has been a philosophers' battlefield for centuries — the actual English word, law, can be used to cover a many different phenomena, ranging from the laws of thermodynamics to the *Highway Code*. Similarly, in the field of canon law there is confusion between what are expressions of theological teaching and what are purely human disciplinary norms for behaviour. A study of the Code of Canon Law would reveal that the word *ius* is there used to cover diverse kinds of law. The laws about the powers of the pope, the episcopate, general councils and the valid administration of

---

[69] D. Knowles, *The Religious Orders in England*. Cambridge, 1956, vol. I, p. 116.

the sacraments are not in the same category as those governing judicial process and the rights and duties of clerics and religious. There is, therefore, a variety of functions that the law is expected to perform in the Christian community. In what sense, then, it may be asked, is the word, law, being used when it is argued that 'law is for the ungodly', or when it is maintained that law is not for mature Christians, but only for children?

Secondly, there does seem to be much that the canonist of today can profitably learn from medieval canonists of the calibre of Cardinal Hostiensis. Admittedly, many of the practical solutions that Hostiensis offered were elicited by the current problems facing the medieval Church and coloured by the mentality of his times. These are no longer applicable. He shared the common assumptions of current opinion in medieval Christendom in which certain elements of Christianity were stressed at the expense of others. The twentieth-century Church has, perhaps, its own set of assumptions and prejudices which a later age may repudiate. Many of the basic principles, however, which Hostiensis advocated embody sound Christian teaching and are as relevant today as they were in the thirteenth century. His emphasis on the close relationship between canon law and theology, his insistence that spiritual values must prevail and the law of the Church be always humanely administered in accordance with the Gospel, and his encouragement that pope, bishops and priests should work together in the government of the Church and take particular care to see that the rights of all are properly protected, are just some examples of how the teaching of this medieval canonist is in harmony with modern Catholic thinking. And there are many others.

Lastly, if a fair account has been given of current demands on canon law, then, in spite of widespread criticism and dissatisfaction, there remains an important task for canon law within the Christian community. What is being rejected, it would appear, is not the law as such, but only those parts of canonical legislation which have seemed to crush individual freedom, initiative and responsibility. So the canonist still has a worthwhile task to perform in the Church. Moreover, there also seems to be a large measure of agreement both between Cardinal Hostiensis and modern thinkers and among modern thinkers themselves about *what* canon law should be trying to achieve. Most would agree that a certain amount of law is needed to ensure order and stability in the Church, to regulate ecclesiastical structures and institutions, and to clarify and protect the rights of the members of the community. All of which constitutes a formidable task for canon law. On the other hand, there is a sharp division of opinion over whether canon law should in any sense attempt to provide a Christian *Torah*, a guide to Christian living. Both sides in the controversy support their case with arguments that cannot lightly be brushed aside. What is the answer? Although the dangers of legalism and a morality-of-law attitude must be recognised as real, they need not be regarded as inevitable. The stronger arguments seem to me to support the attempt to provide, at least in outline, though *not in great detail*, some form of Christian *Torah*. This idea has the support of a long Christian tradition that is firmly founded in the teaching of Christ and of St Paul, and, given the right approach, this could be a valuable help towards living up to the demands of the Gospel. Moreover, the difficulties and dangers that tend to follow this use of law can be avoided if proper care is taken, and they appear to be outweighed by the positive advantages that such a use of law offers.

One last point. If canon law is to be the effective pastoral guide that the first Synod of Bishops asked for, then it might possibly be advantageous to abandon the relatively recent idea of the brief *codex iuris canonici*. There should, of course, be clear and definite legal prescriptions. This is necessary if there is to be what can truly be called law. But these legal prescriptions need not be cut adrift from the *ratio legum*, — the reason for the law, the purpose behind the law and its theological foundation. 'Whenever a law is promulgated', suggest some modern thinkers, 'care should be taken that its relationship to the life of the Church be indicated'.[70] The Code of Canon Law did, of course, depart from a long canonical tradition when, at the beginning of this century, it was limited to command, prohibition and stipulation, and omitted all mention of the reasons for the laws. This was done in the interests of clarity and brevity. Brevity was certainly obtained. So was clarity, but of a rather peculiar sort which has perhaps tended to foster formalism in the study of canon law, and perhaps also a stifling uniformity. This is so because canonical prescriptions can only really be understood and interpreted when they are seen in their particular context of circumstances, motives, purpose, and so on. It could be argued that the decision to omit all mention of

---

[70] From the consensus paper in *Law for Liberty*, (Edited by J. Biechler), p. 20.

these in the law-book of the Church has been a contributory factor in the current rejection of canon law as being of little help in providing a guide for Christian living. All this suggests that it might be profitable to try to produce, not a compact codex of conclusions, but to include the legal prescriptions in a series of positive guides and instructions. Recent legislation has, in fact, provided some interesting examples of this. A number of papal documents have given, not only the reformed law on such things as the Eucharistic fast, abstinence, and mixed marriages, but also introductions on the reason behind the legislation and its theological and scriptural foundation. [71] Why could not the same thing be done for other important parts of the Church's law? A whole series of such brief instructions on, say, baptism, matrimony, and the like, — and they have to be brief and compact, — rather than a patched-up universal codex, could provide the authoritative guidance that is wanted by many and be of very great pastoral value for the whole Church. Such an approach would also help to cut away the legalism and formalism which have had such unfortunate effects on the Christian view of morality in general.

---

[71] Cf. *Christus Dominus* (January 6th, 1953), on the Eucharistic fast; *Matrimonii Sacramentum* (March 18th, 1966), on mixed marriages; *Paenitemini* (February 17th, 1966), on fasting and abstinence, in which the particular legal prescriptions are preceded by an introduction and three chapters on the meaning and importance of the divine precept of penance.